# Blessed Beyond Blessings

## How Faith, Family, and Trust in God Carried Me Through Life's Storms

by Hazel Grace Mitchell-Mattocks

Blessed Beyond Blessings
How Faith, Family, and Trust in God Carried Me Through Life's Storms

Published by Creation Publishing Group LLC
www.creationpublishing.com
©2026
ISBN # 979-8-9857286-2-0
Library of Congress Number # 2026907380

Cover design by Rebecacovers on Fiverr



Published and printed in the United States of America.

# Dedication

dedicate this book first and foremost to God Almighty, my Heavenly Father, whose wisdom, mercy, grace, and unfailing love have guided me through every season of my life.

I dedicate it to Jesus Christ, my Savior, who gave His life for the sins of the world and showed me what it means to love, forgive, and endure.

I also dedicate this book to the loving memory of my beloved sister, whose encouragement and faith gave me the courage to tell my story. Her words remain with me: "Your story is my story, and the story of many other women. Tell it, and trust God to make a way."

And finally, I dedicate this book to my family, whose love, patience, and support have carried me through both trials and triumphs. This story belongs to us all.

# Acknowledgments

First and always, I give honor and glory to Almighty God, my Heavenly Father, for never leaving me, never forsaking me, and faithfully guiding my life. Every step I have taken, every trial I have endured, and every blessing I have received has been by His mercy and grace.

I am deeply grateful to my father, whose example of responsibility, discipline, and dedication shaped the foundation of my life. I thank my siblings, who taught me the meaning of unity, faith, and perseverance. We truly lived the words, "a family that prays together stays together." I am especially thankful for the older sister whose sacrifice and love provided the nurturing and strength I needed.

I extend my heartfelt thanks to my children, grandchildren, great-grandchildren, and great-great-grandchildren. You are living reminders of God's faithfulness across generations. To the members of my family who assisted in bringing this book to publication, your support and encouragement made this possible. You know who you are, and I am forever grateful.

I also thank the many people, friends, and members of the community who encouraged me to share this part of my life's journey. Some of these memories were deeply buried, and your words helped me find the courage to tell the truth with faith and humility.

My appreciation extends to those who assisted with editing, proofreading, publishing, and the many details required to bring this book to life. Your efforts helped make my story easier to read and share.

Above all, I thank God for trusting me with this testimony. My prayer is that every reader who opens this book will find encouragement, understanding, and a deeper awareness of His love.

# INTRODUCTION

## Why This Story Had to Be Told

The title of this book, Blessed Beyond Blessings, is not meant to be clever or symbolic. It is a truth born out of a lifetime of living, suffering, trusting, and seeing the hand of God at work in ways that cannot be explained by human understanding alone.

Many people speak of being blessed when things go well. I have learned that blessings are often revealed most clearly when life does not go as planned. This book is the story of how God carried me through trials, tribulations, hardship, fear, loss, and uncertainty, and how His presence proved faithful in every season of my life.

I was not raised with wealth or privilege. I was raised with responsibility, discipline, faith, and love. From early childhood, I learned that life requires work, sacrifice, and trust in God. I also learned that pain does not cancel purpose, and hardship does not mean abandonment. These lessons were not learned from books, but through lived experience.

This story is written from my own memory and understanding, guided by prayer and reflection. The names of people and places have been changed, but the truth of what I lived remains. I did not set out to write this book for recognition or praise. For many years, I resisted the idea of writing at all, fearing that my story might cause embarrassment or pain for those I love. But again and again, I felt God's instruction to tell the truth and trust Him with the outcome.

There came a moment when that instruction could no longer be ignored. Sitting alone in an airport, waiting for a delayed flight, I began to pray for safety and peace of mind. Instead of focusing on the plane, my thoughts were drawn back to a conversation I had just shared with a stranger, a woman who felt compelled to speak with me about my life. As I prayed, I heard the words clearly and unmistakably in my spirit: Write the book.

I questioned that calling. I felt unqualified. I felt too old. I felt unsure. But the message came again with reassurance: Tell the truth. I will be with you.

This book is not written as a sermon, nor is it meant to instruct anyone on how to live their life step by step. It is simply the testimony of what God has done for me and through me. It is a record of how faith sustained me through poverty, racism, marriage, motherhood, abuse, loss, service, and calling. It is also a record of how obedience, even when difficult, led to healing, purpose, and peace.

My faith is rooted in belief in God the Father, His Son Jesus Christ, and the Holy Spirit. That faith shaped my decisions, strengthened my endurance, and guided my actions. While this book is written from a Christian perspective, it is offered with love and humility, not judgment. My hope is not to persuade, but to share.

If you are reading this book while carrying your own burdens, doubts, or unanswered questions, I pray that something within these pages reminds you that you are not forgotten. God meets us where we are, often in ways we do not expect, and He is able to bring purpose out of even the most painful experiences.

This story is my testimony.

If it helps even one person find hope, strength, or peace, then it has fulfilled its purpose.

# Table of Contents

"Many are the afflictions of the righteous:
but the Lord delivereth him out
of them all."
Psalm 34:19

# CHAPTER 1

## Tough childhood upbringing and other memories

It is January first, 2020. I am an eighty-six-year-old negro woman. Negro is what we were called when I was born. Nigger is what the so-called white folks called us when they wanted to make us upset or fight back. By the time I was old enough to realize what they were doing to my family and me, I was past the stage that we would let their words bother us because we were Christians and behind that. We had control of our feelings.

My mother died when I was six years old. My daddy was left to raise ten children on his own. Of course, some of my aunts and uncles offered to take some of the younger siblings, but my daddy said, "No, we will all stay together." Being six years old, I barely remember my mother. I can remember incidents like playing out in the yard with my younger sister and brother catching doodles. I would remember my older sister doing this for fun. We got some tobacco string, put spit on the end of the doodle hole, and fixed the string in the ground, chanting, "Doodle, doodle, come out and get your supper." We will pull the string out of the hole with a doodle attached to it.

We had caught almost a pint Jar full when our mama called, "Hattie Grace, you all come to eat." When we heard, "What are you doing?" we looked up excitedly. I remember seeing a white apron worn over a blue and white checkered skirt and a blue denim blouse. Every time I try to see a face, I can remember nothing else. We jumped up and brushed off the dirt and grass from our clothes. And she said very disgustingly, "What you got in that jar?" What was in that jar was a lot of white doodles with orange heads and two brown eyes protruding out in front.

"Go throw them in the chicken yard," she said. "But the chickens will eat them," I said very softly. "Yes, I know. What else will you do with them?" And before I could answer, she took the jar out of my hand and sprinkled them to the chickens who came running to peck and swallow.

I remember other incidents like going to school at five years old and mama making me a book bag out of old overalls. That's what most men and some boys wore daily. They had a bib that came up to cover their chest. Some are still worn by farmers or older men. I went to school long enough at five to learn to write and spell my name. I started to read through the pictures in the book. Each page had a picture to explain what was happening in the story and I could find all the words that started with a certain letter.

One day, some white men dressed in suits and ties came to talk with the teacher. They wanted us to be like all other communities. They had a one-room school and all the children from first through eighth grade were taught by one teacher. If the enrollment was not high enough, children five years old could attend the school. These men came with news that caused me not to be able to continue going to school. The state had decided to close down all Community Schools and count all the children who would be transferred to a school in Civic City by bus almost five miles from where we lived.

It would take place in two years, but in one year, all first graders would ride the High School Bus to Civic City until more buses could be purchased by the state. I went home that day very sad, but the only thing that was positive for me was that the teacher gave us five-year-olds books from the library for our own. I remembered carrying the book bag; I had to drag it.

We lived in our own home on three acres of land near a stream of water. In fact, the land was all the way; the water was the boundary on the left side to the east. My Uncle Mark and his family lived on the west side. The road was a narrow dirt road on the north side, just wide enough for a car to drive through; however, not many people owned cars in the 1930s. Most Negroes were sharecroppers and didn't own a mule.

Uncle Mark had his acres, and he also purchased from his four brothers. They had three acres each, totaling fifteen acres. He had enough to have his own small farm, plus he was a preacher and pastored a church. He had a mule and a horse for transportation to and from church. A couple of other families had horses, mules, or cars and owned their own small farm. Families were large and stayed together, so labor was free for sharecroppers, but the whites who didn't have sharecroppers hired laborers.

My older sister and brother always took the laborers' jobs to make money for some clothes. I did, too, when I was old enough to work. Our family always had work to do because we were taught well by our daddy to work and to be honest in all we did. He also taught us to trust God to help us in everything. We learned how to pray and read the Bible at an early age. We went to Sunday school and church every Sunday and were taught to listen to the sermon.

There were four churches in our area. The farthest was almost five miles away from us. The churches include: Baptist Missionary, Baptist Free Will, Holiness Pentecostal, and African Methodist Episcopal Zion.

My family and I attended all four churches, except when it rained. After attending Sunday school at our church, I would walk many miles to the church that was having service on that Sunday. At every church, we heard about the same sermon that God is Almighty, he is the truth, he is love, he is powerful, he hears our prayers and answers when we pray. There were quotes from the Bible, but when you are very young as I was when I started paying attention to the sermons, all you want to know is that God loves you and he will help you. I learned that Jesus saves and that he came to the world to save the world from sin.

At eight years old, I didn't exactly know about sin, but I knew we would get a whipping from daddy if we did anything wrong or didn't do what he told us to do and the way he told us to do it. I thank God today for how my daddy taught us and the way he provided for us. We were taught how to do everything we did in a neat and orderly fashion at a young age. It was not so important to us then, but now we can appreciate how hard he tried to teach us how to be independent.

He was really serious about saving and not wasting. That fact is so instilled in me that I don't waste anything. I recycle, and I will wash and dry the plastic films that cover the meat I bought from the store. The recycle was four times my trash turned into recycle when I first started many years ago at the Marine base where I was hired as a teacher's assistant. God blessed my life through that because of what my daddy taught me.

My father taught us manners, respect, politeness, helpfulness, and all the things a human needs to live a peaceful and happy life.

We govern our lives and shouldn't allow others to control us. With love, mercy, and grace, we can do and be whatever we want to be. I always wanted to be a teacher, and this was my first opportunity to teach in a school. I was appointed supervisor over the recycling program. I planned to involve every student, parent, and God. I never wanted to do anything without contacting God to take leadership and give wisdom, knowledge, understanding, guidance, and strength.

I depended on God and trusted him to take control of the situation for whatever I asked Him. Praise and thanksgiving were always in my heart and mouth. The preacher went home with the announcement of a new project, "Recycling newspapers, macaroni boxes, flyers, junk mail plastic containers, etc. All had to be clean and dry. The class that collected the most would get ice cream on Friday; you make it sound exciting. We recycled old novels, dogs' bones, books, and paper items that had been thrown into the trash before now.

The school was like an anthill; everybody was busy doing their part. Parents were dropping off grocery bags and had a divide between classes because there were two children in different classes. My problem was how to decide which class collected the most. Of course, I went to God for the answer. I met the principal for permission to ask Marines to help judge using weight - problem solved.

Where would I get money for the ice cream? Of course, God sent me to the school cafeteria to inquire what would be served once in a while. By now, I hope you will know that when you seek, you will find;

if you ask, it will be given unto you; knock, and it will be opened unto you; Matthew 7:7.

When I was six years old, I was bullied by two sisters in my classroom. One was in my grade, Hellen, and the other in the second grade, Delilah. They had an older sister in the 7th grade. They would stare at my clothes because they were made from my older sisters' clothes when they outgrew them and hand downs that the community would give us to help us. The sisters would have door button clothes fitting just right, and yes, I longed to have them too.

Eddie would say, "It's not the clothes you wear; it's all about who's wearing the clothes." I always complimented how pretty their clothes were, hoping they would not be mean to me. When the teacher was busy with the other grades and wouldn't see me raise my hand when I tried to get the teacher's attention, Delilah would reach over and pull my hair. My hair did not get combed every day like their own because I didn't have a good grade of hair.

It was long and "kinky."

My oldest sister was out of school when my mother died from complications after childbirth. There were four siblings younger than me. My baby sister was only twenty-three days old when mama died. Everybody old enough had to pitch in and help with the household chores, cooking, and caring for the pigs, chickens, and getting wood for cooking and the heater. My daddy sharecropped starting in January and cleared the ground (land) for tobacco beds. The landowner was not very smart and took advantage of the workers and had them clear grounds in a new place every year, making his farm bigger and bigger.

In January, when daddy and my older sibling cleared land to plant the tobacco beds, my daddy still had to work at night at a sawmill. He fired the boiler at night, making steam to run the mill during the day. I'm not sure how much he made, but it was always enough for us to settle our Sunday school and expenses, buy groceries, and canned milk for the baby.

The bullying got worse when I decided to fight back one day. It was nothing I had planned, pure unexpected impulse. Delilah reached over the person sitting in the next row across from me to pull my hair.

I saw her from my side view, and I reached out and grabbed her hand and stuck my fingernails into the back of her hand so tight that blood came out. She ran and showed the teacher her hand. When the teacher asked what happened, she lied.

However, a lot of other children saw what happened and told the truth. I was free until school was dismissed for lunch. Delilah ran to show her hand to her older sister, who came after me. But to her surprise, several cousins of mine and my older sister Margaret, two years older than me, stood up for me. That ended that war. I prayed my dad wouldn't find out because he taught us not to fight, and he didn't teach us to protect ourselves from others.

Now, I've realized that you don't have to be taught to protect yourself. That is one of the natural abilities God gives us, and when you trust God and live for him, he will always provide a way out.

The bullying stopped for a while until the teacher was doing a group study one day. Of course, we all learned from other grades. That was a plus for having four grades in one room. Every time a question was asked, either Delilah or Hellen's hand would go up. The teacher would usually call on someone other than the one with their hand up. This time, she called on Delilah, and she got the answer wrong. I quickly raised my hand and got the answer right. It made Delilah mad, so the bullying started again.

A few days later, I got permission from the teacher to go to the toilet. It was the old outhouse where a deep hole is dug in the ground, six-by-six and perhaps ten or more feet deep. When you are little and look in, it is very scary and dark. The outhouse had three seats, so three people could use it simultaneously. By the time I finished using the toilet and was ready to go, the door opened, and to my surprise, in walked Hellen.

My instinct, strong as it was, allowed me to put my hand over her mouth and grab her around the waist. She was kicking and wiggling. I was a farmer's daughter, and all the hardwood I carried made me stronger. I was determined to get it done. By the time I was getting her over the hole to let go and about to push her in, I heard a voice, "Hellen, what's taking you so long?"

It had to be God that sent an angel because both of us were saved. Hellen from death, and me from torment. What if I had killed her? I couldn't have lived with that thought. I put her down off the toilet, and she ran as fast as she could out of the toilet. I realized that she had peed on herself. Delilah asked, "Why did you wet yourself?" She replied, "I couldn't get there on time." I agonized about what would happen when they told the teacher what I had done, and I waited until both of them entered the classroom.

I said a prayer asking God to help me and to forgive me. For the rest of the day, the three of us were very quiet and busy with our classwork. At night, when I said my prayers, I cried and asked God to help Delilah, Hellen, and me. The teacher went about her work with the other classes, and every time she looked my way, I thought for sure she would approach me about the situation. The bell rang for the end of the day, and we started packing our backpacks to get ready to go home.

The bus riders had to stay and wait for the bus to come. I began to pray while waiting and didn't want to play the games we usually played while waiting for the bus. What if the teacher is writing a note to send to my dad? I dreaded the whipping I would get, but nothing would be as bad as what I was already going through. "I deserve to be punished", thought would come to my mind. If I had killed Hellen, she would no longer be in school.

What will her family do without her? I also remembered my mama dying and what a sad time that was. When I got home, I asked God to help me. I didn't want to eat anything. I went into our room, changed my clothes, laid across the bed, and went to sleep.

It was time for evening chores. I heard my name being called, and someone said, "She must be sick because she didn't even play at school also. She was very quiet on the bus." My oldest sister Marie came to check if I had a fever. "I don't think so," she said, "but maybe she is coming down with something." I wanted to tell her what had happened at school. Before I could, she left the room to make some tea for me. I heard a voice mostly from inside of me, not with my ears, saying, "You've already asked God to help you, and He will. Trust Him. Whatever you ask God in the Name of Jesus, he would do it for you."

My sister brought an entity made from what we called rabbit tobacco, which was very bitter and hard to drink. I didn't complain about not wanting to drink it. Supper was ready, and I was very hungry and ate all that was put on my plate. Thank God for not letting my dad find out what I had done. I didn't go to school the next day. I spent a lot of time praying and reading my school books. I also brought in a lot of wood for the fire and cooking.

I made up for missing my chores the day before. The bullying stopped after this because Hellen told Delilah to leave me alone. She threatened to tell their mama if she didn't. We became friends in high school, and when I jokingly mentioned the toilet incident, Hellen said she never told anyone about that. My faith was strengthened, knowing that God heard my prayers and answered them.

We missed many days from school to work on the farm because we had a lot of snow in the winter. We would get stuck in the mud after the snow melted because there were only dirt roads in our area. We took our books home every day, and when we stayed home for whatever reason, we read our books and practiced our spelling words too. We also worked on our problems in arithmetic (math). The younger ones got help from our older siblings, so we were always on top of the class and homework.

We all made good grades. My daddy would not have anything else. In fact, he would reward us by going to his money jar and passing out nickels to all of us. It made us determined to continue to do our best. It also made my younger siblings hopeful that they would do well when they start school.

We lived in a four-room house, not four bedrooms; the whole house was four rooms. A kitchen, the smallest, was big enough to have a small table for preparing food. There are no cabinets but a large buffet for the dishes at the top and a place at the bottom for the pots and pans. There were tool stool chairs at the table for the cooking and the helper with preparing the food. More than one person helped to prepare, like peeling potatoes, picking and cutting greens, plus someone had to get the big ten quart pots with the seasoned meat started.

Also, there are the problems of water which had to be drawn from a well located about a hundred feet from the house. Water was a big problem at the cooking time because there had to be water for washing the food, cooking, rinsing the dishes, drinking, outside in a washtub for washing hands before dinner. Everyone else is involved in this water business.

We were blessed with water because most members of our community, especially during the summer drought, did not have water. Our well was always open to anyone who needed water. Sometimes, when the water got low because of all the families using it, you could see water flowing from the springs beneath. After overnight with no use, the well is full again by morning. Back to the cooking, another hard but important chore is getting the stove hot enough to cook. It's very necessary to start the fire in the stove before cooking time. It is also necessary to have sufficient dry wood cut to the right size.

The four-room house also had a large living room with a potbelly heater to heat the house. This combined room housed a large dining table with a bench on either side of the armchair at each end. This table, chairs, and bench took most of the lower end of the room. At the left side of the room were four chairs, wooden chairs with high backs and wicker cane seats. After the table was cleared of dishes and leftover food at night, all of us who had not finished homework or studying took our place at the table. We didn't have to remember to do our homework or study, including reading some of our seven or eight books. Today, children have to be told with lots of resistance to do their homework or study.

Our daddy told us about his dad learning how to read and write after he was a grown man. We took every opportunity to make the best of our lives. Two of the four rooms in our house were the bedrooms. Wow! Two bedrooms for ten people! Well, the bedroom next to the kitchen was a little larger than the kitchen. It contained a back door for walking to the other parts of the house. There was a double bed in which my daddy, my older brother, Odell, who is four years older than me (I was eight by then), and my younger brother Murray, who is four years younger than me, slept in. The other bedroom had two double beds and was occupied by Marie, my older sister, Elsie, my fifth sister younger by two years, my new baby the sixth of my sister five years younger Mattie, and of course, me on the back side of the bed against the wall. On the other bed slept my second oldest sister Marjorie, my third oldest sister next in line Lilia, my immediate and fourth older sister two years older than me, Mae Ann and my baby seventh sister Ruth which was the youngest.

There were no chest of drawers, but we had a cardboard box where we kept our socks, underwear, and whatever other personal items we had. Coats were hung on the walls around the room. There was a trunk for the family towels, sheets, pillowcases, tablecloths, and a few odds and ends.

We were a close-knit, hard-working family. We children stuck together. We would not snitch on each other. We would rather all get whipped than be a snitch. When we did wrong, Marjorie, my older sister, would lecture us and make us promise not to do whatever it was again. We never snitched on each other.

However, dad had a way of finding out what was done wrong. We got whipped for every little thing: accidents, carelessness, stupid things, disobedience, things not done as he told us to do, things we didn't do right, and things we did wrong. In fact, it seemed as if he loved to whip. He would line us up according to our ages and start with the oldest. Sometimes he would be busy whipping us. I would run under the house to my playhouse, which I forgot to tell you about. Our house was built on blocks three feet high. This is where my sisters, the ones near my age, Mae Ann, Elsie, and I, had our playhouses.

There was a big chimney four feet by four feet square, a perfect place to have a private place. In the middle of the house, there were outlets in the living room and the kitchen. We could bend over and walk easily under the house. This particular day, I found myself under the house to refuse the whipping. Daddy didn't notice I was not there, and nobody snitched on me. I decided that if I had not committed the crime, I would not take the punishment.

But the next time, I tried the same thing the same way about the same point in the line. He flogged everybody then asked, "Where is Hattie?" Nobody answered. Somehow he decided I must be under the house, for he had seen us under there before. He yelled, "Come out here. I know you're under there." Not a word for me. I could hear the anger in his voice as I did when he tried to find out who opened the bank of potato slips.

Slips are the small potatoes saved for planting to make plants for another field of potatoes. The bank was broken into because my baby sister was being weaned from the bottle, and all she wanted before bedtime was what she called "eat taters," meaning sweet potatoes. Well, it was early spring, and all the banks of potatoes had been used up. The only thing left was the bank of slips. You might wonder about the "bank" in late summer when it's time to harvest corn, clay peas, beans, sweet potatoes, and butter beans, which is most unusual for most farmers but not for my daddy.

He discovered while saving seeds to plant another year that butter beans and clay peas are on the corn row after the corn has grown tall and ready to produce. Daddy would care for these butter beans in August and let them grow, produce, and dry until frost time in the early fall. Then we would pick them and beat them until the beans popped out of the hulls. They were ready for the wind. Yes, on a windy day, the beans and the clay peas treated the same way are poured from a bucket into a tub, and the wind will blow away the husk and clean the beans or peas. They are put into a barrel and saved for food.

Sweet potatoes are harvested in late summer or early fall and placed in the sun for a few days to make them sweeter. The potatoes are separated according to their sizes and placed in piles to be banked. The banks of the pine needles cover the sweet potatoes and the cornstalk that are put from top to bottom and then dirt covers over the entire pile. That's called "the bank."

My running from the discipline line made my daddy very angry. He went to get his gun and shoot me under the house. I prayed and prayed and prayed, "Oh Lord my God! Heavenly Father, please help my daddy and me this day. I don't know if he had his gun or not. I never saw it, but I did see my daddy walking around the house and stopping on each side to peek under. When I saw him, I would move to the opposite side of the big chimney. He continued calling for me to come, but he gave up when it was time for him to go to work at the mill.

He went up the steps into the house. I watched him get his bicycle from the barn and ride off. I was not sure if this was a trick and he would double back at his brother's house and come back another way. This frightened me even more, so I prayed more for God's help. I sat there under the house with my back to the brick wall. I was eight years old. I decided I knew that God was speaking to me and letting me know he would help me.

My siblings took the punishment willingly, and now they're over it. I was still under the house analyzing, praying, and begging God to hear and help me out of this mess and selfishness I had gotten myself into. Yes, God heard me and helped me to see that I should take my punishment like everybody else. He helped me see that I was a coward and not being fair and honest with my family.

I was wrong to make daddy angry enough to want to shoot me. I don't know if he would really shoot me, but I didn't want to take that chance anymore. My mind was made up, and I thanked God for helping me see the right thing to do and giving me the answer and help I needed. I promised myself and God that I would do the right thing even if it meant that I would be whipped. I would take the punishment along with all the rest, even if I think it was unfair, it was God's will.

As I sat there thanking and praising God, I went to sleep. I awoke to somebody touching my arm and calling me to come out from under the house. "Supper is ready; we are about to eat," said Mae Ann, and I crawled out and quickly washed my hands in the tub of water sitting on the small table outside. The water was very cold and was an awakening for me. None of my siblings said anything about what happened; I didn't eat it.

The next morning, Murray said at the breakfast table, "We all were praying for you." So I said, "I was also praying and God told me not to run anymore and I won't. I will take my punishment like everybody else."

Shores have been mentioned a few times but never told you what they were. We used it to safeguard our firewood from the rain. We had a crosscut saw; it's a long blade with a handle at each end. As we called him by his middle name, my brother Odell did the selecting of the tree to cut. It always had to be Oak and had to be the right size and in the right place. It had to be in the right place not to get caught in another tree or into the stream while falling.

He would cut a few chips out of the tree on the side to determine the direction the tree would fall. I guess daddy taught him this because the two of them went into the forest to cut a lot of wood that would last for most of the winter, depending on the weather.

This was one easy time for us girls. All we had to do was help unload the wagon and stack the wood under the smoke house shelter. Daddy would borrow Uncle Mark's mule and wagon and hall the wood to the yard. In exchange for the use of the mule and wagon, daddy would give Uncle Mark the last load of wood. Of course, we had to go across the fence that separated our land from theirs, unloaded the wagon and packed the wood on their back porch.

Boy, what an easy way for them to walk out of the back door and get the wood without having to climb up steps with an arm full of wood. It may sound like I am a little jealous of having to work while my three cousins older than me didn't even come to the door to see what was happening outside their house. No!! We were not jealous or envious of them because we knew that we were developing life and that blessings come when you help those who can't help themselves.

My cousins and Aunt Shelly may be able, but when you don't have the drive to do the things you need to do, then something is wrong somewhere. They missed so many days from school because they said they were sick. The only days my siblings and I missed school were because of work or bus problems. We could see our blessings in so many ways. Daddy's teachings, discipline, and the love he showed us were paying off in our lives.

"But to do good and to communicate
forget not: for with such sacrifices God is
well pleased."
Hebrews 13:16

# CHAPTER 2

## *Our neighbors*

During the winter and other seasons, Mark's family and other neighbors came to us to ask for food: peas, meat, and vegetables from our garden. Daddy would want us to give to them, but they were always told to come back and ask daddy. That didn't seem to be a problem for them. Some would wait until daddy got home, and they would come back again. Who can borrow food that is going to be eaten? We left out the word "borrow," knowing it was not going to be received back. I am so glad and thankful that I was taught to work, save, and prepare for the "rainy days." I'm also thankful and glad for the teachings of the Bible, God's word. It is a lamp unto my feet and a light to my pathway.

Another important chore was gathering the straw for the hog's bed, especially for the sow; who would be great with a litter of pigs to be born soon. We would go into the forest where there were a lot of pine trees. The pine trees shed their needles in the fall like most trees. We would gather pine straw, as it was called, by raking them into a pile and having a burlap sack in which to put the straw. We would put as much as we could carry in each bag. We would first make the sow's bed and then the other hogs. Our family depended on the hogs for meat and lard. We needed the fat of the hogs, so it is very important to feed them very well in the winter.

We always had killings each year: in November when the weather was cold enough to keep the meat from spoiling and another hog killing in February and early March. Again, it depends on the weather. There were no refrigerators, so the meat had to be salted and cured for about a month, and then the salt washed off. We then hung the meat in a smokehouse and smoked them so that they would not spoil when the weather was hot. Sausages were made from the lean part of the hog and were immediately hung in the smokehouse and smoked for safekeeping.

We always had food to eat and some for those less fortunate neighbors too. It is a blessing and a good feeling to have no needs. "God will supply all of your needs according to his riches and glory." I went through these years doing the same thing year after year and growing in grace and the knowledge of our Lord Jesus Christ. The sermons I heard every Sunday began to seem to come alive. I would listen to what the preacher said and would go home and look it up in the Bible. I didn't want to be disturbed at church. The prayers, songs, and especially the scripture, stayed on my mind at night until I fell asleep. By now, I was old enough and didn't let the disturbance at school during lunch and recess bother me.

We had an opportunity to go to the local store in front of our school at lunchtime. Usually, I was among several girls who went to the store in a group, but only one of us had money. When we got back to the school, some of the other girls without money would have candy or an apple. When I questioned one of the girls, "How did you get that apple without money?" She reluctantly explained how she got the Apple. She made me promise not to tell, and to be sure I wouldn't tell, she encouraged me to just try it. "I've been doing it for a long time, and I never got caught." I knew it was wrong and my dad wouldn't like it. The bible verse, "Thou shalt not steal," kept echoing in my mind.

I just wanted to get away with something once and not get caught. I watched Judy do what she told me how she did it. She stepped away from the basket of apples on the floor in front of the long counter filled with jars of different items, candy, cookies, sweet, dill pickles, pigs' feet, etc. I moved over to the apple basket just exactly what she did, and to my great surprise, I heard a man cough and clear his throat.

I didn't even see the five men sitting around a big heater when we came in. Darrell, one of the men, all white men, begged me to come over to him. Oh, Lord! I wanted the floor to open up and swallow me up. I started trembling and shaking so bad I could hardly walk. What was he going to do? I thought.

When I got near him, all the men were looking at me. I almost turned around and ran out of the store when a hand reached out and put it on my shoulder. He reached the other hand in his pocket and brought out a nickel. He said in a very low voice, so only I could hear him, "If I ever see you do that again, I will tell your daddy, Dallas. Go pay for that apple." As he took his hand off my shoulder, his other hand released the nickel into my hand.

I turned around and started back, then I stopped and said, shaking, "Me… mister…" and he answered, "Green." "Mr. Green, thank you," he nodded his head and smiled. I paid for the apple and said, "This is for an apple; keep it. I've already got it," I said in a voice I barely recognized.

When we came out, everyone who had something started to eat it. Do you believe that I didn't want to eat that apple? Lesson learned! Why did I follow the crowd? Why did I do wrong? The message came to me. Mr. Green cared because he knew my daddy was an honest man, and he would never have approved of his child doing such an embarrassing act. I learned that day that if no one sees me when I do wrong, God sees everything I do, even if nobody else is watching.

My question is, "Why did I let her get away with doing wrong?" I never went to the store again. If I had money, I saved it until I got home to spend it in our neighborhood store. I thank God for I was never tempted to steal again. I know God sees me and everything I do.

The quarterly meeting came on the third Sunday in September. The Monday after starts Revival. I was only eleven. Church rules were that when you are twelve, you can go to the mourners' bench and pray to be saved. The mourners' bench is just a Pew put near the altar at the front of the church. All the twelve-year-olds in our community must go to the mourners' bench. I have decided I want to be saved at the mourners' bench. It was sister Mae Ann's time to go. I'd been praying harder and harder since that incident with the apple. I felt God was not pleased with me for doing such a horrible thing.

There were a few other things I've been praying for since I was growing up. That was since my body had begun to change. We got the Sears Roebuck catalog, and I've been looking at ready-made clothes. Now that I'm eleven, God has provided a way for all to be saved through his son Jesus Christ. I couldn't wait until revival time. I looked at the calendar in the living room and counted the days. There were many things going on in September for me to focus on. We finished with the tobacco by the end of August. Eddie killed a medium-sized pig and invited the community for a barbecue.

We had to spend a week cleaning up the yard. Things were very busy during the tobacco season, so we were not able to cut the grass or rake the parts without grass. We didn't have a lawnmower, Sling Blade, which required muscle to make it work. When everything was ready and clean, including the house, daddy's brother Joshua Odell, he was called Odell, our cousins from next door, and a few other men from the community came and stayed all night to help with the barbecue. Mostly, they all were there to enjoy the night out and to tell any new jokes they had learned since the night a year ago.

Of course, they would be eating and laughing because daddy would have some old hens shut up for a cookout for the yearly occasion. The hens would be just right for a big pot of stew. Daddy always had a joke to play on the men who had to work all day, and we were too tired to stay awake all night. Of course, they would kill the hens and bring them into the house for Marie, Marjorie, and all of us who could give a helping hand to clean and cut up the hens for cooking.

Murray would make a pan full of pastry to put in after the chicken was nearly done cooking. The joke was that one of the men who stayed awake would get some corn from the barn and wash it and put it into the pot. They were careful to ensure that the sleeping men would be first to dip from the pot and see the corn that the men had cleaned. They would think the chicken had eaten the corn and for sure they were not eating this stew. One of the men who were in on the joke had to get his plate of stew and start eating before the sleeping men would know it was a joke. The corn joke had been used before, and everybody was wise not to fall for it.

They decided to get leaves of collard green and cut them up into small pieces to make it look like the hens had eaten them. The joke worked well and you could hear the laughter from the house. The barbecue was ready by morning, and the meat was being chopped. The women from the neighborhood started arriving by mid-morning. Each brought a covered dish. One brought slaw, another brought potato salad, one collard greens, one string beans with potatoes and dumplings. A boy brought an apple cobbler and one a cake, another a cake and blueberry pie, another corn on the cob.

The men were busy chopping the meat while others were making a makeshift table by putting the saw racks that make the table's legs about 20 feet apart. They used chicken wire at the top of the table; it's about six feet wide. Everyone worked in harmony to get the work done. A few women brought tablecloths to cover the table. The children had to go to the front yard to play a game. Things were so exciting and we had time to focus on the game.

Ring around the Roses got our attention because Sally had to do a dance when she was chosen. We would hold hands, make a circle, and sing: "Ring around the Roses; A pocket full of posies", and Sally had to be inside the circle stooping down. "Rise Sally, rise and wipe your weeping eyes. Put your hands on your hips, and let your backbone slip, shake it to the east...." I don't remember the rest of the song (shake it to the East, shake it to the West, shake it to the one that you love the best...

on and on), but Sally would close her eyes, turn around, pointing her finger, and stop turning. The one she was pointing at when she stopped had to run around the circle and Sally ran trying to catch the person. If the person gets back to her position without being caught, Sally had to go again. When she is caught, she has to replace Sally.

We played this game until we heard Marie call, "Dinner is ready." Marie got the honor of calling for dinner because she took momma's

Place. Usually, the wife would get the honor. There was not enough space at the table for the children. We had to stand in line and wait to be served. Then we take our plates and sit on the grass or on a block of wood. We could not eat until Uncle Mark, a Pastor, asked the blessing for us all.

As always, the blessing turned into a long prayer. He prayed for a safe summer, for the good crops, for all who participated, for those who could not come because of sickness, that the Revival and all who needed to be saved be blessed with salvation. He prayed for everything he could think of, I don't think he left anything out. He started to thank God for everything he prayed for and thanked God that he is our great Jehovah, our heavenly father.

He thanked him for the grace, mercy, and for loving us. He thanked God for the sunshine, rain, and all he could think of. Finally, he said thanks for this food we are about to receive for the nourishment of our bodies and so forth and so on, at last, amen, amen, amen. I think all of us children took a long, deep breath and started to eat.

The food was delicious for all of us, including the grown-ups, too. There was a game each year, after the cookout. We all went to the front yard for games. Some of the men went into the barn to get sacks for three leg races and sack races. The women gathered eggs for the egg race and potatoes for the potato race. I ran to the smokehouse shelter to get the grape vine ropes used for the jump rope contest.

We ate so much that the thought of competition didn't get us excited enough to get energy for the games. The adults were excited and wide awake. Even the men who stayed up all night were ready to root for (cheer for) and push their children to win. The three leg race was first. That was the one my daddy and many others wanted me to be in. The year before, I was the winner, along with my Sister Mae Ann, I had to actually pull her along when the game was ready to start.

Uncle Mark shot the cap pistol which he purchased for the occasion. My sister Mae Ann, usually very quiet and shy, took off like a bullet, yelling come on, Hattie Grace, we got to win. At first, she had to literally drag me along, and then I saw Willis and Lucy pass us. A burst of energy pushed me, so I began to hop with all my might when suddenly I saw a blue shirt, Willis's blue shirt in line with us.

Mae Ann yelled, "Let's do it, let's win again."

Plopp, I heard Willis and Lucy fall. That moment, I saw Rose and Sally almost in line with us. I yelled out loud, "Come on, God, help us do it" when I saw the finishing line. We were just a few steps ahead of most of the racers. I heard daddy yell louder than anybody else. "You've done it again." I didn't compete in the other races to save my energy for the jump rope contest. I had to compliment Mae Ann for the effort and for pushing me along.

I didn't know she had that spark in her. The sack race was next, then the potato race. Different children and families were excited. The most fun was the mothers carrying the babies race. Think of a mother of a fifteen-year-old baby who tries to carry her. They both finished on the ground, but it was fun seeing them try. Marie carried Ruth, who was five years old, on her back, and she was the winner. Again, I've never seen dad getting so excited.

He yelled out, "All that hard work, carrying wood and big buckets of water paid off." Everybody was pleased with the outcome of the races. There were lots of comments and joking throughout the afternoon. The jump rope winner was Rodger, Aunt Sally's son, the first winner in her family.

Labor Day celebration was a great success, with one of my uncle surprising us with late watermelon from the field. Some of the families stayed a while; the men especially went to sleep, some on the ground and daddy sitting in his rocker as he did every night before going to bed.

"Train up a child in the way he should go:
and when he is old, he will
not depart from it."
Proverbs 22:6

# CHAPTER 3

## Church upbringing and school friends and rivals

There were three things the neighborhood had to focus on now. The first was school opening and going back to school. The second service was hard to stay awake, especially if the preacher didn't put a little pep in the sermon or raise his voice. This was when I had to keep hunching the person sitting on either side of me. I wanted to hear what the preacher would say about God and his son Jesus. Also, what he would say about the Revival.

All he said about the Revival was when it would start tomorrow night. He asked everybody to pray for the preacher Reverend Rogers, the weekly preacher. He also asked everybody to fast and come early for a donation before the Revival time. He reminded us not to forget to pray all day for the Revival that God would save all who needed salvation.

I was very happy to hear his last remarks. It sounded like he was talking about me who needed salvation. For the last three years, I had really survived by depending on Jesus to help me in everything I did. I prayed and thanked God for his guidance before I made any decisions. I waited to hear God's voice on what to do. Sometimes I wanted to be different, but I always obeyed the voice. Every time I didn't obey the voice, there would be incidents that let me know I was wrong about not obeying the voice.

At eleven years old, I heard the voice Monday night telling me to go to the mourners' bench, but because of the church's rules that you had to be twelve, I hesitated. Again I watched my peers, all twelve years old, go to the mourners' bench. When all had gone, there was still room. I looked desperately at the space as the church began to sing. I got up quickly and rushed to the space. I kneeled and put my head down in my hands on the bench.

I thought one of the women would pull me up and take me to my seat. To my surprise, this did not happen.

Immediately, I started to pray, "Oh Lord, help me not to be picked on. Let the children in my class like me and let them stop laughing at my clothes. Thank you, Lord, for helping me to accept my mother's death. I know she is in heaven with you and has no more pain or sickness. Thank you for letting my daddy live and take care of us. Thank you, Lord, for my brothers and sisters. By that time, I felt somebody's hand on my shoulders. I heard a voice saying, "God is listening, and he heard you ask him to save you."

Since eight years old, after the toilet experience, I thought I had put all this behind me. I was learning to deal with my troubles. God knew what I needed, and he turned lose all the things that had bothered me for these past years. My prayer point changed to, "Save me, Jesus save me." I was as sincere as I could be, with no embarrassment or shame. Tears began to run down my cheek, but I didn't care, and in the twinkle of an eye, my voice got louder and louder. Literally, my mind and body took me to a beautiful place where I was happy with unspeakable joy.

When I came back from where I went, I praised God, shouting with a dancing rhythm. Others were also shouting and praising, both the mourners and some adults. The Holy Spirit had come in and poured out into the majority of the church. What a glorious Hallelujah time! Kids say I was in heaven, but if heaven is anything like where the spirit took me, I surely want to go there when I die. If I had not subconsciously accepted my mother's death, I was sure I had now. What a place to be if for a short time.

Tuesday night, all the mourners who did not get saved were asked to come back and sit on the front pew. The sermon was very short but to the point. The scripture and the subject of the message have left my remembrance, but I do remember the message because it answered the question I needed. God sent his son to earth to give his life for the sin of the world. He died on the cross with all our sins in his body.

They put him in a borrowed tomb and guarded the tomb because he had said to his disciples and many others that he wanted to be killed and buried, but in three days, he would rise again. The priest and other leaders didn't believe he could rise from the grave but believed his disciples would take his body and they would say that he arose. Guards didn't see or hear anything when they discovered that Jesus was not in the tomb.

They were afraid of what the leaders would do to them. They made up a tale to clear their intentions. Matthew 28: 1- 15

## Jesus Has Risen

After the Sabbath, at dawn on the first day of the week, Mary Magdalene and the other Mary went to look at the tomb. There was a violent earthquake, for an angel of the Lord came down from heaven and, going to the tomb, rolled back the stone and sat on it. His appearance was like lightning, and his clothes were white as snow. The guards were so afraid of him that they shook and became like dead men. The angel said to the women, "Do not be afraid, for I know that you are looking for Jesus, who was crucified.

He is not here; he has risen, just as he said. Come and see the place where he lay. Then go quickly and tell his disciples: 'He has risen from the dead and is going ahead of you into Galilee. There you will see him.' Now I have told you." So the women hurried away from the tomb, afraid yet filled with joy, and ran to tell his disciples.

Suddenly Jesus met them. "Greetings," he said. They came to him, clasped his feet and worshiped him. Then Jesus said to them, "Do not be afraid. Go and tell my brothers to go to Galilee; there they will see me."

## The Guards' Report

While the women were on their way, some of the guards went into the city and reported to the chief priests everything that had happened. When the chief priests had met with the elders and devised a plan, they gave the soldiers a large sum of money, telling them, "You are to say, 'His disciples came during the night and stole him away while we were asleep.'

If this report gets to the governor, we will satisfy him and keep you out of trouble." So the soldiers took the money and did as they were instructed. And this story has been widely circulated among the Jews to this very day.

Jesus showed himself to Mary. The women went to the tomb to anoint his body. When they found an empty tomb, an angel said to them, "He is not here for He has risen as he said." Then two disciples and Mary Magdalene also went to the tomb. Even his disciples questioned his presence, so he proved to them that he is alive and not a ghost as some thought. He told them, "I'm on my way to prepare a place for you; where I am there, you will be also."

The preacher stated and made it clear that to be where Jesus is, you had to live right and be saved, washed in the blood of the Lamb. I'm sure that the place I went on Sunday night as I was praising and shouting is the place Jesus went to be with his father. There would be no place on earth like the place, even if it was transformed for a short time. The Revival continued throughout the week. At the end of the week, all the mourners had confessed salvation.

The baptism was scheduled for the following Saturday, a week later. All of the candidates were called to go to school every day, but we never talked about what had transpired in our lives. Most of the candidates in the school were my cousins, and we stayed away from the students who were not going to our church.

I only told Ruth who became interested in me after I had the incident with the apple. I can't say she was a friend who was nice to me. I helped her with her spelling some days at lunchtime. Ruth lived near the school and always went home for lunch. Most of the bus riders would eat in the same place every day. There was an old church bench from the church next door. Next door means that the church was not our church, but a different denomination within a stone throw of the school.

The church put several pews outside near the woods. We asked our teacher if we could have one. She contacted the church leaders, and they agreed that we could have two of them. We were like ants carrying a big piece of bread trying to move the bench to the end of the school building. However, we no longer had to sit on the ground to eat our lunch.

Ruth asked me one day, with nobody else hearing her, "What is wrong? You've been quiet and acting strange this week. I told my mother about you, so she wanted me to bring you to our house if you would like to come." I told her; "I will have to ask my daddy if it would be all right."

I told my sister Marie, and she said she would ask daddy for me. This is the season that daddy was at the mill at night and was not at home when we left for school. Marie said, "I think it would be all right. I will take the blame if it's not alright." Since Marie was older, daddy and Marie had a better relationship and she stood up to daddy about whipping us so much. "Let me do the discipline.

You hold me responsible for everything anyway." Dad stopped whipping us for every little thing, and Marie started telling him who was to blame for any problems we had. It's only the person responsible for whatever happened got whipped. Sometimes Marie would scold us and threaten to tell daddy on us, but she never did. Trust was what our daddy needed, and he was happier and relieved after he began to trust. I went home with Ruth, and her mother was happy to see me.

She said, "Ruth has been telling me about you and how Delilah and Hellen had been picking on you. I told my sister, Queenie, who is their mother, about the problem. "Things are better for you?" "They are," I said. She continued, "Ruth thought you were having some problems this week. Is there anything you want to tell me about? I can help you with it." "No," I said, looking away from her. "Do you know?" she said, pulling me over to where she had sat in a chair at the kitchen table, "young woman," then I knew what her concern was and immediately found a voice and said, "I know about that.

I have not started yet." "Want something to eat?" she asked, looking at my lunch bucket, "you can eat with Ruth if you like." "No, thank you," I said, "I have my lunch from home."

Ruth saw that I had a sausage biscuit, and she wanted to share her grilled cheese sandwich as a swap for part of my sausage biscuit, so we shared. When we finished eating, Mrs. Becton went to the oven, took out two sweet potatoes, handed me one, and said, "Careful because they are really hot." I put my potato in my lunch bucket and said I would eat it later. "Mrs. Becton," I said, "thank you for the potatoes and for inviting me, but I'm not having any problem. I got saved this week and will be baptized next Sunday."

She grabbed me in her arms with a real tight hug. "Oh!" she said with a loud, exciting voice, "You got saved?" "Yes," I said. "Did your church hold their Revival last week?" "Yes, it ended Friday." "I've been talking to Ruth about being saved when our church holds their Revival next spring," she said. "She will be twelve then. Are you twelve?" she said. "I'm eleven," I said, "but I didn't want to wait for another year." "That's all right," she said, "for I think you are more mature than eleven. You have had to grow up being tough." Ruth and I walked back to the school.

We got back just before the bell rang to start class. I was very excited. I got home and told Marie Marjorie about my new experience and visit. I told Mae Ann about it on the bus. She said, "Did you tell her I got saved?" "No," I explained, "I had a hard time telling her about myself." Homework and studying went quickly, and we finished our chores in a jiffy. All my family seem to have a light shining in a dark place.

The Revival was really a blessing to my family and our neighborhood. The bus ride to and from school became a joy instead of the dread that it once was. And the bus driver was so relaxed with his driving he missed most of the bumps on the road, which made the trip even more enjoyable. Instead of talking and yelling at one another across the Isles, most of the students started doing their homework. I couldn't wait until Saturday.

Eddie and the church's deacons had gone to the creek to check out a good place to have the Baptism and to do some work on the road to the creek. Mae Ann was just as excited as I was. We couldn't sleep at night. We would keep whispering to each other, "Are you sleeping?" Of course, if we were sleeping, we would not hear the whispering. "Mae Ann," I would say, "be quiet, close your eyes and say your prayers again." Or she would ask me to count 100 backward. That did the trick. Before I could get to 70, I was already asleep. I remember thinking over and over what comes after 70.

Lilia's voice woke me up. She was calling each of us by name to wake us up to get ready for school. My brother Odell and Marjorie already went to check the rabbit boxes they had set in the woods the evening before. We were anxious to see if we had a rabbit or two. Mae Ann opened the shades out of the window and peeped out. "I see them coming," she said, "but I can't see if they have a rabbit." Marie called out, "You all need to hurry and get dressed.

Already have your water ready to bathe in." We brought the foot tub with the water in the bathroom. We washed our faces, arms, and private places. We hurried to get dressed and brush our teeth because there would not be enough time after breakfast before the bus came. Sometimes we had to still be chewing while running to the bus. The bus made a lot of noise over the dirt roads, so we could hear it before it got close to our house.

We could also hear the motor taking off after each stop because our community always got the used buses whenever the county bought new ones. We would each get our lunch buckets and books and head to the stop. Odell and Marjorie were the last to get on the bus because they got two rabbits and had to wash and change clothes in a hurry. As I munched my food on the bus.

I was happy there would be rabbits for dinner tonight. A big change of meat! We liked the change from pork every now and then. September is the month for hunting. We were blessed with many wild animals, such as rabbits, squirrels, raccoons, deer, bear, and wild turkeys for Thanksgiving. When a deer or a bear was killed by someone in the neighborhood, all the neighbors who wanted some would be welcomed. The meat had to be cooked and consumed quickly, for there was no refrigeration and only ice once a week.

When a truck would come along and sell blocks of ice, we had a hole in the ground lined with leaves and burlap bags on the Shady Side of the Barn to put the ice to keep it from melting so fast. The hole would be covered with leaves and a wooden lid on top. Most of the white people had ice boxes and store-bought ones, but nobody in our area had electricity. Everybody lit their houses with kerosene lamps, which were sold at the grocery store. We had only one lamp, which had to be moved from room to room according to what was being done. We had to do homework before dark because the light was not bright enough for all of us to study at once.

I would read at night by the light from the heater. The front of the heater had an air vent with several openings for the air to circulate. The light from the heater was brighter than the lamp. The problem was there was only space for one person. Your book had to be directly under the space where the light hit the floor. Another thing was you had to lay on the floor on your stomach to be able to read.

I often use the lamp because I like to read my class books ahead of the class assignment, and nobody else was reading. I was always on the floor in front of the heater. You might think that with the air vent giving out light, we might have some illumination. The vent was forced to go to the back of the heater toward the chimney. The air blowing down from the crack under the doors and the windows made the floor very cold.

I could stay there only long enough to read one chapter of a book.

This was my task every night because I had six subjects to cover. My coat kept me warm for a little while and then I felt the chill. In the night, the house would get cold enough that all the water brought into the house for the next day would freeze. We were always warm in the bed from our body heat, plus we all had enough quilts on each bed, three or four heavy ones. Most of the quilts were made from old clothes. Families, white and negro, would give us their hand me down. So many of the clothes would not fit anybody, so they were made into quilts and later on rugs.

The high school's home economics teacher taught a class in quilting and rug making, passed down from generation to generation. In fact, ladies would have a quilting party that lasted a week or two. It is long enough for all the ladies to have their materials ready for the last phase, all of their quilts done. Daddy bought mama a Singer sewing machine from the money made from the crops. She had gotten real good at making clothes and other things for the house. The family was so big it was hard for her to keep up with the sewing by hand. As soon as the girls in the family were tall enough to reach the paddle, which had to be operated by foot, they were taught how to sew.

"Lo, children are an heritage of the Lord:
and the fruit of the womb is his reward."
Psalm 127:3

# CHAPTER 4

# Marie and Little Mark

Marie had to drop out of school when mama died. But everybody else continued in school until it was necessary to help out and take the leadership role. All of us finished high school, except Marie. She had started courting and was ready to get married, but she waited until Marjorie finished high school before she got married.

She moved out of the home with her husband, Robert. He immediately got a sharecropping farm, and they were doing good. The first year she was married, she became pregnant with her first child. The baby was a little girl named Sally. They were doing well until the winter of the second year, December 1942. Robert was drafted into the army. He had to leave right away, not enough time to move his family or furniture out. Misty Brook, the landlord, agreed to keep the furniture in the house and take care of it until they get another sharecropper.

We went to help Marie move her personal things back to our home. Daddy decided we needed more room and made plans to add four rooms to the house. From daddy's big family, 6 boys and 6 girls, there were many different talents among them. One of the talents, Uncle Rubin, was a carpenter. He was very willing to lay the foundation and put up the raptors and the studs. Most of the men in the community gave a helping hand. By the time spring came, everybody was busy again and the house was ready.

We enjoyed the extra space. Instead of having a bed to ourselves, now we had a whole extra room. Dad took a room for himself, one of the front rooms. We all agreed that we would like a living room.

The other front room was the living room. Marie and Sally took a room, and Mae Ann, Elsa, and I, had a room. Unlike the old rooms, these rooms were big enough to have space after putting in two beds. Building the addition to the house and the uplift of the Revival and baptism uplifted our strength to a higher Peak. And we began to encourage others to live right and trust in God. Everything looked brighter, and daddy was not whipping so much. He could trust us more to do and be what he had taught.

Taking a girlfriend made some difference in this matter because whenever he rode away on his bicycle, his dress was different from work. He wore his Sunday hat and wouldn't tell anyone where he was going when asked. "Be good and mind your sisters," he would say. "I'll be back soon." We would never be awake when he got home. Maybe Marie would hear him come in because she slept in the room closest to him. He even stopped being so serious and would occasionally make a joke with us now.

He bought a .22 rifle and taught Odell how to shoot it. The hawks had gotten bad about catching our young chickens. They would sail around in the air for a while until they spotted the chick they wanted to get. What great divers they were! They would swoop down so fast we could barely get a glimpse. Every time they scooped down, they would get a chick. The first thing to protect them was to keep the hen house close until all of us were at home.

We took turns watching and waving a flag made of old clothes tied to a fishing pole.

The next safety measure was the .22 rifle. Of course, all who were old enough had to learn to shoot. It was a long time before I got a chance to learn. You had to be sure when you shot not to waste a bullet. We all learned to get him with the first shot. It would be a few days before spotting another. Whose time is it to shoot? Sometimes we would lose track of whose time it was. Odell, the one in charge, would shoot because there would not be time to figure out the problem. When things were over and there was another dead hawk, we all had to agree he was right.

He had to put in money to buy bullets, which didn't cost very much, but because we didn't have much money, it seemed like a lot. Once the chicks grew too large for the hawks to carry away, they stopped coming until spring when there was another hatchling of biddies or chicks. We all learned to shoot very well, and sometimes when we could afford the bullet, we would practice target shooting. All of us were expert shooters. Everybody could hit two of three shots. We had to be good in order to hit the hawks when they were flying.

Hawks were not the only things that we were good at shooting. We'd make deals to go squirrel hunting, one of us at a time. If we were not back in an hour, he came to the creek and called for us. Sometimes while hunting and doing other chores like gathering straw for the pig pens or cutting bean poles, or even picking blueberries, it is very easy to stray further than you think and get lost in some cases. I quickly learned the paths by breaking some bushes along the way or cutting a different tree from all the rest. Two squirrels would be sufficient for dinner, so the hunter tried to at least get two or more each time.

My family went through a lot when Hoover was president, and times were very tough for everybody, especially the Negroes. I was born right after President Roosevelt was elected, but before Roosevelt was elected a long time afterward you had to live off the land and learn to eat whatever extra God provided. Hunting and fishing were very helpful. God provided abundance fish, more than our family could eat. Daddy would always remember those who couldn't provide for themselves, especially his three widower sisters.

One only had a child, and he was blind. He also remembered the sick and other big families like ours. We would mud the ponds without a hose or rakes until the water was not clear and the fish would come to the top of the water to get air to breathe. We would then throw a bucket out and catch the fish.

All of us had our buckets and carried as many as we could. I, being the youngest at eleven, could not carry very many. We would walk along, thanking God for the bounty fish. When we took some to our neighbors, they would say, "Thanks," and we would say, "Give thanks to God, and you are welcome." God did miraculous work in our family; He increased our faith and we trusted his words. I can recall when I first started to listen to the preachers on Sunday at the church.

I was seven or eight while being picked on as it was called in my day. Wood started his sermon by telling the church what God would do if we, the church, would get our souls and lives right. I remember him saying, "You got to love everybody, you got to treat everybody right; if somebody harms you, you must forgive."

There were other things he mentioned; these are what I remembered, "How can I love somebody who is treating me badly? How can you treat someone right when they are pulling your hair, kicking your shins, and spitting on you? You must 'forgive.' What does forgiveness mean? Let me tell you what I learned when God, 'Jesus' saved me. I could say to my enemy, "You might have pretty clothes, hair with ribbons, and bows, but I've got 'Jesus,' and he is more than all the world to me." I heard that in a sermon at church.

Some girls that were bothering me would look at me very seriously and ask, "What is that? What is Jesus?" they asked, as if Jesus was a material thing. "It's not what? It is Who? He is." To get over on them and to let them know that I knew something that they didn't know. I smiled and said, "He is my savior!" One girl, began to ask other questions and I told her to go and ask her mama.

It took me a few years to learn to live right, treat everybody right, and forgive.

I felt special over my peers and older sisters because I was blessed with everything I did. I was a straight-A student, but I had to study hard. The teacher in the 5th through 8th-grade room was paying more attention to me; it made me relax more. She would call on me to help the other students when they didn't understand the direction. She would also ask me to call the spelling words to another grade level, check the papers, put the mist word on the blackboard, and dust the blackboard eraser. The eraser chalk dust is dim when used to erase work or writing from the blackboard. They needed to be cleaned daily or they would not erase very well the next day.

## Little Mark

One day, during summer vacation, my older cousin, Mark Jr. (we called him little Mark), asked daddy to allow me to help his wife, who had given birth to twins, a boy and a girl. His job would not allow him to take off work. There were two other small children to take care of. Boy, did I feel special that day. He asked for me instead of one of the older sisters because they could go to the field and do better work than me.

And another reason was I had to take care of my three sisters and brother, plus three cousins so their mama could work and earn money to support the family. Mark Jr. had observed my caretaking skills from their home while working on Uncle Mark's farm the year before. He said, "This girl has a lot of talent."

I had a lot of practice with my dolls in my playhouse under the house. Daddy reluctantly let me go, for this was definitely a case of need. I learned how to take care of real babies. Taking care of the other three children made it possible for their mother to do what needed to be done when I'm not there. These days, when a woman had a baby, they had to stay in bed for nine days before she was allowed to get up and do anything. She told me what to do, and I did it. Being only six when mama died, I had not taken care of a newborn, although I had seen the diaper and band put on around the baby by our neighbor.

The twins had not been named when I came to the house to finish her papers to be filled at the courthouse and give the mama and the babies a final check-up. Kathy asked me to help her name the twins. I named them Darnell and Denise. What a great and rewarding experience this was. God was at work in my life because I knew how to clean house, cook, bathe, and dress children. I also knew how to wash and hang clothes. I was always eager to learn at home by helping. God gave me a desire to help others and be sympathetic toward others' troubles and problems.

When little Mark came home, he was surprised and expressed it in such a way I knew he was appreciative. He went in to greet Kathy and to check on the babies. He was excited that everybody had already eaten, and the other children were bathed and dressed for bed. "I had a hard day," he explained, "the oxen would not behave, so it took one man to continue managing them." He worked in the woods. Oxen was used to pull the logs out of the woods so they could be loaded onto a wagon to take to the Sawmill.

When the oxen worked together and each pulled together, it made the work easier. One would not listen to the directions by the driver. It made the other oxen work harder and sometimes tangle the logs up in the standing trees or bushes. The oxen are very intelligent and can be trained to pull the logs out of the woods without anyone helping. The direction would be given, and they obeyed orders. I understood when little Mark said he had a rough day.

All the work I did made me very happy. He started toward the kitchen and then looked back at me and smiled. He said, "This is the first time in months that I don't have to come home and cook and take care of children. Thank you and God bless you. Will you come back tomorrow?" "Yes, I will. I will be here at the same time as today." All at once, my tiredness left me, and I began to skip instead of walking. Thank you God for giving me the strength, knowledge, and know-how to get things done. Thank you for daddy and my older sisters teaching us how to work and for you giving us the mind to help others. Thank you for using me today to help somebody who needed my help.

Little Mark had three sisters at home with his daddy and stepmom. He knew not to ask them to help him because they were lazy. I hate to say that, but they had not learned the work habits as we did. Thank God for his inspiration, love, and willingness instilled in my family.

Sometimes I think, would we be different if momma was here? Then I would know she would stand by her strict rules, and we would obey. We would be the same. The prayer and thought took me all the way home in such a short time. At the dinner table, after everybody was served, daddy began to ask about our day. The day went well for my older sisters. They took care of the tobacco plantation, removing the grass and all.

They will be going back the next day and the rest of the week. I was next, and I was so excited to talk about all the work I had done. When I mentioned bathing the babies, everybody gasped with unbelief. "How did you know what to do?" one of my siblings asked. "Well, I've been watching when you did it to Ruth and I practiced with my dolls in my playhouse. The only thing was my dolls didn't wiggle and move about when I played with them.

These babies cried and kicked their feet and threw their arms around. I finally had to put them on the floor to get the job done."

Kathy said that was a good idea. Everybody was happy for me and said they didn't expect me to get so much done. "The Lord was with me," I said, "so I did what needed to be done." I couldn't tell why, but I didn't mention making a fire in the stove two times. Dad said, "God will richly bless you," and continued asking Odell about his work. Marie said, "Don't anyone want to hear about what I've done today?" "We see what you've done and we're also tasting this scrumptious dinner," Dad said. Even though I had become tired after eating, I had to help Marie with the dishes.

We went to bed early every night, right after dinner, as soon as everybody got a bath. There was no argument about going to bed, unlike today with the younger generation. We worked from sun to sun doing hard work and then the daily chores; it was easier to get in bed as soon as possible. There were no sleepless nights. Even if someone was snoring, you would listen to the rhythm and fall asleep.

Morning came quickly, even if it was in the summertime. The sun came up at about 5:30am or 6:00am. As soon as it was daylight, everybody had breakfast and morning devotion. We took turns saying the prayer and a bible verse. Never the same one that was said yesterday. That kept us busy studying the Bible to get new ones. We had devotion every morning in primary classes at school: Pledge of Allegiance, The Lord's Prayer, a bible verse, and the national anthem.

Sometimes we would sing The Negro national anthem. It was always something to learn. I'm happy there was. Today, the young generation probably does not know what the Negro national anthem is because after the schools were integrated, these things were lost. I tried to teach my children and grandchildren some of these things I learned and thought they ought to know, but to no avail, for they were learning things that I don't have average knowledge of.

"Before I formed thee in the belly I knew
thee; and before thou camest forth out of
the womb I sanctified thee."
Jeremiah 1:5

# CHAPTER 5

## Sunday school and the call to preach

When I was twelve years old, I was selected to teach the children's Sunday school class. As a young person, I can't say I was a child or adult because neither of these fit my ability and talents. My determination to please and do my best at every task and my dependents and trust in God made my jobs come easy and of some perfection. All of my siblings were equally able to manage their tasks as I was because we all had the same training. We were self-disciplined, an appreciation for the opportunities that God granted us to make the best and do our best with every circumstance that we were afforded.

No job was too hard or too little that we didn't eagerly take advantage of. We knew that we had to give daddy half of everything we made. Daddy would sometimes test us to see if we were keeping up with who gets the odd penny. We would make a big fuss over just $0.01. How much money we made and saved depended on what remained after buying our school clothes. Yes, we had to be responsible for our clothes as soon as we were old and smart enough to work for pay. The pay was not much, but it was sufficient for the times. We're also reminded that it's not what you make but what you save that counts. I'm happy today that I learned that rule early in life because it is what I live by today.

We learned to be careful about what we need and what we want. God can help you, as the apostle Paul said, "I learned to be content in my every situation." Another good thing I learned early in life is our brother Odell would say, "Nobody can control how you feel or how you act. God has given each one the choice and ability to control ourselves. You can't help how someone treats you, but you can control how you treat them."

It's alright to get mad, but staying angry or upset is not alright. You can choose to change how you feel about every situation. If you choose to stay upset, you only hurt yourself. You do not hurt anybody else. Choosing to get rid of the ugly, unpleasant feelings puts a smile on your face and forgiveness in your heart. Saying I'm sorry if you are not at fault lessens your stress and makes you feel good. Asking God to help the enemy to do right, praying a forgiving prayer and trusting God to work the problem out with you and the hostile one, talking about the problem, and coming to an agreement to settle the matter keeps your heart at peace.

I've never had any trouble agreeing with my peers. God will work it out if you only believe. My Sunday school class grew after I started teaching. Merely because of my age and energy and because the previous teacher was an elderly lady and didn't have the patience to put up with all the squirming and wiggling. It was hard to keep their attention for an hour when they had not started school. The way I would keep their attention is that you make the learning from the book very short and only give them one thing to memorize. Have them repeat after you; things like: The Lord's Prayer, bedside prayer, table Grace and certain other things that little ones need to know.

For the last part of the day, I would take them outside for a walk around the church. They had to learn to walk in a line to make it exciting. A leader would be chosen each Sunday. When we finished the walk, each child would tell me something they saw that God made, but it didn't take long before everybody pointed out things like the sky, trees, grass, birds, water in the ditch, the sun, and the wind. When asked, one boy said he made us.

"Oh yes," I said. When a little girl said, "My mommy and daddy made me." I could usually get away with saying, "Oh yes, that's right;" without being questioned. I had to go home to ask for help with this one. At twelve years old, nobody had told me about the birds and the bees. I was advised to tell them to stick to things we could see and touch. The class was very eager to please. They accepted what I said without question.

The class grew. Other parents started coming and bringing their children. It was hard not to disturb the youth class stationed on the opposite side of the church and the adult class beside the choir. Soon, the youth class was asked to move to the front of the church so we would not disturb their class.

I taught this class until I left the community. Every time I went back to the church for a visit, these little ones would call me their teacher. That's what I wanted to be, and that's what God gave me as one of my talents. Even though my grade was as good as could be, I never imagined going to college. Nobody encouraged me, including family members, neighbors, or teachers. My teachers knew I was capable of college because they always chose me to do extras like supervising the Glee club when no other teacher was available. I also practiced and supervised the drama and talent night program once every year.

We chose Tom Sawyer School and students played different parts. I wasn't given a part because of my mini day absent from school. Plus, how would I get to school at night? I was not supposed to come to the final week of rehearsal. However, some students were absent. Victor would send for me to act the part because I had been supervising and knew all the parts. The main student playing Tom Sawyer got chickenpox, so I had to take his place.

With just one day to study, I mastered all the actions. The only problem was speech. Whenever I had a problem, I would pray. This particular day, at school with all the practicing going on. I began to pray every time I had a break from the stage. "Our Father in heaven, if it is your will that I come to school on Friday night and act as Tom Sawyer, please make way for me to get here." The next time there was a break, I prayed and thanked God for hearing my prayer.

I believed that God heard me and that he would make a way for me.

When the practice was over, all the children met with the teacher so she could tell us what time to be at the school before time for the assembly. Shaking and afraid of who is directing and in charge, I asked my Aunt Sarah, my daddy's sister, to let me stay at their house and bring me to the school Friday night. Another problem was how I would get to Aunt Sarah's house, which was two miles from the school.

I prayed again. This time, I asked God to work out everything. There was no doubt in my mind that he could and would. There were no telephones in our area or the school area. No sooner after praying, my teacher answered a knock at the door, and it was Mrs. Jacobs asking him to drive me to my aunt's house. Uncle Thomas was excited to have me stay. I rode the school bus to her house on Friday, and she was waiting to greet me.

I was met with another problem; another student who had a part in the play was absent. I was a girl. We had a very small part at the end of the play. The only thing was when the play was over, I had to be very quick in changing my clothes from a girl to Tom Sawyer. I had to tuck my two long braids under my cap, pull up the skirt and put on pants, take off the blouse and put on another shirt with help from the director or any other staff member.

I would have missed the introduction of being Tom Sawyer. Uncle Thomas and Aunt Sarah were very happy to see me act in the play. They could not believe that the part was not assigned to me from the beginning. I had to change my voice from a girl to a boy.

The next time Uncle Thomas visited our home, passing by from church service, he told my family all about my acting and the excitement they had at the school with me. Their three children were all grown and either in school or working. And going to school filled the empty place in their hearts left by not having their children around.

For the next two years, I was very busy at school and home. The basketball coach, Mr. Adam, posted forms to all the high school classes to find girls interested in being on the team. I reluctantly took a form home to ask my daddy for permission to be on the team. "What if you get hurt?" was the first thing he said. "I'm not going to get hurt," I said. "What about uniforms?" was the next question. "The school provides them." "How will you get home after the games?" "All the games are during school hours; we will ride the bus to the games and my regular bus back home." He stood up and left the room without another word.

I filled out the form and went to Marjorie, the oldest sister at home. Marjorie had to be in charge because Marie had moved with her husband Claude after he returned from the Army. "What did daddy say?" she asked. "He just asked me some questions, and I answered all of them. He didn't say anything, just walked out." "What did he ask you?" I repeated all his questions and my answers to her, and she said, "He doesn't want to be responsible, but I think he doesn't care if you play." Marjorie signed the form stating she is my sister and has permitted me to play.

Of course, my prayer that day and every day for two years was, "Dear God, please protect me and all my teammates from getting hurt. Help us to play fair and do our best."

For two years, we had a winning team. When in high school, the basketball court was marked off, which meant you could not cross Center Line. Defense would only try to keep the opponent from scoring, rebounding, and getting the ball to their offensive team. There were three defenses and three offenses. I played both positions according to the school team we played. I can't take credit for what was done because I prayed throughout the game, "Lord, don't let me get hurt and let me play my best.

Just let that ball go in the net," and it would. When I played defense, my prayer would be, "Help me get the ball," and I would. Sometimes I would not have a chance to see the net and would just throw the ball toward the net, to the yelling of the crowd. I knew that it was an unusual basket.

Thank you, Lord, my God. I always remember to give thanks to God for answering my prayers, no matter what it was. I needed a pair of white tennis shoes. Knowing how daddy felt about my playing, I could not ask him to buy them. When I brought the problem to Marjorie, she was determined to help me. We entered the grocery store and all the stores had white tennis on the shoe rack. Daddy had given Marjorie and Odell permission to charge not more than $25 a month for anything we needed.

I tried on the shoes and they were tight. I'd rather have them too big than too small because they hurt my toes. "Two pairs of socks," Marjorie said, and that's what I did. The next day, when I dressed at the school before getting on the bus just before the end of the basketball season, my tennis shoes came apart from the sole. I brought them home and fix the sole by wiring the sole back with hairpins. At least, it was not dangerous for me.

Two members of another team we were playing laughed at my tennis shoes. It made me think of how I was teased when I was six years old. It brought back the way God had helped me through that ordeal. I put my hands on my side and said, "You are laughing now; I will be laughing when the game is over."

I prayed, "Hold me up, Lord." I knew that was all I needed to say. When the game was over, our team had the last laugh. Of course, we seriously greeted them and played a tough game, a good one. You can catch more flies with honey than with vinegar, hoping they learned from their mistakes. Always thank God for His word and faithfulness, and he will be with you always, even to the end of the Earth. He cares about every one of His children. If you think you are not His, you need to do something about it. While I was trusting and depending on God for every area and situation of my life, He decided he could depend on me. He had given me the courage and strength to trust him and his word.

I was moved one day on the school bus to read my bible while thanking Him for how he allowed my debate team to win. I heard this voice say, "I want you to preach my word just as strong and sure as what you did today." With a positive reason, my hair stood up on my head – the feeling you get when you are suddenly startled. My body shook with uncontrollable movement. "Preach," I said under my breath, not wanting anybody to hear me. "Preach," said the voice. Tears ran down my face and I tried to wipe them away before anybody noticed. When I look up at the person seated next to me she. She was wide awake and chatting loudly. I knew then that something very unusual was happening.

"Preach," I whispered. Preach? I only know one woman preacher; she is an older person. "I'm just a child, God. I'm in school. I play basketball and baseball. I know you'll help me do my best, should I preach?" I didn't hear from God or the voice anymore that day. It was time for me to get off the school bus. That experience was like no other I had before. Why did I not realize I was asking for an answer? The answer came a few days later. I was unable to eat and sleep. I didn't have a mind to read or study. "I don't know where to start, Lord," I prayed. I've been hearing, "Tell your daddy."

When I told my daddy, he gave me a look as if he had seen a ghost. "Fine," he said, "tell me all about it." I started from the beginning. I told him about the debate and how my team had won the tough debate. I told him about the voice I heard during my thanksgiving prayer in the bus. I told him how I questioned the voice repeatedly. "I'm sure of what God said to me," I concluded. He pause for a while, then looked up at me and said, "I've been hearing you teach Sunday school and how you correct and advise your siblings here at home.

To preach is a very different thing. I don't think what you are talking about is real." Then he said, standing up, putting his arms around me and hugging me tightly, which was very unusual for he never showed any affection to any of us, "God doesn't call women to preach!!!" My heart felt as if I would stop beating, and maybe it did stop for a while. Tears began to flow. He said, "That's why women are not strong enough to be a preacher."

What he said didn't stop me from crying, but it did make me go to God for help. My help came. I was asked to watch a first-grade class a few days later. The teacher was sick and had to leave school. In cases like this, one of the students, mostly seniors, would watch the class. I know in my case, God had made way for me not to doubt him and what he told me to do. I was reading a book to the class.

I would often explain what I had just read so that the children would understand it better. When I finished explaining and began to read, a little boy raised his hand and said, "Teacher." "Joey," I answered. "You sound just like a preacher!" That strange feeling came over me, and I could barely speak when I asked Joey, "What do you know about how a preacher sounds?" He answered, "Like you, except he is a man." I was sure, without a doubt, what God wanted me to do.

How can my daddy be sure that God, with all his wisdom, inexplicable power, omnipotent, omnipresent, omniscient powers, makes a mistake? How can I misjudge what I heard over and over again? Did I want to preach? The thought had not entered my mind; I was really enjoying the fellowship with God and what he was doing in me and through me. I never liked talking about myself because I don't want to sound boastful.

Sometimes some folks need to know who God is and what he can do. He can take a-nobody and make somebody out of that humble heart. Not many years earlier, I was angry, bitter, mad, upset, and felt like I had no friends at all. It was Jesus, God's son, who had mercy on me and let me know that His grace is sufficient for me. Now, the very one who was picking on me being mean and thought I was a nobody is asking for my help with her lessons because she was not as smart as the teachers made her out to be.

All through my life and still now, God has been my source of help and strength. I can always depend on him; he never lets me down. His love is greater than a mother or father. He is always near if we keep him in a clean and pure heart. I'm so glad I surrendered all to Jesus, or my mother and father could not do for me what God did through his son Jesus. I thank God for the trouble I had and the hardships I faced.

I know if I hold on to God's unchanging hand, God will keep me in his hands.

God made opportunities for me to do his will and work. You don't have to be in a church or behind a royster for God to use you. You just have to be willing and obedient. I learned later that my dad was obeying the rules of his church. I did not want to disobey my church rules, and I didn't have to. God worked out the plan, so I was able and willing to do what he called me out to do. I love to say that when I don't know what to do, I allow God's will to be done. His will was done for me all through my life.

I was troubled with sickness that nobody knew what the problem was. Sometimes my family believed I was pretending to be sick so I could get out of work. When this happened, I would pray and get the work done but not as best as everybody else. After I was married and went to the doctor, I discovered that I am allergic to a lot of things, including tobacco, especially dried tobacco and cigarette smoke. I was allergic to all kinds of smoke and most of my neighborhood burned trash and wood in the cookstove and heaters. If the smoke went up into the air, it was fine. When the wind caused it to come down to the ground level, that was when I had problems.

After I was married, we had to stop burning kerosene for heat, and when I was growing up, kerosene was the only light we had. We had to stop hanging clothes on the line because of the pollen from the trees and flowering weeds, especially the buzz from the dandelions, which is a year-round weed. I glorify God for His all-knowing, mercy, and grace. God let me suffer enough to always pray, depend, and trust him. But I could always stand the test with God's help.

I never went to a doctor until I got pregnant the first time, so my family was not educated about the effects of the body or medicines. My daddy's mother was an Indian and knew a lot about herbs and natural remedies. She knew what was good for headaches, stomach problems, and high blood pressure. If there was diabetes or cancer during that time, nobody knew about it.

My uncle Ruben could fix a cut when it needed stitches. He would use an ordinary needle for sewing and strings from what we called beargrass which he kept in a half gallon jar, which he said was sterilized. He would heat the needle and let it cool, then he would stitch the cut with one or two people holding the part to be sewn. I know all this because I had to get my finger sewn. Uncle Ruben doctored my finger by putting salt and what else on it. I didn't look because the salt hurts so much. I closed my eyes and started to pray. Another thing that got me through was thinking about what daddy would do to me for disobeying him.

For a long time on Sunday mornings, my siblings and I would prepare for Sunday school early so that we could go to Clara's house to help her get ready for church. Clara was crippled since young adulthood. She had one son, an only child, Charlie, who lost his eyesight when he was a teenager. Charlie was sent to a blind school to learn how to take care of himself and help Clara do things around the house. He learned a trade of weaving.

He could make baskets, flower pots, belts, but his biggest job was putting the bottom in chairs. Oh yes, chairs; mostly dining room and even rocking chairs; Wicker is what it was called. Charlie had no problem putting in the Wicker, but he could not get the Wicker out of the chairs when a customer brought him work.

In hindsight, it would have been easier for him to tell the customer to take the Wicker out of the chairs before they brought them to him. My siblings and I would go early to take out the Wickers from the chairs before Sunday school so that he could work during the week to make money. My daddy found out what we were doing and asked us not to do this on Sundays. "Go another day," he said, "I don't want you working on Sunday." When we got to Aunt Clara's house, we told Charlie what daddy had said. He begged us to do just two chairs so he could get them back to the customer as promised.

My siblings said they would not take the wig out of the chairs. I was so sorry for him and decided to do just one chair, making an excuse for my daddy's suggestion of working on Sunday. The first time I raised a big butcher knife to cut the Wicker out, it came down on the middle finger of my left hand, cutting the first joint through. The only thing holding the tip of my finger was the skin. It didn't bleed much at first.

Somebody ran to tell Clara what had happened. She immediately read from the 16th chapter of Ezekiel 6-8, and the blood stopped. She put on some spider webs from under the corner of the porch, and it made it feel better. I was determined not to cry, even though it hurt badly. She wrapped it tightly with a clean white cloth, and I was able to teach my Sunday school class.

It didn't hurt much because I prayed and asked God to forgive me for not being obedient to daddy's request. Also, I prayed, "God, thank you for taking away the pain. Please, heal my finger. All was almost well until I went to bed at night. I woke up yelling because the pain was so great; I could not bear it. Daddy found out what I had done and didn't argue or scold any of us for what happened. After looking at the cut, he just said, "Ruben can fix it. Go early tomorrow before he goes to work.

Ruben was daddy's brother. When daylight came on Monday morning, Odell and Lilia went with me. Uncle Ruben started the process I narrated in the previous section. Then he stopped and said,

"Let us pray." I had already been praying, but I said out loud, "Yes." We prayed, and I believed my finger would be alright. I said out loud thanks to God, Uncle Ruben, Odell, and Lilia. Every evening, I had to go to Uncle Ruben to wash my finger and put on new bandages. About nine weeks later, I didn't have to change the bandages anymore. When it was time to take out the bandage the next day, Uncle Rueben took out the stitches and all was well.

Two lessons I'd learned from this ordeal: not to disobey daddy and not to work on Sundays. These two were lifelong guides and have helped shape my life in the right way. My siblings went on Monday to help Charlie, and when the work on the farm got busier, we went whenever we had a short day of work. Not all of us went at the same time, whoever was free to do it could go. We were glad to help him and whoever asked us for help. Not just because we would be blessed later in life but because someone needed our help. This was one of daddy's teachings, "The more you give, the more is given unto you." We were already blessed because we were healthy and happy, at least most of the time.

My finger healed with barely a scar. It was well enough for me to go blueberry picking in the woods next to our house. These fruits added to our food and money supply. They were ripe before any other fruits, and we had plum, apple, peach, and pear trees in our orchard. Also, there were wild strawberries along the side of the road. They were free for all. Anyone smart enough to pick them got a special treat. We would pick enough for our family to eat and would have some to sell to the white people who were too proud to pick for themselves.

With this money, we could buy something special from the store, like bath soap or karo syrup to sweeten the berries. Sugar was rationed for a long time, and the price was so high we couldn't afford to buy it. Rationing meant that every person in the household got a coupon for one pound of sugar per month. We had at least ten people in our household, sometimes more. We never used all of our coupons because of the price, so we had a coupon to trade to the rich for flour, coffee, and other items we could not afford to buy.

"To everything there is a season, and a time to every purpose under the heaven."
Ecclesiastes 3:1

# CHAPTER 6

## *Life continues*

Daddy always planted cane with which he made molasses. So we had plenty of sweets to make gingerbread and cookies. At the bottom of the Barrow where the molasses were stored would be sugar, but we could not get it until all the molasses were gone. Every year, the molasses was made and shared with the neighbors. Most of the men in the community looked forward to the time, for that meant their household would be supplied for a while.

A 50-gallon barrel would last our family for a year, from one season until the next season. The men who helped chop down the stalks and carry them to the barn got 10 gallons, or however much they could put in the cans they brought. Of course, if they gave out before harvest time, they could always come and get a gallon at a time at the harvesting.

The hogs would be turned loose in the cane fields to feed on the scrapings that were left from the cutting. This was a good time for them to get fat before killing time. Peanuts were also planted between the cane before letting the hogs in. We would dig the peanuts, wash and dry them for winter and snacks, but not before we would boil a pot, a wash pot full of green peanuts. We had only three acres of fields, so daddy used his godly wisdom to make the best of it all.

Corn was planted in about one acre, and when the corn was tasseled, where the peas were planted between each stalk of corn.

The peas would grow and run up the stalk of corn, which made it easy to pick. When these peas were picked, some of them were deep green and filled out. Some were picked for roasting to be eaten with the corn.

When I was old enough, my sisters and I would can some jars. There would be peas in the winter months, and when the frost came in the fall, we would pick the rest of the peas that had dried and prepare them for the winter. The dried peas and beans that were planted in the garden had to be put in a cloth bag, and we would really enjoy beating them with a stick to make them pop out of the holes. When the hose was removed, the peas and the beans were each ready for wind calling rending winnowing is when you pour the peas or beans from one pale into the other on a windy day. This process causes all the husk and the trash to be blown away. This process cleans the beans.

We also enjoyed doing this because we made it fun. These foods lasted all winter and we have some to share with our neighbors. I am happy that I was taught how to provide for my family. What I learned as a member of the Matthew's family and still use today include sewing, and after I married and left home, I made my clothes, and I made them handsome. And when my children were small, I made their clothes too, boys and girls. I didn't have a public job, so I could save money by doing the things I learned at home.

I made a garden and planted all the things that daddy had planted. I didn't have to plant as much because my family number was not as large. I started the gardening using a hoe, but when Jurius, my husband, saw what I was doing, he borrowed his dad's mule and plow and made the rows up for me. I planted in the spring, summer, and fall. The fall garden consisted of things that would last all winter long. They were not only for my family but for some of the neighbors and the extended family members who wanted some. I used the same habits I learned growing up. When one really learns a lesson and life skills, it is not so easy to strike away from them. Just as bad habits are hard to break.

In high school, I was a member of the four H club, which taught about cooking, canning, and sewing. This club gave its members an opportunity to exhibit and show what they've learned throughout the years of being a member. I always looked forward to the time we had to exhibit and prepare my projects in advance and kept them in my room to ensure they were safe. When it was time to can through, I always canned in quart jars, for that was what the exhibition required. My family being large, always canned in half gallon jars.

Blueberries and peaches were my fruit the first year when I was a freshman. String beans or green beans and burdock beans were my vegetables. After this year, I was sure that my team would have won along with my fruit and vegetables. My apron won first place in sewing. I had made ruffles for the bottom, cut out a red heart, sewed it all by hand, and put it on the bib of the apron. Seeing some of the exhibits that won first place and second place, I was very sure I could have won.

My sophomore year was very challenging. Most of the girls like me learned some skills. I made a jacket for a project this time and as the saying goes, I "bit off more than I could chew". The teacher taught us how to use a sewing machine, and our project had to be sewn with the machine. The biggest problem was that we had only one machine, and waiting for your turn was very time-consuming. I had already cut my jacket, so there was nothing I could do but wait. All the work had to be done at school. We had a sewing machine at home that belonged to mama. I was tempted to cheat and take my jacket home too, but I remembered every time I broke one of the golden rules, I got in trouble.

When one of the girls took her pants home and finished them, it looked very good. When Mrs. Jones, our home economics teacher, questioned her about that and how she finished the pants without being assigned a time at the sewing machine, I knew she was in trouble. I began thanking God that he gave me the wisdom not to cheat. Mrs. Jones made her take out all the sewing that she did at home. She had to start from the beginning. Mrs. Jones gave all the other girls permission to help her take out the stitches because she would not have enough time to finish the project before show time if she didn't get help.

My jacket won second place, and I was very pleased. I was glad to finish. During the second semester, the girls had to take agriculture for the quarter of the year, and the boys had to take home economics. This was a whiz for me because I had already been doing these things on the farm. The class was about farm animals, chickens, pigs, cows, ducks, sheep, etc. We didn't have all these animals, but I had seen them and come in contact with them on other farms that I worked on.

Identifying tools was very easy, but some girls didn't know a wrench from a screwdriver. I aced this class and was able to help others pass also. Hard work and being kept busy as a way of living paid off and made my schoolwork easier. There were so many days we missed school to work on the farm. Some days we missed because the school bus would get stuck in the mud. All the roads in our area were dirt or gravel roads no pavements, and when it rained a lot or snowed, the bus would not run; if it did, it might get stuck.

Sometimes all of the children would get out of the bus and push until it was free. A lot of the children would get muddy from the spinning wheels, other times we would get off the bus and walk to school or back home, whichever was closer; there were no telephones either at home or school. By chance, someone who lived nearby might have a truck and would let the school know what has happened. Sometimes another bus would be sent to take us to the school, depending on how muddy the roads were.

Much of the time, we would wait for the bus until farmers would come and put down brushes in front of the tires and the wheels would get traction and help us get freed. We would miss half a day from school and always had to catch up on work on our own.

I missed so many days that I learned to always read and study ahead in all my subjects. Homework was for me every day. School or not, reading was one of my strong points from first grade onward. I still read a lot. I read all the directions on my medicine and everything that has an ingredient notice. Reading the nutrition facts helped me decide if I should buy the product or not. The two ingredients I mostly pay attention to is salt and sugar and sometimes how many calories in total fat. Also, I want to see how many good ingredients are in a product: vitamins, proteins, fiber etc. It pays to know what you're putting in your body at all times. It could save you a trip to the doctors.

My junior year was unforgettable. This was the year for our first term paper. I had already decided what I was going to write about. My summer was just the same old things: work, work, and more. However, this was the year that daddy got married and brought his new wife and mother home for us. She was someone we had met on several occasions but didn't know he was courting her. Very seldom did he even joke about her. Daddy promised not to marry; not really a promise, just a statement.

I was the oldest at home at this time. All my older siblings had married or left home, usually they moved to the northern states to find work. Our brother Wilbert had been drafted into the army. Odell had lived with us when he first married but had moved into a house of his own. Marjorie married and moved out. Mae and Lilia went to New York. They were invited to come and stay with Wilbert's mother, who had recently moved there for work and found that work in diaspora was plentiful.

The oldest at home had to step up and be the responsible one, taking charge of the cooking. I did the washing and planned household duties. As the woman of the house, my sisters Marjorie and Lilia ensured me that I could do what needed to be done or else they would not go. "We will make sure you get the things you need for school and all the other sisters and brothers also."

I worked hard in the evening after school to make sure everything was ready for the next day. Our stepmother Sarah was very supportive in helping to cook breakfast and getting the younger ones ready for school. Daddy thought it was too much for her to do the washing for the family, so she only washed for the two youngest kids. She was very helpful in keeping the house clean, except for our bedrooms, which each of us had our own room as everybody else moved out.

We got a new washer and dryer for the Home Economics class, and the teacher asked for volunteers to bring clothes from home so we could learn how to separate clothes and how to use the machine. I already knew how to separate clothes because I had been doing the washing at home for a long time. But I raised my hand to bring clothes and all the other girls agreed that I bring the clothes. They knew that I spent all day on Saturdays washing, and if the weather was bad, I couldn't get it done. There was no other family who didn't have a mother to do the washing.

I believed that God would make a way for me. I couldn't read and do all my homework when I was responsible for the house and family chores. I have not mentioned it in a while, but I still prayed about everything and praised and thanked God for how he would work things out for me.

My stepmother was born and raised in a little place named Hallandale near the East Coast of the Atlantic Ocean. Her father was ill, and we went to see him as often as we could. We would clean the house, wash, cook a meal, and visit other family members. I met Jurius during one of our visits. On Sunday morning, we went to church with him while daddy, Tom, and Miss Cera went shopping for her father's weekly needs. We met several other young people who stood back and looked at us strangely. It was different the next time we went. The young people were more polite and introduced themselves, and we talked about school and other things. Most of the young people were family to Cera. In fact, most of her brothers and a sister lived there.

We visited several family homes and had dinner at a different home each time we visited. There was a boy who liked me, and we walked from church to the house where we were to eat dinner. Jeff was not a member of the family and was a brilliant and polite fellow. He told me he lived with his grandparents. His mother had died, and his father went north for work to help take care of his parents. They had lost contact and had not heard from him in a couple of years.

He was a school bus driver and a senior in high school. I understood his situation; it was a little worse than mine because I had a dad at home who was helping and teaching us how to survive. I never got a chance to talk with Jeff again because I didn't go to Hallandale again for a long time.

Miss Cera and her brother Mark worked out a plan for someone in the family to take care of her father. Her son, who used to drive us to Hallanville, got a job that made it inconvenient for him to drive the distance on weekends. Cera's sister, Susie, would come to report on their daddy's progress, and Jurius came along with them. We thought we were cousins because my dad married his relation, but he discovered we were not keen. I had already asked him if he wanted to go to the prom with me, and he wasn't sure. I told him cousins or not, he would have to, he would have a good time because he loved to dance and was a good dancer.

Finding out we were not cousins put a damper on things for me. I had told him I could not dance except the Walt, which all the juniors and seniors had to be taught for the opening dance. This dance featured the boy in the senior class and the girl in the junior class with the highest grades. Nobody knew who that would be until the night of the prom. That was the first thing to be announced, and my name was called.

I can't say I was surprised when I knew all my grades were As. I couldn't think of anybody whose grades were better. The only way somebody would beat me would be by popularity. The teachers were fair in their judgment, and even then, I would have been OK with Linda being chosen, except it would not have been fair.

I didn't have much time, but I slipped in a short prayer and thanked God for letting the teacher be honest and fair. I also thanked God for Lilia sending me an outfit. She had sent me a deep pink dress with short sleeves and a skirt that was popular in those days. Long gloves up to the elbows, a pink bow with a side comb attached for my hair, a pair of silver slippers, and a silver purse with a long strap.

Of course, a necklace and earrings of silver and diamonds were not real diamonds, but to me, they were. These were my first jewelry earrings at all. My cousin Rose did my hair. Two braids, one on each side, except this time she combed the hair up and twisted the braids on top of my head. The pink hair bow was fitted in front, making me look like a princess if I say so myself.

I was not the only one who went ahhhh when I slipped out from behind the crowd. Everybody was surprised, even the teachers, for they knew how I struggled with wearing homemade and hand-me down clothes. I never felt less dressed after the incidents of being laughed at and teased in the first and second grades. I know we were doing our best, and my clothes were always clean and ironed. Nobody could laugh at me now; I felt so beautiful and special.

Thank God for sisters who wanted me to have better than they had. My prayers went up to God the very minute I opened the package that came through the mail and saw what was in it. Pink is one of the colors that I get compliments about whenever I wear it. "God, please don't let Lilia and Mae go without anything they need because they spent so much on me. Please, God, provide for them with whatever they need.

Thank you for the clothes, thank you for loving, caring sisters." I wrote each one a letter, thanking them and letting them know how happy I was and all the compliments I got every time.

I've got to go to two other proms. These schools were invited to our prom, and we were invited to theirs. I didn't invite Jurius to another prom because he was jealous of me doing the opening dance with someone else. He didn't want to understand that schools have these rules, and it was an honor for me to be at the top of my class. I should have ditched him right after I saw his attitude.

"Whoso findeth a wife findeth a good
thing, and obtaineth favour of the Lord."
Proverbs 18:22

# CHAPTER 7

## *Encounter with Jurius*

I wasn't really interested in boys or dating. I was too busy taking care of my younger siblings, our home, and schoolwork. He kept coming, and it seemed he was willing to do all he could to make me sympathetic for him coming a long way to see me. When I talked to my stepmother about the situation, she convinced me that he was not what I described as his attitude. "God," I prayed, "help me to get out of this mess." It seemed like the more I prayed and trusted God, the further away He was, and sometimes, I almost lost all faith. My stepmother and her sister Susie encouraged me to give him a chance.

School's out, and now work had begun to get harder because there were farmers who wanted us to work in their fields. This work is where we get our school clothes. Daddy was no longer sharecropping, so we had to work every day for pay. We still had to give daddy half of what we made because he had to buy seeds and fertilizer for our fields, and there would need to be food for the family. My youngest sibling, Ruth, was nine years old, and all of us pitched in to make the workload easier.

Dallas junior, Elsie, and I went to work in the fields along with some cousins who promised to supervise us to do the work right, not knowing that our work was done better than anyone else. Ruth and Mattie were not old enough to be hired for a pay; thus, they kept up most of the work at home. They fed the hogs, make their beds, and kept fresh water for them. This had not been daddy's work for a long time.

He paid no attention to the family getting smaller. He just expected that everything would get done as usual. Our stepmother would constantly remind him that this was too much work for those girls. She was very concerned also about Ruth and Mattie drawing water from the well, and she would help them. She complained to my dad that the bucket of water was too heavy for the kids.

Sometimes we worked after dark to get all the work done. One of us would stay home to bring in firewood for the stove, help with the cooking, and ensure there was enough water for bath, breakfast, and cooking. Everybody was willing to do their part, but sometimes we thought that daddy was not doing his best to help. When we spoke to Odell about dad's strange reaction to certain things, he said he would be sure to come and help with the chores. That worked for a while, but when his wife was pregnant and expecting another child, his help got scarce. It took all his time with his family. We didn't complain anymore and thought it necessary not to complain to daddy anymore.

We saw that the arguments were getting worse and more often. We would get the work done and pray for God's guidance. Our stepmother thought we were crazy. Even though she never said it, her questions and comments suggested that she didn't expect anything to change. It rained the next week, and we couldn't go to work in the fields for two days, so we spent that time catching up with our chores. And when we did go back to work, we didn't work as many hours as we used to. We always got home before dark, and praised and thanked God for hearing our prayers and answering in our favor.

Daddy decided he would sell some of the pigs to a cafe in New Hope because he didn't need as much meat since the family grew smaller. He decided to give us some of the money from the sales for school clothes. It was as if he had awakened from a long sleep. He also started to help water the hogs and plant the fall garden. What he had not done for a few years was butchering cows for some farmers who raise their own cows along with hogs. Dad had asked for money for his work instead of the scrap parts of the cow: the head, the lungs, the kidneys, and the stomach, which is tripe when it is cleaned and processed.

The farm owners could not find anybody else who was skilled in butchering. They got together and tried to do it themselves. They found out that they made such a mess and could not get it done before some of the meat was spoiled. One farmer came to find out how much they would have to pay for him to butcher a cow for them. When daddy told him, he told the other farmers, and they thought the price was reasonable.

Dad had all at once come to life and began to be a valuable member of the family. Our stepmother didn't believe it when she heard daddy pray at our weekly devotional Sunday mornings. "Thank you, God, for the faith to trust and believe that we can depend on you." These were not his exact words, but the meaning is the same. God hears our prayers when we pray with a pure and clean heart, and with faith, nothing is impossible for God.

She heard daddy praying the same prayer requests we told her that we would pray for. We wanted God to inspire us to get the work that we needed to do done.

We only prayed about our chores, but God gave us much more – He gave us our Daddy back. I never found out his problem, but I was so happy that God solved it. Maybe God wanted to restore his faith. Susie and Uncle Roy came again and brought Jurius along. I had to give him some attention even though I didn't want to. I had to show him, I thought, how Christian friendship should be. We were in the house talking, and the older folks were outside under the walnut tree having their weekly talk about this Sunday service at each their church. Jurius decided he wanted a Pepsi cola.

Aunt Clara, daddy's sister, ran a little store in the neighborhood, just drinks, candy, cookies, salt, and cooking stables that one might need in an emergency. I thought we could walk to the store when I heard him asking Uncle Roy if he could drive his truck. "Well, yeah boy," he said, reaching his hand in his pocket for the keys. "You know, boy, that's our ride back home. Take care and don't try to show off in front of that girl." "I didn't know you could drive," I said. "Yeah, I've been driving for a long time." "A long time?" I said. "How old are you?" "I'm 19," he said. Something about this didn't add up, but it didn't matter so much.

I wanted to call him out about being 19 when he told me he was in the 10th grade. I quickly dismissed all this from my mind. We went to the store and got drinks and candy for everybody at home. I introduced him to Aunt Clara, and she said he looks like a nice young fellow. I was happy for what she said, but then my mind returned to him being 19 and in 10th grade.

I was very quiet on the way back home. When he pulled to the side of the road, I asked, "Why are we stopping?" We stopped near the house where Odell's family lived on one side of the road and Mark Jr., my cousin, lived on the other side of the road, about the same distance. He answered, "I want to talk with you." "Talk?" I answered. "Let's go to the house and talk. The sodas will get hot." He cut the truck motor off and began moving closer to where I was sitting.

He reached over and put his arms around me and said, "I've been coming all this way to see you almost every week, and you act like I'm not your boyfriend." I started to say, "You didn't have to come anymore-" when he cut my words off by kissing me and beginning to put his hands up my dress.

I didn't know what he wanted to do, except I remembered a time when I was raped by a man who had been in the army before he finished high school, and now he was back at school to graduate. He drove a school bus. His bus was sent to pick up the children when the bus we were riding broke down along the way to school. When we arrived at school, he yelled, "Everybody stay in your seats." He got up and started walking to where I was seated about halfway down the bus. I was seated next to the window, and another girl was seated next to the aisle. He told the girl to go, and he stood in front of the seat where I was seated so I could not get off the bus.

After everyone was off the bus, he quietly closed the bus door and began driving the bus to the parking place. As soon as he moved, I jumped up and started to exit, but I was not fast enough. "What are you doing?" I yelled. What is he trying to do, I thought? He has a girlfriend, a senior who he stays with all the time at recess and lunch. I had heard how they go out every weekend. I don't want anybody to see me walking with him from the bus. All the other children had already entered the school, and there was no one to see me. I found out that he had something other than walking through the school in mind.

I was still standing with my arm full of books when he got up from behind the driver's seat. "Open the door," I said softly. When he reached to take my books, I pushed and struggled to hold on to the books.

Finally, the books began to fall to the floor as he pushed me onto a seat. He started to pull up my skirt, and I started hitting him. I've scratched him in the eye, and he let go for a few seconds and then continued to push me onto the seat. I hit him, kicked him, tore his shirt; all the time he focused on what he wanted to do. I don't know if I had ever heard of rape before, but this is what happened to me. He got off the bus without saying a word or looking at me.

At first, I decided to stay on the bus because my clothes were torn and wrinkled. I fixed them the best I could and decided to get off the bus when I heard the bell ring for the second class. I walked quickly and got in the crowd in the hallway and got in class first before anyone found my seat and sat as quickly as I could. A few of the students in my class asked me about homework and my answers for a few math problems.

That was the next class we would go to. Everybody acted normal as usual and said nothing about my clothes or why I was late coming to school; nobody, teachers or students. I then remembered my praying while I was being raped, asking God to have mercy and help me. I know God heard me, and I believed he helped me the only way he could. He didn't allow anybody to notice my clothes.

At lunch, I stayed on the doorsteps. I didn't want to walk around too much where somebody might see my clothes. After I ate my lunch with a few girls who joined me on the steps, one of the girls said, "I wonder what happened to Marvin. His eye is red and his face scratched up. Somebody really did a work on him." One of the other girls said, "You know it had to be Patty Lee; nobody can't get a hand on him but her." "No, it wasn't Patty Lee," the girl said, "I heard her asking him what had happened. He looked around and began talking so nobody could hear, so I walked away."

I thought, after hearing this, Lord, should I tell? This is a good time to tell somebody what he has done. "Restroom time for me," I said, knowing that was the answer from God. We all went to the restroom, and one of the girls started to tell me what I missed in the first period class and what homework was. When I got into the stall, I found that my period had started. "Thank you, God," I prayed silently, "if what got into me was like what got on my clothes, please wash it out with this period." Not knowing what to do, God solved the problem, and I told nobody until after school.

I heard that he was jail for raping a girl in my class, not Patty Lee. I told Marie about it when she read about it in the newspaper. "Just do your best to forget about it," she said, "maybe he will know not to do that to another girl." The victim's father indicted him and took him to court. I know my dad would have done nothing if he knew. I didn't want anybody blaming me because I knew I was not to blame.

God helped me through that, and now it was clear in that truck with Jurius what was about to happen. I tried to open the door, but he grabbed my free hand, he had already pinned my left under him. I was able to cross my legs, but he forced his way to what I thought was not a penetration, and it was over. Well, that part was over. Over for a little while, when I missed a monthly period and told my stepmother, she advised me to go to the doctor. My siblings and I had never been to a doctor, only daddy. The doctor's office was in New Hope. I could get there by bus or train. Since I was going alone, I took the bus since the walk was closer to my house.

I got off the bus at the station and started walking in the direction we used to go when we went to school clothes shopping. I remembered the name my stepmother told me as I passed the doctor's office. He was my daddy's doctor. I walked into the office and saw only the nurse seated behind a desk. She was dressed in a white uniform and had a funny-looking hat on her head. She looked like the nurse in one of my books before I started school.

"May I help you?" she asked. "Yes," I said, walking closer to the desk, "I would like to see the doctor." She looked strangely at me and said, "Do you have an appointment?" "No," I managed to get out before clearing my throat. "You will have to wait a while," she said, "the doctor is with someone now, and I have another one waiting. Then you will be next." "I'll wait," I said. She got my name, age, address, etc.

Then she looked up at me and said, "Why do you want to see the doctor?" "I haven't had my period this month." "When was it due? When was your last?" she asked. It was June 20th when Jurius had the affair. I didn't say all this to her; I just said May 28th. "May 28th," she repeated, reaching for a calendar from her desk. "As of this date, you are about five weeks late, and that is not quite enough to tell, you could be late for other reasons."

That statement sounded real good to me. Then I recalled every month since I started at 12 years old. I didn't know much about birds and bees. My sisters didn't talk to us about that at all. I learned from eavesdropping when they talked with cousins gossiping about the news they heard from others gossiping in the community. Even in school, the homemade teacher didn't teach anything about this. We took a course in health in the ninth grade, which talked about health problems but nothing about sexual health. I was about to believe that was a dirty thing.

When an older girl moved into the neighborhood to live with her grandparents who lived across the road from our home, she would come over on weekends to play sports with us. Her grandparents were very old, and she wanted to mingle with some younger people whenever she could. She also walked to Sunday school and church with us every Sunday. As they say, she was a little wild, a bit mature for her age. She was a year older but in the same grade as I was.

The nurse called me to go in to see the doctor. He was a very pleasant gentleman. He commented about me being brave to come here alone. He asked me my age and about my mother. I told him my mother died when I was six years old. "Oh," he said. He picked up my folder that the nurse had placed on his desk when we walked into the office. "I see you are Hattie Matthews. Are you related to Dallas Matthews?" I could barely get my voice. I was surprised that he would mention my dad's name. Then I remembered my stepmother telling me that this was daddy's doctor.

For a minute, I had forgotten the conversation I had with her. This would be my secret period now. I know she will want to know what the doctor said when I get back home. "Yes," I said, "he is my father." "I should not have asked you," he said. "I can see the resemblance. How is Dallas doing?" he said. "I haven't seen him for a while. I hope he is doing well?" "He is doing well," I said. The nurse came back into the room and stated, "I've got room two ready if you are ready." "I will see you in a little while," Dr. Allen said, still smiling.

The nurse took me into a room and asked me to take off all my clothes. "All of my clothes?" I repeated. "You can put on this gown. I'll go out while you put it on," she said. She could see the embarrassment on my face. "Call me when you are ready. You can lay on this bed when you get dressed." When I got dressed and tried to get on the bed, it was so high I could barely get on it.

"I'm ready," I called out, and before I could get out ready, she opened the door. I think she was standing behind the door listening to everything going on with me. She walked in and reached under the bed, pulled out a drawer, and took out a sheet. "Covering you up might make you feel better when the doctor comes in," she smiled. I also laughed, not knowing how I managed to get it out, but this was the most embarrassing moment I had ever been through, except when I walked into school after being raped on the school bus.

The doctor came in, still smiling. He picked up the bottom of the sheet, pulled up a stool, and sat down at the table's end. Oh my God! What is he going to do?

Then I remembered to pray, "God, please help me endure this terrible thing that the doctor is doing. Help me be OK," just as the nurse said, "Let something else be the problem for my lateness." The doctor stood up, not smiling this time, and I was confused. He left the room, pulling off his rubber gloves. The nurse pulled back the sheet, handed me some tissues, and said, "Clean up yourself and get dressed. You can come into the room when you are ready." I cleaned up, put on my clothes, and walked into the doctor's office. That was the first time I noticed his deep blue eyes, and they looked very sad.

"Have a seat," he said, and without catching his breath, he said, "I'm almost positive that you are going to have a baby. I want you to come back next month." "Is that because you are not sure?" I asked. "I'm sure," he said. "But you said you are almost positive," I said. Then the smile came back. "That's what I have a habit of saying," he smiled bigger. "I never miss."

I walked to the bus station as fast as I could go without running, passing the hotdog stand where we always stopped to get something to eat before going to the bus station. I didn't want anything to eat today, so I went to the ticket counter and purchased my ticket. "Your bus will leave in an hour," he said. Usually, when we had as much as an hour to wait, we went to "Roses" a 5 and dime store near the station and bought things like nail polish, lipstick, and maybe some more loose leaf paper because, at Roses, they sometimes had a school opening sale. Today, I didn't want to do anything but get on the bus and go home.

I sat near the side of the station where the bus would come to load people traveling. I wanted to be on the bus as soon as possible, or just be alone. Usually, I would enjoy watching the sailors who traveled by bus to and from the Navy base nearby. All I could think about was the doctor's words and his voice when he said, "I never miss." I tried to pray that God would let him miss this time.

Somehow I could not even pray. All I could say was, "Thank you, God, for being my God, my heavenly father, my savior, my Lord, and knowing all about me and what was happening to me. Please forgive me all the sins I have committed against you. Help me not to commit these sins again. Thank you for your love, mercy, and grace, for you are faithful in your word toward us. Thank you for owning me as your child.

Create in me a pure heart and keep me in your path of righteousness forever."

When I opened my eyes and looked up, the bus had started loading. Somehow all my worries and fears were gone, and I felt a peace like I've only felt a few times before. The ride home was quicker than usual. Walking from the bus to home, I began to think about what I would say to my stepmother and the letter I would write to Jurius. Mail was the only form of communication we had. I didn't want to see him again, and I didn't know if he would come again.

I didn't know what to say to my stepmother when I got home. So I busied myself with all my chores. She had already cooked dinner and was calling everybody to come for dinner. Daddy had been working outside and came in to wash up and get ready to eat. Everybody else was already seated at the table. I tried to get my stepmother's attention to ask her not to mention anything to daddy at the table. She had already begun serving her plate and passing the food to the ones already seated. I passed by her back and whispered, "Don't say anything about me at the table." She looked at me and nodded her head. Daddy saw me whisper to her as he was coming into the room.

"What's that about?" he asked. I spoke up real quickly, "Just girl talk." I didn't know if she had told him about going to the doctor or not. Nothing else was said about it at the table. We had a pleasant talk about what went on with the others, and nobody noticed that I was just playing with my food and not eating. It was all I could do to sit there. The smell of what should have been a delicious meal could not let me hold back the sick feeling in my throat.

I reached for a glass of tea near my plate and deliberately knocked it over, grabbing it before all the drink spilled out. I quickly jumped up from the table and out the back door. Elsie got up and went into the kitchen to get a towel to clean up the mess I had made.

I could barely get outside when it all came out. As sweet and caring as she was, my stepmother didn't say anything. She just tried to comfort me. When we went back inside, she went to the table, and I went to my bedroom. Everybody knew that when we went to New Hope with anything, we always stopped by the hot dog stand and got something to eat. Sometimes we would just get popcorn or ice cream cones. Elsie mentioned that at the table.

I was glad she did; that was an excuse for me. I could hear the conversation because the dining room was close to my room. After a while, dad pushed back his chair from the table, and I could hear footsteps getting close to my bed. I was lying there with the covers over my head to keep out the smell of food.

"Do you feel any better?" he asked in a very sympathetic voice. I pulled the covers off my head and said, "I feel a little better." "I'll go out and get you some ginger root before dark," he said. Being half Indian, he could find all kinds of herbs and medical remedies for whatever sickness there was. He went out the door and in a few minutes, I could smell the aroma of ginger, which was very relaxing. A few moments later, Elsie was bringing me a cup with the ginger tea, which was very hot and spicy.

The tea was too hot to drink right away, so I just held it close to my face to inhale the steam from the hot cup. When the tea was cool enough, I started sipping it. Not many minutes went by before I was feeling sleepy.

Elsie helped me get undressed, got my nightgown on, and got me another cup of tea. "Daddy said you should try to drink another cup," she said. I slept all night and felt very restful, but when I smelled the aroma of ham and eggs being cooked, I hurried back inside my room and called for ginger tea. Every day, this was a routine - six ginger teas. I wrote the letter to Jurius, and he replied right away. "Are you sure?" he asked "I will come this weekend to see you, and we can decide what to do," he wrote back. Decide what to do? I thought. What can that mean?

Another letter came in a couple of days that said how much he loved me and wanted to marry me. He talked about him telling one of his sisters, who was already married, and she thought him wanting to marry me was the right thing to do. The letter was long and full of how I need you and don't want to live my life without you. You are all I think about every day and night. While I was reading his letter, all I could think about was that day he parked along the road and I begged him to stop doing what he was doing.

I saw a person I had not seen before and one I could not get out of my mind. I didn't intend to write to him again. I had already let him know what he had done to me, and if he came this weekend, I would make it plain how I felt about him taking advantage of me.

I prayed and asked God to help me make the right decision, whatever He wills for my life. I trusted God for my prayers and knew I could trust Him in everything he approved for my life. I knew he would never leave nor forsake me. "Oh Lord my God, my heavenly Father, my protector, my keeper, my hope and peace, your word says you will be with me until the end of the earth." My mind changed, and all the evil thoughts disappeared.

Who am I to judge? The same judge will judge all of us. His judgment will be true and righteous. I believed God would change my mind. I promised God that he could use me anyway and anytime. He brought to my remembrance how he had worked out and solved other problems and troubles that came my way. I had to do nothing except to be obedient and trust him. The weekend came, and another morning of sickness and weakness.

I had not missed a Sunday teaching my class. Somehow, the children brought me an extra surge of strength and energy.

I felt stronger and uplifted after teaching my class and hearing the sermon from reverend Johnson. His message was about not giving up. He encouraged us, the church, to continue to fight the battle until the end. "You can't win if you quit. The way might be hard, but God will give you the strength to press on." We went home after the service was over, changed our church clothes, and put on something comfortable. I helped warm the food, set the table, and made the tea. All of us chipped in to get things done in an orderly manner. One got fresh cool water from the well while another made fire for the cooking.

By the time dad and our stepmother got home, everything was ready to put on the table. We had just finished dinner, cleaned the food away, and started outside to relax under the walnut tree when the truck rounded the curve and in our driveway. I stood in the doorway while everyone else continued outside to meet the visitors. "We just finished dinner," daddy said after greeting everyone. "The food is still warm; we can go back in so you can eat." "No," Susie said, "we just finished eating and hit the road." "We had to come in a hurry," Uncle Roy started, "or I don't know what we had to do with this young man over there," he said, pointing at Jurius.

Then he let out a big, "Ha ha ha ha ha ha! Just something very important to tell your girl. You know, ha ha ha."

Jurius had already come into the house and I was about to be seated when daddy called out to me, "Bring Susie a glass of water or some tea if there is some left." I hurried and came back with a pitcher of water and two glasses. I put the pitcher on the window sill, filled one glass for Susie, and asked if anyone else wanted some. Uncle Roy said he might as well take a glass. I went back into the house where Jurius was still standing. "Have a seat. You're not getting any taller by standing," I said. I have heard dad say that many times when greeting visitors. I'm sure it came to me from God. Well, I had no idea what to say. This started us with something to talk about right away.

"I would like to be a little taller; it's hard to reach the top of the Raptors to hang the nets," he said. He worked at a fishery part-time, and when the boats came into harbor with a load of fish, the workers did hang up the nets to be cleaned and dried. Jurius had told me about that when he visited me the first time. He told me about unloading the boat, separating the fish, and the whole work. "I would like to be a little taller too, especially playing basketball." "But you are doing alright the way you can jump," he said. This conversation could go on all afternoon, I thought. I needed to change this. When he started a conversation, it would go on in very little detail.

"I got your letter," I said quickly, changing the subject. "I was surprised to get the second one." At least we were on the subject I wanted to talk about. "Did you remember what I told you about in my letter?" I asked. "Yes, I remember," he stated. I wanted to tell him how he had messed up my life, and now I begged him to stop. "Do you realize you took advantage of me against my will? Is this what you call love?" I had planned to go on an-all-out verbal attack, but I was not able to talk about any of these things.

When he opened his mouth, he said, "I need to talk with Mr. Matthews. I need to ask him if I can marry you." I was shocked out of my mind. Why is he going to ask daddy about marrying me when he cheated me the way he did? Before I could say anything, he was at the door calling for daddy. Dad jumped up quickly as if something was wrong and headed into the house. "I want to talk to you," Jurius said. Daddy opened his bedroom door, which was right behind where they were standing. He invited him in and followed, closing the door behind him. They were in the room for what seemed forever but only about 15 or 20 minutes.

Daddy went back outdoors to the visitors. Jurius took a seat beside me on the couch. I was eager to know what this was all about but was determined to let him start the conversation. When I could not hold out any longer, I started to ask if he wanted to take some water. He started out at the same time, then we were both stopped and looked at each other and smiled. I imagined the awful feeling talking with my dad about what he had done. I said, "You go first." He said, "No, you go first." "I was just going to ask you if you wanted some water, that's all." "No," he said, and then he said, "yes, the drink would be good."

I went outside to get the water I had put on the windowsill earlier. Everyone outside stopped talking and looked at me. Nobody said a word when I announced, "I'm just getting Jurius some water." They started talking again, and I took a while to pull the water in the glass and put the pitcher back on the windowsill. I asked Jurius what he was saying earlier. I handed him the water, and he took a sip and put the glass on the table.

He was probably stalling as I was getting the water. "What were you trying to say before I interrupted you?" "Oh, I just asked your father if I could marry you. And he asked me a lot of questions. The first was if I loved you, and then he said I put it in to say what did you say? I told him I did very much. Then he asked me if I had a job and where we would live." I started to interrupt to ask his answer to the other questions.

Before I had a chance to ask, he said, "Let me finish and then I will tell you my answers."

I could see by this time he was sweating very much and his hands were shaking. He continued, "He asked me about my schooling, and I told him that I had not graduated. He said you were doing well in school and would graduate next year. He wanted you to graduate. I promised him that you could still go to school after we are married. He made me promise again that you would be able to graduate." "Did you tell him about the baby?" I asked. "No, I want you to tell him that." "Why me?" I asked. "He might have questions for you about that when it happened.

Did we both agree to do this thing that caused you to want to marry me? He should have asked you why you wanted to get married now," I said. "I should not let you get by without telling him."

It came to my attention what I was saying and that I should be quiet and not put him down. I began to silently say a prayer that God would help us. "Help us decide if this is the right thing to do." By this time, I had doubts about me being able to choose. I trusted God to help me decide what to do. I can't say for sure God made the decision or not, but I decided to trust that he did.

Daddy was calling to come outside. I went quickly to my room, got a clean handkerchief, and gave it to Jurius to wipe the sweat dripping off his face as if the glass of water had been poured over him. Dad called again, "You guys come out here." "We're on the way," I said, stepping out of the door with Jurius close behind.

"I told these folks the news," he said, "that another one of my children is ready to jump the broom and make it family for herself." Mentioning the word family made me wonder if he knew about the baby. Jurius and I just stood there smiling, looking like a happy couple. Everybody congratulated us and asked about the date. "Nothing's been decided yet," I said, "we'll be sure to let you know."

The next month, I was busy helping my sister Marie, who asked me to help care for her two children after she gave birth to her third baby boy. Again, I helped with the name Columbus Martin. I had to stop working on the tobacco because the smell made me sick. I had just gotten over morning sickness and didn't want that feeling again. She gave me a stipend for helping her so I would have some money of my own when I got married.

Daddy and stepmom also gave me a wedding gift, even though I was not married yet. I borrowed a suitcase from Marjorie. She bought it when she got married. I started packing my suitcase and putting in my best clothes. I will come back for others later. All my toiletries were packed in a box. I didn't have very much, so it didn't take me long to pack it all.

My cousin, Ruby, from my mother's side, gave me a shower. She was very considerate, knowing I didn't have household items to start keeping house. The whole community gave me things for my kitchen, like a sifter for sifting flour and cornmeal and a grater because we grated sweet potato pudding. There were pots, pans of all sizes, utensils sterling silver, and all kinds of cutting knives. I still have some of those items. Oh, I forgot cake pans and flat pans for biscuits and bread, a dishpan and a bread tray, whose handle was made of wood. There were also sheets, pillowcases, all kinds of towels, tablecloths, and napkins.

I always wondered if my cousins made a list of things I would need and asked each one to choose what they wanted to bring because there was not a duplicate of any item. I can't remember all I received, but I needed to buy nothing to start keeping house. All the household items were already put in boxes for me to bring home. Seeing this big party which was held at the church and all these showers by the whole community really let me know I was getting married. Even though I had a lot of encouragement from people who were already married and knew my housekeeping skills, nobody mentioned the most important fact for two people joining together – love!

An important factor in all this was nobody knew, not even me, who (I)was going to marry. I sincerely believe that God would not let me make a mistake that would ruin my life. I relaxed and started reading the letter he wrote to me about his love for me and how he could not go on without me. Maybe I was the one who was not letting myself be sincere and honest. I started praying for God to help me see exactly what I needed to do.

I was praying all along, but now my prayer points changed to more serious ones. A lot of things were at stake. What would I do if I didn't get married? My basketball and baseball were over, and I promised dad that I would finish my schooling and graduate. God, please work out every problem we are facing according to your will.

Jurius must be having some problems also, my conscience reminded me, or was that God speaking to me? You can't just think about yourself. There are two others for sure that you need to think about. Two families needed to be considered. How will my dad, stepmother, and younger siblings carry on? The Miller family will need to make a lot of adjustments in their home with me moving in. "Thank you, God, for reminding me that I'm not the only one to be considered. Thank you, God, for helping me not be selfish. I thank you from this day forward, God. Remove every ounce of selfishness from my life, body, and thoughts. Please, God. Our Heavenly Father, forgive me for letting myself get in your way of blessing me the way you want it."

I felt free, freer than I had felt since Jurius' proposal. I knew that God would take care of whatever came my way. 'Of me trust in me with all thy heart and lean not on your own understanding. In all your ways, acknowledge me and I will give you the desires of your heart.'

That's all I needed to do to keep my heart right with God, and there would be nothing that he would not do for me.

I remembered teaching about God's love in my Sunday school class. Why did I let the facts of what I was going through get in my way of knowing who God is and have some doubt about my God? There is nothing too hard for our heavenly Father. It had been two weeks since I heard from Jurius. The letter came letting me know that he was coming this weekend. He wanted us to set a date for the wedding.

Again, the feeling came as usual, but I dismissed it from my mind. And this time, peace came to me quickly. I started to think about a date and a place. The church came to mind since I knew that the bride's family should make all of these decisions. I thought we could afford a church wedding. But maybe just to marry in the church, since it was the only place large enough to hold the community. These ideas turned over and over in my mind.

Jurius and Daniel came walking up to our house on Sunday. I was expecting Uncle Roy to bring him as usual. Daniel was one of the young men we met when we visited Hallandale, where my stepmother was born. They had caught the bus to New Hope and another bus from New Hope to Civil City and then walked the two miles to our house. They started at 9:00 am to catch the bus at 10:00 am in Belgrade. It had been a long day for them, but they still had smiles on their faces.

When I saw them, I retraced my feelings and believed this was the first time I felt love for him. We had just gotten home from church and were warming dinner. Daddy and stepmom were on their way. Daddy always stayed to make sure the pastor was taken care of and the money was distributed correctly.

I greeted the young men, and so did everyone else. Then I excused ourselves to finish the dinner. We knew our younger brother Dallas Junior who was called Junior, would be entertaining them well. He always teased me about telling Jurius about my life. I hoped what he would say would be true, or at least halfway. Instead of talking about me, he was trying to hook Else up with Daniel. Daniel would come along every time Jurius came. From then on, he and Elsie got married two years after we did, even though she insisted that he was too short for her.

We ate dinner without much talk other than about the food. Our stepmom had helped in preparing the okra. Daddy had a contract with a couple of restaurants in New Hope. The okra had to be harvested every day, even on Sundays, except daddy would have us cut them on Saturday evening instead of morning. This made us have a lot of okra to share and cook. We had eaten okra until we wanted no more, all except Miss Cera.

She would cook them differently. This day she decided to fry some and steam some. She made okra, onion, and tomato soup. We baked the ham, made potato salad, and baked bread. She insisted we didn't need another vegetable. Elsie and I looked at each other while hiding our feeling about all the okra. We didn't want to say anything that would hurt her, so we accepted her suggestion.

We made a great sweet potato pudding last. It would be put in the oven until everything else was taken out. We left the pudding in the oven while we were at church because the fire would go out of the stove but would stay hot long enough to cook the pudding. We had done it many times before. There was no way it would ruin. Jurius looked at the okra and said, "No, thanks. I don't like them; I just can't eat them." But Miss Cera was determined that he tried the fried ones.

She reached over and put a couple of pieces on his plate. "Try these," she said, "I bet you've never had them fried." Jurius dropped his head and started to eat the other food on his plate. Miss Cera continued to encourage him to try it.

I spoke up and said, "Leave him to eat his dinner in peace. If he doesn't like it or wants it, it's alright. Maybe the next time he will try it. Miss Cera was still telling him how he never had fried okra, and to my surprise, she was holding her fork with an okra on it right at his mouth, like you would feed a baby. I could see the embarrassment on the face of everyone at the table.

He finally opened his mouth and took the food. "Not bad," he said, and immediately she put more on his plate. He slowly consumed all on his plate and said again, "Not bad." From that day on, he loved okra. At first, only fried, and then he tried it cooked other ways. When we later planted our first garden, he planted a lot of okra.

We left the table and went into the living room where we started to talk about the wedding plans. "My family want to plan the occasion at Hallandale," Jurius said. Daddy and Miss Cera came into the room at that time and asked, "What is this about an occasion in Hallandale?" He repeated what he had said, except he said one of his sisters wants to help us plan it at my church. "Church? I thought you were going to the courthouse and get it done.

That's what we will do. Don't make too much fuss over it. Save that money to live off." We dismissed the subject of where to have it and talked about a date. Jurius stated, "My sister thinks that Labor Day weekend would be the best time if that's alright with you." He was looking at me. Dad said, "Do what you want to do," talking to Jurius, "just don't forget the promise you made to me."

I spoke up and asked, "Daddy, what promise did he make to you?" I was so glad I asked because Jurius had told me he had promised to be sure I graduate. Daddy said, "I want you to finish school because you are doing so well, and I told him he knows where he found you and if he decides he doesn't want you, he should bring you back. He shouldn't mistreat you. Just let me know and I will come to get you." Those words from my daddy with Miss Cera agreeing with him made a big difference in my life. We set the date on Labor Day weekend and that was final. We also decided to have a wedding at his church, as he and his sister wanted.

"What therefore God hath joined together,
let not man put asunder."
Mark 10:9

# CHAPTER 8

# Marriage with Jurius

Sunday, September first, Jurius and his dad came. They had stopped in New Hope to get the license, and dad had to sign for him too. My dad and Mr. Mark signed the marriage certificate in front of the Justice and had the license notarized. They put all my things in the car, and we headed for Hallandale. There was a strange feeling in my heart, and I began feeling as if something was not right. Then I began to pray, and before I said just a few words, his dad glanced back at me and said, "You are going to be alright. I'll see to it." The ride seemed longer than usual, but finally we arrived at their house.

There was a group of people there, all his family and some close neighbors. We said our hellos, and I immediately went into the house. Mr. Mark, Jurius, and one of his brothers were bringing my things into the house. I quickly took the dress that I was going to wear and followed Jurius into a room at the back of the house. I had read from my home economics book that you should not wear white if your life has been damaged.

So, I felt that since I was going to have a baby, I should not wear white. I chose from the mini prom dresses left at our home by my older sisters. The dress was pale blue with lovely long sleeves, a high collar with ruffles down to the waist, and a full skirt. I looked like a typical medieval young lady. It was not as beautiful as my prom dress, I thought. I didn't wear my prom dress because Jurius had already seen it.

He had not seen the dress that I was wearing. Somebody came to the room door to get him. He had already gotten dressed in a white shirt, black suit, and black bow tie.

I had already seen the suit before, but it didn't make a difference to either of us. I hurriedly got dressed and took off the scarf I wore on my head. One of his sisters and three other girls came to do my makeup. Lipstick was the only makeup I had ever worn and very scarcely. When they finished, I sat and listened to them say, "Eyebrow pencil, rouge, and powder." I asked them what I looked like and one of the girls handed me a mirror.

When I saw who was staring at the mirror, I didn't recognize myself. "Thank you all," I said, "I will be out in a minute." They left the room, and I washed my face as fast as I could, except for some of the lipstick. It was not the color I usually wore, but I didn't wash all of it off.

When I walked out of the room with the jewelry, bag I wore at my prom, and my silver slippers, the girls who did my makeup said, "Why did you take off the makeup?" I clearly stated that was not who I am. I wanted to be real for my wedding. Mr. Mark had driven Jurius to the church and was on the way for me. A large group of people was waiting at the church. Jurius had already gone in, and the pastor was waiting to talk to both of us.

He asked for the marriage license and began to read it. "Alright," he said, "we have a problem, which is, I can't marry you today. Go get your parents Jurius," he said. "I see both your parents had to sign for you to be married. So that tells me you both are underage." "I am," I said, "but Jurius is not."

He had told me when we first met that he was nineteen, and I remembered having some questions in mind about that. Now, the pastor is saying that he is underage. I refused to let my mind dwell on the thought that he started out lying. Jurius came back with his parents. The pastor explained that the license was from a county different from the churches, so he could not marry us. He continued to explain that he could do some of the ceremonies, but he could not sign the license or pronounce us married. All agreed because many people were waiting for the wedding.

We went through with the ceremony as planned, and the next day, Monday, was Labor Day. The courthouse would be closed. It meant we could not stay together that night. Jurius' sister walked to his parent's house with us. As we walked, she began to let us know how sorry she was about the wedding, but nobody knew that it was not complete except the preacher and us. "You don't have to tell anybody. This can be our secret," she laughed. I did tell some of my sisters, the ones I could trust to keep a secret. Even if the truth did get out, it was alright with me.

Tuesday morning, we were in New Hope as soon as the court house was opened. And for sure, we were married in a short time. We didn't dress up for the occasion as we did for the church wedding. Nobody seemed to care. The Justice said we couldn't do this without some music. So, he put on a record and stated that everybody has to hear this before they marry. We drove back home with his daddy, who took me to the house where I stayed for the night to pick up my suitcase.

I was very frightened and embarrassed to be in the same room with Jurius. When it was time for me to undress, I tried to think that he was my husband. I convinced myself that taking off my clothes with him in the room was alright. I had a pretty pink nightgown which I got from the wedding shower. I sat on the bed, holding it in my hands. Jurius was already laying across the bed, fully dressed. He got up and asked, "Are you ready to go to bed?" "No, I'm not sleeping yet," I quickly said, "you please go out so I can put on my gown?" He started to say something but stopped and went out into the room where some family members were talking.

I hurried and took off my clothes, put on my nightgown, and got under the covers.

When he went out into the other room, I lay there wondering if he had told them that he had to leave the room so I could undress. He stayed awhile. I could hear them talking and laughing, but I could not understand what they were saying. When he came back to the room, he was unfastening his belt and just pulled off his pants and started unbuttoning his shirt, not saying a word. He pulled back the covers and said, "Are you asleep?" I wanted to say yes, but I said no, how could I be asleep and talk to him? I realized that I was tired. We snuggled and fell asleep.

The next day, we walked to Uncle Roy's home just to be together. Mr. Mark came out and took us to look at things we needed for our room because we only had a bed in it. We immediately decided to get a kerosene stove, a table, and four chairs at the furniture store. I had never seen a kerosene stove before, but I knew I wanted to get it and have my own means to cook. When the stool clerk added up all our purchases, he asked, "How much do you want to pay down?" Jurius whispered, "How much do you want to pay down?" "How much do you have?" I asked, "Twenty-five dollars," he said.

"Then we will pay all of it," I stated. I opened my purse and took up the balance of the money. The table, four chairs, and the stove were something like $60.

Mr. Mark and Jurius were surprised that I had that much money. We did get some money for our wedding gifts. You got about $20. My family gave me money too before I came. His daddy said, "If you don't pay all of it, we can stop at the lumber mill like we talked about." "Jurius, how much will you need at the lumber mill?" I asked. "Well, about ten dollars. That should get all we need." "Well, I've got that much.

Let's keep the bill as paid," I said. The store clerk was very happy and promised we could always get anything we needed with or without money. On the way home, we stopped at the lumber mill. I stayed in the car while Jurius and Mr. Mark went to the back of the mill to buy whatever they had planned. It seemed as if they didn't want me to know. So I didn't ask any questions. Maybe Mr. Mark needed lumber for something.

Jurius came back to the car and said. "I forgot the money. May I borrow ten dollars? I'll be sure to pay you back. Not until you give me and I owe you." I laughed. He laughed also. "Money being funny," he said. A part of him came out that I had not seen before. "Thank you, Lord, for helping me see something good and different in him," I said in my heart.

Up to this point, I had not told him I loved him even though he had said it to me many times. I thanked God for changing my mind and heart. At that point, while sitting there in the car all alone, I began to realize how I had been feeding him. No kissing or any kind of affection had I shown him. We talked about how I felt taken advantage of and trapped. "You need time to get over that," he said. This gave me more reasons not to show affection. Lord, you took all that away from me before we got married. Now it has shown its ugly head again. Please, Lord, help me. I need your help at that moment, I thought to myself.

They were back at the car, and a man was helping them put the lumber on top of the car. They tied it with some cords they ran through the inside of the back seat and out to the side of the car. The stove, table, and chairs were inside the back seat and the car's trunk, and the trunk was open and tied down also. Mr. Mark threw his bag into the back seat, and again, we all got into the front seat.

Cars were made bigger in those days than they are today. Plus, the gear level was on the floor, and the front seat was one piece with divided backs. It was easier for three people to ride in the front seat. We all were seated and ready to go when Mr. Mark remembered we forgot to get paint. Back to the hardware store, we went.

While he was in the store, I looked at Jurius and said, "I love you." He smiled and put his arm around my shoulder, and reached in for a kiss. "I love you too," he said. There was the start of a love affair with us. Our love grew stronger each day. I learned to appreciate many things about him that I didn't know about. Mr. Mark got busy on the farm and didn't have time to build whatever they had planned to build.

One morning, I awakened to find he was out of bed. I asked his mama if she knew where he was. She said he was out in the barn helping his father. I was OK with that, even though he was not supposed to go to work until the 15th of the month. I cooked breakfast like a good wife. I took his breakfast to the barn. He had done this for his dad every summer when he had to stay at the tobacco barn. I fixed two plates for him and Mr. Mark, including orange juice and water.

When I got to the barn, he was alone and busy nailing and didn't hear me come into the barn. He looked up in great surprise and said, "What have you got?" "Your breakfast," I said, and he headed over to where I was standing in the doorway. "Where is your daddy?" I asked. "He's getting things ready to process the corn," he said, "and I'm going to help him." "I have a plate for him also," I said, handing him the food bag.

"Have you eaten?" he asked. "No, I'm not hungry," I said, "after smelling the cooking, I didn't feel like eating. He handed me one plate and started eating the other. "Go ahead and try. You might eat it. This tastes good to me." At that time, I started sneezing, several times in a row, one right behind the other. I jumped up and went outside without saying anything. I couldn't say anything because I felt another sneeze coming. Three or four more times, just as before.

I was breathing deep and bent over for a minute or two. He was standing beside me, looking scared. I am allergic to dried tobacco, and the scent was in the barn. "I'm going to the house. You can bring the plate later." At the house, I lay across the bed for a minute and began to feel better. Then I started sneezing again. I slept so much until Mrs. Polly, my mother-in-law, came to check on me. She asked me to wash my hands, arms, face, and legs and change the clothes I was wearing. After I did that, the sneezing stopped. Jurius came to the house about 10:00 o'clock. After a little rest, he went back to the field so he could help Mr. Mark gather corn.

I started thinking about cooking dinner, except I was too weak and tired to do anything but lay on the bed. Mr. Mark came for lunch and said Jurius was still breaking corn. They were trying to finish before the rain came tomorrow. He was going to take some food to him. When he went back, they loaded the corn in front of the barn and asked Polly to tell the children to put it inside the barn when they come home from school. He instructed that they move the lumber and tools over to the right side and be sure not to cover anything with corn.

Jurius got back to the house when it was about dark. They had finished moving the corn. "I'll be working with the project in the barn early tomorrow morning," he said, "but I would not wake you up if you are sleeping." "What is the task?" I asked. "Well, I might as well tell you. It will be a cabinet," he said, "some place to put the dishes and other kitchen wares." I was so happy about that because we needed it.

"After we finish the cabinets, I'm going to make a cradle for the baby." He did just that, and then made a bookcase for all my books. You wouldn't believe what a good job he did. This was one of the things he enjoyed doing in high school. He also made a wardrobe to hang our clothes. It was not fanciful, but it looked better than what most people had in their homes.

Our room was crowded, but we didn't mind. We had the conveniences we needed and were very satisfied. Jurius started calling me Grace, my middle name. I had never been called that name before, so I was very excited about that. We lived happily as husband and wife. Although I needed no practice, I had been doing what I needed to do for a long time. I just had to get used to being a wife and having a husband who was raised differently from my upbringing.

Living in the house with his parents was quite a struggle to get used to. Polly asked me personal things that I didn't want to talk about, like my father and his wife, Miss Cera. My answer to her questions was, "Well, all are one big loving family who loves and serves God. I would say I didn't want to talk about her other questions and would say nothing else.

I didn't like her calling me Girl. One day when she called me Girl, I was a little bit pissed off and not feeling well. I said to her, "Please, Polly, don't call me Girl. My name is Hattie. I thought you knew that," as nicely and politely as I could. "You don't tell me what to call you," she barked, which frightened me too. "I'll call you nothing. Well, you are nothing to me." I turned around and headed toward the door.

She continued, "You should not have married my son." I stopped, looked back and said, "He married me. He was the one begging to marry me. Why don't you talk to him about that? Maybe he will get a divorce." I didn't hear anything else from her that morning. I stayed in our room the rest of the day. My prayer was for us to love each other and understand our roles in Jurius' life. I prayed that we could get along as a family should.

"Dear God, our Heavenly Father, please help us to be a loving family."

The next day, she was washing clothes and had a lot of work to do. I went out and helped her. I fetched water and helped her wash and hang the clothes. We didn't talk about anything. Everywhere was quiet, except the wind blowing, almost drying the clothes immediately. When we finished, she didn't thank me for helping; however, I didn't need anything. I told her to let me know if she needed help with anything. I thank God for giving me the mind and the spirit to reach out to her.

Jurius started working at the fishery and only came home when the boats were catching the fish at the sea. He was at work for three or four days and nights. When he had days off, he would go grocery shopping, and I would buy food and eat without much cooking. I found out that I felt better when I didn't use the stove. A few years later, I found out that I was allergic to the fumes from the kerosene.

I finally told Jurius that we had to move out of that house because his mother was telling her children that I was eating her food, which I could not eat if I wanted to, because I had a problem with my stomach. I was not cooking very much, and she must have thought I was eating her food, or she just simply lied. The fishing season would be over by the end of December, and Jurius would have to find another job. I would be glad because I was getting heavy, and it was hard to do things, including getting on the bed. It was higher than usual, and I needed to step on a stool to get up.

We talked about moving into our own home. He said the place he saw a job could keep a few men for the full-time work, but there would be a cut in the pay. With a pay cut, we could not afford to get our own place and would not have transportation. However, God worked out everything for our good.

There was this man who owned a farm near our house. He needed a sharecropper. Jurius talked to his dad about the deal. His dad asked him to go for it. I was very happy. We would have a house with electricity. We could have a different stove and a refrigerator, which would help my condition. However, the deal failed, and we were stuck in staying where we were for a while.

"For thou hast possessed my reins: thou
hast covered me in my mother's womb.
I will praise thee; for I am fearfully and
wonderfully made."
Psalm 139:13–14

# CHAPTER 9

# Arrival of Junior and Doctor's Prognosis

Jurius got a job with a furniture company in Centerville. He worked mostly on a truck hauling furniture. Everything worked out except transportation. He had to ride a bicycle five miles and then catch a bus for fifteen miles. It was nearing my due date, and I was hoping that it would be on a day when Jurius was not working. I hoped and prayed that I would know what to do when the time came and who to trust to help me. I asked Jurius what I should do. Maybe ask his dad to be more stand-by for him. His mom laughed and said, "He was never on standby for me all these years, why do you think he's going to be faithful now?"

Anyway, his dad was dependable as he promised. He stayed close to home and would often check on me. He was nice to me and encouraged me. God heard my prayers, and I went into labor on a Tuesday when Jurius was off from work because he worked on Saturdays at the furniture store. This was no luck or coincidence. It was the work of God. Junior was born on the 20th of March. The doctor was checking on me while attending to another sick and laboring patient. Jurius went to work the next morning, and his employer gave him a few days off.

Junior was 24 and 3/4 inches long, 9 1/2 pounds. Right away, Jurius' mother decided he didn't look like Jurius. Also, one of the heading Miller's women in Hallandale decided he was not Jurius' complexion. I pointed out the color of Junior's eyes, but she still insisted that he didn't look like Jurius. I needed Jurius Junior to carry on her family name. I had no problem with naming him Jurius. However, Satan was trying to put ugly thoughts in my mind. His name is Jurius Samuel Miller, as the doctor wrote on the birth certificate. "Is everybody happy with the name?" I asked as I looked directly at Jurius. He was smiling very broadly and nodding his head.

I was very tired and exhausted, so I turned over to relax my body and the doctor said, "There will be no more children for you, Mrs. Miller." I turned to face him and asked, "What did you say?" We both spoke at the same time. "I can tell by the afterbirth," he stated, "no more children. It is a miracle that you had this morning." Miracle? I thought. "God promised me four children," I spoke out loud. Then in the next breath, I said, "God, you promised that if I ask anything in the name of Jesus, you would do it." I felt at peace trusting God's words.

I missed telling you the year was 1951; Junior was born and I was eighteen years old. Eighteen in those days were like thirty in today's world. I stayed in bed for nine days, sitting up in bed to care for the baby and eat. Jurius was just a bit older, and we had no experience taking care of a baby. I was too stubborn to ask his mother for help. I thought she would come in and offer to help.

We made it through the nine days. I was directing Jurius on what to do. He had to put everything I needed at arm's reach from the bed. He knew how to cook and clean, and I told him to wash the diapers. Yes, there were no disposable diapers then. We had purchased the buckets we needed and the baby soap for washing his clothes before time.

On the 9th day, we paid our bill and came back to the house. Late in the afternoon, Jurius' mom came into the room. "Why aren't you out of bed?" she said. "Well, I didn't want to do anything wrong." She came to the room and told Jurius to get a silver spoon. She put it in the baby's right hand and carried him around the house. I was surprised to see that because none of the families I've helped care for their babies ever did that.

So this ritual was carried out. This was the first time grandma saw the baby after the first day everybody came to make their opinions about him. It might sound cool for me to say that, but when God told me to write this book, he said, "Tell the truth so people will know who I am." I pray as I write, that God will help me tell the truth as I remember here.

My life was as hard as it was coming. The only way I got through was the love, mercy, and grace of our Heavenly Father. Still, I need him every day of my life. I would not and could not intentionally do anything to displease him by thoughts, words, or deeds. If I think I have displeased him, all I need to do is ask his forgiveness, and he will do it. This fact was proven to me at an early age when I was struggling with my mother's death. And likewise, when I was separated from my siblings in the 1st and 2nd grades. When you feel as though you have no one to help in times of trouble and you really need someone, God is there where you are.

My dad seemed to be a tough person to live with, but I learned early also. He trained us for what we would have to face in life. He taught us to read and learn the bible verses, taking turns at our Sunday morning devotion where each of us had to pray. We learned that God is to be honored. We could not call each other a liar or say that others are fools. No curse words came out of our mouths.

If daddy found out that we said one of the bad words that were forbidden, he would punish us with a whipping. None of his ten children had any problems with breaking the law, was put in jail, or was arrested. We were trained in such a way that nobody had to worry about that part of our lives. I still thank God for my mother and father and how they loved and cared for us. Their training has lasted all our lives.

I was determined to be a good parent to my children. My mind was made up from an early age. I mostly depended on trusting God to give me help and understanding. I also relied on God's word and did teach my children what I had learned and how to do what God expected of them. I mentioned my children when I was to only have one…. Yes, God ordered my request of four children, and I had four children as I asked for. Two boys first, and two girls. There were some challenges we had to go through, but nothing was too hard for God.

We still lived in Jurius' family home, and in September, I would enroll in school. Jurius had asked one of his sisters, Ada, who lived nearby to take care of junior. He had not talked to anyone about my plan to go back to school. He told me he was alright with the plan, but when Mrs. Polly found out, she was very upset. She made a big thing out of it and blamed me. She said I didn't want her to take care of the baby.

Well, it was my Plan B because earlier that summer, she wanted a DNA test to make sure the baby was Jurius'. Or maybe she was a little more relaxed about the baby because the test was positive and he belonged to jurors. Anyway, the problem was solved when Jurius told her it was his, and he had decided that Ada would take care of the baby. He told her I didn't even know anything about their plan until he told me of it.

She convinced us that the baby would better stay in the house in the morning and not having to be taken out, interrupting his sleep. That decision sounded good to me. She was keeping one of her daughters' two children, plus another child she had raised from a baby who was four years old. I had to ride the school bus to school and had to leave early in the morning. School was usual for me since I had good study habits, and I used every chance I could to read and study.

The ride to and from school was a little more than an hour, a good time for me to get all my homework done, including some reading. At home, I had more time to get dinner ready and spend a lot of time with Junior. I got some washing done for Jurius and I would hang the clothes at night while we catch up on our talking about how we spent the day or just a little loving and close time.

We would tease each other by offering a shirt or something and then snap it back.

Most of the time, he was hanging the clothes and I was passing them to him. I liked my clothes to be hung in an orderly fashion, all the diapers side by side and T-shirts together. When he handed the clothes and I pinned them on the line, he would hand them to me as they were piled in the basket. I could pin faster, so I pinned most of the time. When he handed me a piece of what I didn't want, I would drop it back, and he would try to keep me from getting the piece I wanted; we would laugh and play.

If people saw what we were doing, they would say, "You children need to grow up; you have a baby now." I hoped we would be able to play with the baby when he grew up so that we could have a good bonding relationship.

I can remember us playing with daddy while working in the fields. This made the work easier, and the time went by faster.

We never had a watch to know what the time was, except the 12:00 o'clock sun. The sawmill sounded an alarm again at 1:00 o'clock in the morning and evening. We always went by the sun. When the sun rise above the trees, we were already in the field working, and when the sun got to the top of the trees in the evening, it was time to go home. We worked about twelve to thirteen hours. I wanted our lives to be patterned after my home life.

Everything was working in order. We were lying in bed talking and the baby was asleep when Jurius started talking about his life growing up. He blamed his poor education or lack of it. He would be working on the farm while his dad would be drunk or had a hangover from the weekend. As soon as he was old enough to realize what was happening, he vowed that he would never drink any strong drinks. And as far as I know, he kept that vow.

He even talked about his parents fighting when his daddy was drinking every weekend. He told me about going with his daddy to a little place called Over the Creek, where his dad would get drunk and flirt with the homeowner that sold the liquor, and he didn't take his money off him. He would wind up getting robbed of all of his money. That would cause the fight at home.

I didn't know if I should believe what he told me. He was not truthful about not going to school. From his siblings' discussions, I learned that he would go to school and pretend to be sick. He would return to the field where his dad was working. His mom was a teacher before she was married and continued to help other adults to learn how to read and write. I didn't really know what the problem was in his family.

Perhaps, the lack of education. His dad couldn't read or write, and a few of his siblings the same. One of his older sisters went to college and became a teacher, and his youngest sister also went to college for a teacher's training. Jurius told me about his father's intoxication, fighting with the mom, and cheating. The cheating carried over to Jurius because he was cheating on me.

"Fear thou not; for I am with thee: be not dismayed; for I am thy God."
Isaiah 41:10

# CHAPTER 10

## Second pregnancy and the surrounding circumstances

was doing well in school, and by the end of the first semester, my grades excelled all others seniors. There were some questions about how she was excelling in French classes in the second level when at the other school, Spanish was the foreign language. I had to be tested in French and I passed with flying colors. Something else came up.

Unexpectedly in December, I found out I was pregnant. "Nobody is to know that, even Jurius," was the voice I heard. If the school knew, I would have to drop out. "Lord, I need your help." I wanted to share the news with Jurius, but I was afraid that he still wasn't used to his family. I was so happy and thankful that it was hard to say anything about it. I kept hearing God's voice saying, "Leave it to me."

I had a few days of morning sickness, and I had to stay home from school. As I trusted God to work it out, I was not sick until Jurius went to work, and I never vomited in the house. I thanked God for his faithfulness because some other students were sick about the same time, and measles and chickenpox were high around the school. There were also colds and flu.

When I returned to school, nobody asked me why I was absent. I had to be checked in through the counselor's office. A short time after lunch, I got sick and had to run out of the room without asking permission. My mouth was full of what was coming up. One of the girls in the class followed me into the restroom and heard me vomiting. She decided to tell the guidance counselor who told the principal. I heard the girls in my class talking about it at recess one day. They did not say my name, but I knew they were talking about me. There was nothing I could do except trust God. He worked this problem out as he had all the others.

The principal called me into the office just before school ended that day. He asked blankly and sternly, "Mrs. Miller, are you pregnant?" I smiled big, not knowing where it came from. "The doctors said I can't have any more children," I said, "I have a son already." He nodded his head. "I know. How are you managing your home life and doing so well in school?" he asked. "I have help from my family." He urged, "Just bring me the doctor's statements tomorrow." "Miss Willis, I won't be able to get the statement until next week because I have no transportation until the weekend," I answered.

I knew dad would take me to the doctor's office, but I knew Jurius would want to make the arrangement. I had seen a spirit of jealousy in him about certain things I did or didn't do. I want to keep our family life as true as possible. I have not had it confirmed, I thought, plus God had not told me to announce it publicly.

We went to Doctor Bill's office first on Saturday morning, and he suggested we also get Doctor Brown's diagnosis. That was what we did.

Monday morning, I took the two letters from Doctor Bill and Doctor Brown to the Guidance Counselor's Office. She had accompanied the principal Miss. Willis when she requested the doctor's statement. "These letters are from two of the doctors' offices that said I could have no more children. There is another Doctor who also said no more children. If you need his statement, I will get it for you." "This should be sufficient," she said, "I will give them to Miss Willis and then put them in your file." I cried a little before going into my homeroom.

"Thank you, God, for working on this problem without me having to lie about it." I would have to be able to say, I'm going to have a baby. But instead, I continued to trust God, knowing that he never makes any mistakes. You don't know how he will fix things, but you can be very sure he will fix it.

At home, after school, I could hardly wait for Jurius to come home. When I was on the school bus, I heard from God, "Tell Jurius. Make him know how important it is that he doesn't tell anybody because your schooling is in jeopardy." Only four more months to go. I told Jurius how I pray, trust, and depend on God to lead, guide, and direct me in all I do. He seemed to believe me. However, when he needs to trust God to do the impossible, he talks as if he can do it himself.

He has asked me a lot of times how I know it's God's voice I hear. "There is no other voice. Do you not know your daddy's voice when you hear it?" I asked him. Also, I trust him to do what he promised me. He promised that anything I asked in the name of Jesus, he would give me. There is another thing that one must do - believe and have a pure heart. This means that you have to do right and live right all the time.

The farm owner came back to talk with Jurius about sharecropping. "The house is available now, but you will not be able to start your work until a few months later. I can supply you with money to support your family until we are able to bring in money from the crops. Oh, I forgot to tell you. I rented my tobacco allotment out so we will only have corn, soybeans, watermelons, and cucumbers. I will be there working right with you. I realize you are a young farmer, and I need to continue to stay busy. The market for cucumbers is big this year, and they have a market in Bellevue, just a few miles up the road," the farmer said.

Jurius told his dad about the offer, and he thought that would be a good offer. "If we move now, what about furniture and baby care?" These were two things I had not thought about. "Just a few more months and school will be over, and you can continue working at the furniture store and will be able to pay and get the things we need." We planned on how we spend money so there would be money for the furniture. Things were looking up for us. And finally, we would be able to move to our own place. I've been patient and told myself that Jurius' condition was not deliberate.

It seemed like taking care of Junior was just too much for Mrs. Miller. I would find him in the same diaper I put on him in the morning before I left for school. The bottle would be empty, but the food was just as I kept it. To keep my sanity, I had to tell myself she gave him food when she cooked. I also told myself nobody would mistreat their own flesh and blood for no reason, especially a child who could not help himself.

I thank God that Junior never got a diaper rash from being wet and dirty all day. I thank God also for keeping him safe from any harm. These were the sacrifices I had to make for getting my education. I thanked her every day for keeping our son. I occasionally gave her money, but that was just a token of our appreciation, which was from my heart.

We gave her half of what his sister gave her for keeping her two boys. It was hard to see Junior not changed, but I never said anything or told anybody else about it. I prayed that God would take care of him. And he did. I also thanked and gave glory and praise to God for all the other children in her care. I didn't know about her condition. And maybe she was doing the best she could. This was surely a help to Jurius and me, for it made everything easier for us.

My dad told us to always see the positive side of everything. He would say there is some good in everybody, and if you can't see it, maybe your eyes are not seeing right. When I was much younger, I found out that it helps to be at peace, happy, and appreciative for anything we can, no matter the situation. Getting upset or mad only hurts you, not the other person. At school, I could really be relaxed about our baby because I put him in God's hands.

There are angels that I have not mentioned before that I trust to surround my loved ones who need to be protected. I called on them to do whatever needed to be done throughout the day. We can be content and at peace if we can trust God that his will be done on earth as in heaven.

I graduated at the top of our class in June, which meant that I should have been a valedictorian. But because I was a transfer student, that disqualified me. So I was told by the guidance counselor. Nevertheless, I didn't want to stand before that auditorium full of students, parents, and the whole town and make a speech. Another problem for me would have been time to practice what I was going to say. I've never been good at reading before crowds; I was always nervous. Nervousness probably would have caused me to give birth early.

I didn't fuss about it. But a few of my teachers and classmates had questions about it. I said that the council's decision was alright with me. Melissa Hardy should get the honor because she had been in the school for twelve years and maintained an A-average. All I needed to do was to graduate and get my diploma. I was the only one from our neighborhood to graduate that year but was very surprised that many of the people from the church attended. Some of them even gave me gifts, and others gave me cards. Any attention they gave me was appreciated and made me happy.

What really made me happy was that the family members seemed genuine about my grades when the professor who had our diplomas announced before giving me mine. "To Hattie Grace Miller, a transfer with the highest grade in the senior class." There was a loud applause. "Winner from the Hornets." That last statement would seem to me like forever standing there, all eyes on me. "Please, God, help me stay." I was shaking like a tree when the wind was blowing. A big smile came on my face. And I know that God's spirit was nearby, and I would be alright. I went back to my seat, thanked and appreciated my fellow graduating students for their care and support.

Jurius had already planted the crops, and the cucumbers had already started to put out vines. This crop required early morning work every day. The cucumbers would be ready for the market by the end of June. This means that Jurius would need to find some helpers because even if I worked every day, he could not keep up with the picking. This time, I was beginning to get heavy with the child. There would be little that I could do. The cucumbers were very heavy and would be difficult for me to carry. I could pick them easily and put them in someone's basket, but that is what I did for a while until the doctor suggested that I stop.

I worked on the tobacco farm for a couple of days a week, which was easier. The farmer that my brother-in-law and his sister, Thomas and Ellen, worked for needed someone to help care for his tobacco farm. His whole group of about ten people could not keep up with the work. They both came with the farmer to ask me to help. I told him I could not help because I had a small child to care for and was expecting another soon. The farmer, Thomas, and Ellen promised me I didn't have to do anything. I didn't have to lift the heavy tobacco; they mostly needed my expertise. The farmer also told me I could bring Junior with me and take all the time I need to care for him.

I saw how desperate he was. So, I decided to help. I went into the house to get a change of clothes and some snacks for Junior and we were on our way. Looping tobacco was a very complicated means of putting the tobacco on the sticks for hanging on the tobacco barn. It was hard to learn, and not many people could do it fast enough to keep up with the amount of tobacco being brought out of the fields. Thomas and Ellen knew that I could, so they wanted me to help.

Not only was I helping Mr. Hill, the farmer, but it would also help us as we would be moving into a house of our own. We needed a bed for Junior and money to pay for all the furniture Jurius had laid away at the furniture store when he worked there. We were making payments, but small ones. My work will help us pay more and possible pay off by the end of the season.

Junior was not giving any trouble at work, and Mr. Hill was pleased that it didn't require any time away from my work. Every time we finished a cart of tobacco, another one was waiting. I would teach the girls who work there how to loop tobacco. My two days a week turned out to be a full six days a week. Thomas and Ellen got me working everywhere. They also worked and helped me with the baby. Jurius was very happy with the cucumber sale and was able to pay off all the money we borrowed. This meant that whatever profit he benefitted from the farm would help us throughout the year.

We planned to work the farm for another year. It was the best year so far since we got married. We moved into the house at the end of summer after Mark Christopher, our second baby, was born. The one that we were not supposed to have, according to three doctors. Everybody was saying that the doctors had made a mistake, including Jurius. I knew that the doctors were right. I also knew what I voiced every time somebody said that the doctor was wrong.

I would say they could have been wrong, but they were not because there was a physical reason for my being sterile, but God never makes a mistake, and there is nothing that he can't do. I choose to believe him because I know that he made this world, the heaven, and the earth by speaking it into existence. He also made man from the dirt of the earth. I have faith and trust in Him, and I choose to praise and glorify His holy name.

In return, instead of doubting the doctors' intelligence, I gave God that thanksgiving for the child. I'm going to trust God to let His will be done, as He asked for a long time ago. I know He can do it, and if He doesn't do it, I thank him for doing what he knows is best for us all.

### Arrival of Mark Christopher

Mark Christopher's birth was a very easy one. The easiest of all my labors. Just like when Junior was born, his name was chosen by Mrs. Polly, my mother-in-law. I accepted the name. Mr. Mark gave the middle name Christopher. Mr. Mark tried to convince Mrs. Polly not to name the child after him. He said, "We've already had two children named Mark, and both died." She would not give in or change her mind. His name was Mark Christopher, I had no objection, and I voiced none.

However, I could not help but wonder why she wanted to name him Mark if she already had two children named that, living or dead. I was surprised at the way she demanded, not thinking about anyone else's opinion. What was it about names that meant so much to her? I wondered but kept quiet and said a prayer and asked for help for all of us.

I didn't say anything because I believed she would misunderstand and make a big fuss over it. I was keeping peace with her for all our sake, especially for the kids. Jurius and I started as a happy couple, being able to have discussions without fighting, agree on most things, and be reasonable over the few things that we didn't quite see the same way. Most of the things we didn't see eye to eye on were that every weekend on Friday and Saturday nights, he had to take his daddy to Steeling and would get back late at night when the children and I were already in bed and fast asleep.

He wanted to wake me up late at night and make love. Even though I would not feel like it, I always gave in to him. My prayers would have already gone up to God to keep everything safe and to protect our home from evil. My prayers were mostly for him and his dad, but also for his mother. I had seen firsthand what happens when they return home. I believe it would be the same way for me or us if I didn't give in.

Maybe I was too trusting in God and didn't do my part in developing more of a stable family relationship. When Junior was three months old, I thought back to when I found out that Jurius was cheating on me. I decided to leave and go home. When he went back to work the morning after I confronted him the previous night, I packed a bag for us, mostly diapers and a change of clothes. We slipped out of the back door where we thought nobody saw me.

The trip to catch the bus was eight miles, but I was determined to walk the distance carrying the baby and diaper bag. I had walked about two miles when a truck came up behind me. I looked back to see Mr. Roy's truck. He pulled up beside me on the road and said, "Sweetheart, get in." I kept walking and. He drove slowly beside me. In those days, there was not much traffic, so we were safe and not in any danger. He kept asking me to get in, and I kept refusing. "Let me take you where you are going," he said. When I considered the distance where I needed to go, I came close to the truck, and he stopped. I got in, and he drove forward for a little while, then pulled over on the side of the road and said, "Let's talk." "There is nothing I want to talk about," I said. "I just want to go home. Can you take me?" I asked.

"After I understand what the problem is, I will do what is best for you. What reason do you want to go home? "Just to visit?" "No! No!" I said, "I don't want to be married to Jurius anymore." "What caused that decision?" he asked. "Uncle Roy, I don't want to talk. I want to catch the bus. Are you going to take me or not?" He started his truck and made a circle to turn around. I asked him, "Please, let me get out, I've already walked a long way and I've just had to walk this distance again." He didn't say anything else, nor did I.

We rode the way back to Hallandale quietly. Instead of making a left turn to go to my house, he made a right turn toward his house. He stopped the truck. As he got out of the truck, he said I've got to get somebody else's advice. At that time, I looked up and saw Mrs. Polly and Aunt Susie coming out of the back door. Mrs. Polly yelled out, "Gal! What do you think you're doing?" Uncle Roy quietly said to her, "Wait a minute.

We all need to make a decision." This was the first time Mrs. Polly had called me gal since I asked her not to. Her voice didn't sound good, and I was pushed by the devil in me and yelled back at her. "You're no good cheating son has been cheating on me ever since we got married. And you know all about it. Oh, you don't care because your husband, his dad, is doing the same to you." She turned around and started toward her house without saying anything else.

When I yelled, I woke up Junior that had been sleeping since he left home. Susie opened the door and reached out to get the baby. Poor me. By this time, I was crying. "I'll take him to the house. You can come too." She took the diaper bag and went into the house. Uncle Roy got back in the truck and said, "I'm sorry about that." The devil was still in me, and I felt really empowered. I snapped back at him, saying, "What are you sorry about? What did Mrs. Polly say about what I said? You need to be sorry for bringing me back here." I looked at him and could see that his face showed sympathy. And when he spoke the next time, I could hear the humility in his voice.

"Let's go inside. The baby is still crying. Maybe you need to feed him," said Susie. By this time, he got out of the truck and rushed around to help me, but I was already out and started toward the porch to go into the house. As I reached the door, I looked back to see him sitting on the tailgate of his truck with his head bent down almost to his knees. "Oh Lord, God," I said, "what have I done?" I paused for a moment at the door, even though I heard Junior cry like I'd never heard him cry before.

Maybe it was because he was with a stranger, somebody he had never seen before. Or maybe he sensed the problems we were having. "Oh, Lord," I continued to pray, "help all of us to make the right decision. And God, please forgive me for letting myself get out of control. Heal the hurt in all of us, and let us say and do the right things that you will be pleased with."

I opened the door just as Uncle Roy called out. "What's wrong, sweetheart?" That was the second time he called me that, and I felt that he really did care. I nursed the baby. Aunt Susie had already changed his diaper. In a little while, he was fast asleep. "You can put him on the bed in that room," Pointing to one of the bedrooms. "Are you hungry?" she asked. "No, thank you," I said. She went to the door and called Uncle Roy.

He came and said with a big smile, "I was afraid to come in." We all laughed," and I said, "I want to apologize for what I said and for hurting you when all you wanted was to help me." "I accept," he said, "all is forgiven. I apologize, too, for the choice I made. I knew Polly was upset; I should not have brought you here." "I'll be alright." I said a prayer standing at the door. "Oh, I think we should pray before we talk," he said.

So we did.

"Well," Uncle Roy announced, "I do know the reason you wanted to leave, but I would like to know how you found out. And did you talk with Jurius about it?" "Well, I found out when he told me what his dad was doing. If he was not involved, he would not be taking his dad to cheat on his mama. Also, Lucy told me he was messing with somebody at her house. When I asked him about it, he would say nothing.

He didn't deny that. He didn't even consider that our marriage was on the line. I'd rather he told the truth, but if he had to lie to save the marriage and make me feel better, so be it." Uncle Roy said that my source of information was not enough to make him believe that. I should not end the marriage because he didn't believe. Jurius wouldn't take a chance on losing me. He talked very positively about our relationship and that some people would do anything to break us up.

God's words and Uncle Roy's words convinced me.

I changed my mind about leaving. Uncle Roy took us home, where I began to pray. I kept remembering Uncle Roy pleading for the baby. "You started a family now, and both of you need to do all you can for the sake of this child. He needs both of you in his life or his life will not be complete without you both.

My mind went back to my childhood. I remembered our life without a mother. "God help me to make a sacrifice or as many as I need to make for my baby and my marriage." Uncle Roy really made a great impression on my life when he said, "There are no perfect marriages. There is going to be problems of some kind or another. It's up to the two of you what you do with these problems. If you go home, there will be problems. Try and run from them. You will have to trust God to help you work them out and give you the courage and strength to get through them."

I decided that I was going to do my part to make things better and leave the rest that I couldn't do to God. He took me to my home and waited until I got inside. Then he drove away. Junior had fallen asleep again, and I was lost about what to do. The day's journey would not leave my mind, and I started thinking about what I would say to Jurius when he came home. I didn't feel like cooking, so I sat in the room in darkness. The Sun was going down and the trees near my side window blocked out what little sun was left. The back window had been shaded since noontime. I didn't light the Lantern. So the room was just right for thinking and praying.

Mrs. Polly was outside in the front yard where she was when Uncle Roy brought me home. I tried to dismiss the bad thoughts from my mind. No such luck! I tried to pray, but my mind would just keep going back to the things I said to Roy and Mrs. Polly and how I allowed the devil to take control of me. Then I heard the little voice say, "That's the way you need to stand up to Jurius.

Let him know you will not put up with him like his mom puts up with his daddy." I had heard her say a lot of times that he was fornicating around here. All the time! There was no doubt in my mind that she knew what he was doing. And that she knew what Jurius was doing also. I wondered why she had not stopped Jurius from going with him. Then I remembered her say if it weren't for Jurius driving him, he would have killed himself because he always got himself drunk.

All I could think to say was, "Oh Lord my God, my heavenly father. Please come and help us get right with you and with each other." Footsteps hit the steps leading to our door. The door opened quietly. I could barely see the shadow of a man as he entered. "Why are you in the dark?" he said, reaching for the light from the match. I could see there were no wrinkles on his forehead. Usually, when he is upset or troubled about something, his forehead is deeply wrinkled.

"How are you and the baby doing?" he asked, reaching over to me for a kiss as usual. "Oh, Junior is down for the night." I said, "I hope not, but he has been sleeping a long time." "What's for dinner?" was the next question. I tried to keep my voice calm and as sweet as possible when I said nothing. "Nothing?" he replied, sounding surprised. Usually, he would come in and try to guess what I was cooking by the smell.

At this point, I heard the outside door open and close. For sure, Mrs. Polly had waited outside to talk to Jurius before he came into the house. "How are you doing?" he asked again. "I'm OK, but I had a very rough day," I replied, "sit down, and I'll tell you all about it."

"You know things didn't go well with me after we talked last night?" He nodded his head. "Well, after you went to work this morning, I decided it was best for me to leave and go home." He didn't act a bit surprised. "I started walking to Four Corners to catch the bus," no astonishment, no change in his facial expressions. I stopped and looked him straight in the eyes and said, "You already know all about it, don't you?" He nodded his head again.

I said, "What do you have to say about it? Who told you?" He dropped his head and said, "You know who told me. The one who is always watching you." "Who's watching me?" I wanted him to say the person's name, but he said, "That's why we have got to get out of this house. Maybe then you can be happy." "Happy!" I yelled louder than I wanted to. "You don't get the reason I want to leave and go home.

Not this house nor a spy, but the one I made vows to that I would love and cherish until death do us part." "You made those vows," he said, "so, why are you so quick to break them then?" "Me break my vows? You don't get it, do you? What do you think caused me to want to leave? Since you couldn't or wouldn't be honest and answer the question I asked you last night, then when do you plan to be honest and give me a reasonable answer?

As soon as the question was asked, the answer I expected was a simple yes or no. When you want to be fair and respectable, then we have something to work with. You simply refused to give me the respect of an answer. I simply cannot deal with that kind of attitude, and tonight when I asked you who told you about the day I had, you gave me no answer. I'm here tonight hoping that we can come to some understanding about our lives.

If you want to stay married or if you want to act like a married man and stop supporting your dad in his drunkenness and cheating on your mama. You need to decide. For I'm not willing to stay in this mess."

"I'm sorry," he started, "I should have told you the truth on both incidences. It's just that I've been hearing that you don't have to answer to a woman. From what I have been thinking about and what I hear from you, we are in a partnership and should consider each other's feelings. I'm not used to answering to anyone, for as long as I can remember. I didn't have to answer, so I didn't answer. To answer your question about me cheating, the answer is yes. The other question about who told me about your day, was momma. She met me at the highway and told me as we walked. She also told me you had been disrespectful to her. Now that I have told you the truth, do you think we can work things out?"

I'm sure we can with God's help if you really want to. Maybe you need to take some time and think about it. As I see it, many changes need to be made. I don't want you to change your life because of me. I think you need to change because it is right and because you want your life to be pleasing to God. Also, you ought to want self-respect for yourself and me right now. I am ashamed that others know what you are doing, and you claim to be a married man and a father.

Would you be proud of yourself if Junior was old enough to know what was going on in our family? Are you proud of yourself for knowing what you and your daddy's been involved in these many years? Are you proud or happy with your daddy letting you know what was going on with him and not teaching you that it was wrong? Is this the way you will teach Junior when he is old enough? Do you think God is pleased with you breaking so many of his commandments and laws?

What about who God is? Knowing everything about us, nobody has to tell Him anything, and He still loves us and provides us with all we need. The things nobody is capable of providing but him. Yes, I know we both need time to think about trying to work our marriage out."

His mama knew I had not cooked anything, and I could smell food cooking from her kitchen. She knocked on the door to ask if we wanted to eat with them. This was the first time she had ever invited me. Surely, God was at work in all of us. I called out with a loud thank you. And thank you, God. I felt that even though I could not eat a bite, I needed to play a role of appreciation. Yes, God was at work solving our problem because Junior started crying, and I had an excuse to take a plate of food and go back to the room. Words of

Thanksgiving to God went up from the depths of my heart while I attended to Junior.

It was hard to stay calm and not infect my stress and emotions on the baby. To my surprise, I believed he sensed what I was thinking, and to let me know God had also heard and answered, he had a huge smile on his face. What an awesome sight to behold in such times as this. God is always near and lets us know he cares. Anything that was not right and comforting at this time disappeared from me. Freedom and peace came over me, and I had "No Fear" or worry that everything would be well in my life.

For sure, Jurius and I didn't know each other before we married, but I am happy to say that I know God and He knew me. He has proved to me many times that he is with me and will be with me until the end of life, as long as I continue to be faithful and trust Him and never leave nor forsake Him. He promised to be with me and make ways that no man can make. He will open doors closed in my face. Close doors that are open against me. I'll keep the faith and trust and depend on God, our Heavenly Father. My prayers went to God for Jurius, that he will know the same and let God rule in his life.

My mind was made up that I will let nothing separate me from the love of God. I decided to be a good wife, mother, person, and friend, one that God is pleased with. I would show my love to everyone I come into contact with. I would worship God with all my heart and continue to pray and praise him for all his goodness. I would continue to love my husband with all my being, just realizing that I didn't want to leave him, no matter what he did.

"Dear God, please accept my marriage and make it what you would have it to be. Bless everyone who is a part of this family, either by blood or connection. Heal, oh Lord, the broken hearts and spirits and give us the kind of love you told us we should have. Help us understand your Word and to live accordingly. Let us always remember to worship your Holy name and give you glory and thanksgiving for all you have done and what you will do for us.

Make us strong for the task before and give us help and courage to continue life's journey for your glory and honor in Jesus' name."

The next few days were make-up. Jurius and I spent the weekend from Friday night through Sunday night together. His dad was also at home with Mrs. Polly. He was doing repairs on the house that she had been trying to get him to do for a long time. All of us were a little uneasy because we all knew the reason for the change. The change was very good to the point of all of us going to church on Sunday morning.

Jurius used to go to church before just to please me. However, he went this time because he wanted to go. He talked about the Sermon on the way home. He was surprised to know that I had joined the senior choir and had been going to Sunday school. These were things I missed a lot from being in Civil City. I had been singing in the choir and Sunday school for a long time. Satan was not going to steal my joy.

While he was doing his things with his daddy, I decided I was going to be a part of a community and church.

Right after we were married, I told Jurius about God calling me to be a minister of his gospel and a preacher. He did not hesitate to say, "No wife of mine is going to be a preacher." I said, "I don't have a choice, and you have no choice. God calls whomever he pleases, and there is nothing I, you, or anybody else can do about it. I had already accepted, even though my dad thought God would not call a woman to preach." The conversation ended, and no more was said about that from either of us. As I knew he would, God made a way for me to spread the gospel by teaching church school to the adults.

There were very few young adults coming to church school, and none of them was qualified to teach. None of them had high school learning; no one even wanted to try. Most of the older members were coming to church school. The pastor taught the class, but he could not always get there on time every Sunday. When he wasn't there, the adult class just listened to the other teachers teaching the youth and children. I started going to prayer meetings when Mrs. Polly was afraid to go by herself and there was no one to go with her. "I'll go with you," I told her. "What about the baby?" she asked. "Who will watch him?"

"I'll bring him along with us." So we did. Prayer service included three or four songs, one after each, prayer and scripture. The scripture is read by an appointee selected by the preacher's steward. "Mrs. Hattie Miller, will you read the scriptures?" He had to specify which Miller because there was more than one in the congregation.

At the end of the reading, I explained, with the help of God and by the Holy Spirit, what the meaning was. Most of the members there stated that they liked the explanation.

Every week, I had to choose a scripture, pray, and study for the next explanation. The word got out, and more adults came each week. Finally, the pastor came one week to see all the fuss and joyfulness in prayer meeting. He decided that part of the period should be bible study. Jurius came after he got home from work a little late. Studying for the bible class increased my knowledge of the bible as well as the members. I knew God had ordained the plan to let me know he would work out any problems that came my way.

All I had to do was be obedient to him and willing to do whatever he asked. The members who were laughing at me and teasing me about my hair and how skinny and tall I was, were not laughing anymore because they were getting into the word of God.

"Trust in the Lord with all thine heart; and lean not unto thine own understanding."
Proverbs 3:5–6

# CHAPTER 11

## Jurius and the captain

Jurius also got a big blessing from God after he got serious. He had been working at the Marine Corp Base for a few months when there was a change in the Head manager. One day, the captain talked with him and found out that I was pregnant and had two boys at home. The workers at the hospital worked on shifts and went to work very early some days and got off early and went in later and worked until late, other days. They stayed at the barracks when their shift was working. Jurius explained to the captain that he had no transportation except one of the workers who lived near our community. In fact, three others rode with him and the car owner.

A few days later, the captain called him into his office. He and others who heard the request thought he was in trouble for something. Instead of being in trouble, he was blessed beyond belief. The captain asked him if he wanted to buy a car from him. "I have a 1940 Ford Coupe in good running condition. Do you want to see it? I drove it today. But after my wife and I talked about it, we decided that we didn't really need it, and you do." Jurius said, "Yes, I want to see it, but I don't have any money to buy a car.

How much do you want?" "I don't really know," he said, "I'll need to talk with my wife, and then we will decide." "The next day will be shift change, and then I will be off for three days," Jurius said. "Well, I will give you an answer tomorrow, and you can decide about the pay." "I was so excited," Jurius said to me, "and my heart was beating very fast." "Calm down," the captain said, "this is not a life and death situation." By that time, he was also sweating a lot.

"Yes, I know, but you don't understand; I don't have any money." The captain said, "I've been watching you work, how you interact with your coworkers, and how you treat the people you serve with kindness and respect. I know I can trust you to pay me for the car. You're not going anywhere, are you? You are going to work here for a while, aren't you?" "Oh, yes. For as long as they will let me." No phones to call and share the good news with me.

He could not tell his coworkers because this was between him and the captain.

He told me that he lay awake that night wanting to talk with somebody about the Big Blessing. "Thank you, God," he prayed, "for blessing my family and me with a car and with the plans to pay for it." That's how thankful and sure he was that the car was ours. He had been thinking if there was an emergency at home and he needed to be there. He prayed until he fell asleep that night.

The next morning, their workday started at 5:00 o'clock. He was up and dressed before anybody else. Somebody asked, "What's wrong with you, Jurius?" He's been acting strangely for a few days. Another person said, "He's been acting strange ever since Captain Anderson called him into the office. They continued to wonder what had happened, and no one dared to ask. At the end of the day, when Jurius told the driver he would not be going home with them, it really made all his coworkers who rode together with them very suspicious. Captain Anderson talked with Jurius as the workday ended and asked him to keep the business of the car sale a secret from all the other workers.

"Well, my wife depreciated the car and came up with $50.00. Is that alright with you?" "$50.00," Jurius replied, "I have no idea of what a car costs, but I thought it would be more." "If that price is alright with you, here are the keys. This set was my wife's, and she said to give this set to your wife. The keys are color-coded. The red one is for the engine, and the blue one is for the trunk.

This set is yours. They were my set. I didn't need to mark them. I just knew which one was for the engine and the other for the trunk. There are two bags of clothes Kathy thought your boys could use." The Andersen's had two boys, a little older than our boys. "Oh," Captain Anderson said, reaching his hand into his pants pockets again and pulling out a piece of money. He handed it to Jurius and said, "You'll have to put some gas in at the filling station.

You get to. My wife always drove on empty. He handed Jurius the $5.00 bill and said, laughing, "Don't forget, or you will be walking to find gas.

He turned around quickly and waved his hands for Jurius to stop as he walked away. Coming back to the car, he said, "I almost forgot to tell you. You need to get the car registered to drive on the base. You will need to stop at the MP (Military Police) station at the gate going out and ask for a sticker to get back on the base when you come back to work. The car registration is in the glove compartment over there," pointing at it.

"And you will need to show them your driver's license. You do have one, don't you?" "Oh yes," Jurius replied, reaching for his wallet; he showed his license. "I don't need to see it. I didn't want to have sold you a car and you can't get it home. When you come back to work, I will go with you to get a permanent sticker." When Jurius drove the car in front of the house, he was grinning from ear to ear.

I went out to the porch to get a better view of the car. "Here it is," he said, "I can hardly believe it. Am I dreaming?" Before I could say anything, he was getting out of the car. Both of his hands were up in the air, saying, "Thank you God! You are so awesome. So loving and kind, there is nothing you can't do for your children. That's why I worship you, praise and glorify your name." He was standing on the ground, and I was on the porch trying to get down where he was.

I began to thank God and his Son, Jesus Christ, because this was the first time I had heard Jurius pray like that. We went into the house, and he told me all about the car and Captain Anderson trusting him and letting him bring the car home without any down payments or even a promissory note.

Jurius was sure as I was that this was the work of God. "Captain Anderson has only known me for about three months, and I was surprised when he said he had been watching me in my work," Jurius said. "Captain said it as if he had been watching all the other workers also, and he decided to sell me the car for that reason." "You don't know who is watching you without you knowing. You are right," I said, "that's why we must always do our best and live right at all times. We decided to take a ride to see how it drove. When we started to get into the car, I saw the two bags. "Captain Anderson's wife gave clothes for our boys."

Jurius took the bags into the house while I put the boys into the car. There was only one seat in the coupe that was made for three adults. So there was enough space for all of us to fit comfortably. The first place we went was to his family home. They were excited, especially Mr. Mark. Mrs. Polly was always negative about anything we did. Jurius accepted the job on the base. We had to move out of the house we were living in.

She thought there were no other houses in the area and that we would have to move back into their house. All her talk about it were very negative. Aunt Susie, who had moved with her children after Uncle Roy died, told Jurius he could move into her house, just for the upkeep of the house. What she didn't tell us was that her younger brother had been looking out for the property and staying there part-time. Uncle Corey had a house of his own, and Susie assumed that he would move out of her house completely and into his house.

Uncle Corey's house had three little rooms: kitchen, one bedroom, and a living room. He moved all his bedroom furniture, including his double bed into the living room. He told Jurius he planned to come back to his house as usual, and we could use his kitchen and the bedroom. We prayed about the arrangement and decided that this was better than going back to his parents' house. We fitted almost all our furniture into the three rooms. Jurius said, "This is for a little while. I'm going to build us a house."

My third pregnancy had not gone well. It was a tubal pregnancy, which usually ended in miscarriage. I was very sick, weak, and always tired for two months. I was still having a monthly period, which puzzled my regular doctor for two months. When my symptoms got no better, I went to the doctor in New Hope, where I went for my first pregnancy. After a physical examination, he made a few other tests and an X-ray. We went home without any answers about what the problems were. My weight dropped a lot, and my blood pressure and blood count had also dropped. I couldn't teach church school or sing in the choir. People who visited me had no idea what was wrong, but they had discouraging stories to tell about someone they knew with similar symptoms.

Finally, we received a letter from the doctor telling us about the tubular pregnancy. He gave us two choices, but he might as well have given us one. We knew we wanted to do anything to save the baby. The first choice was to abort the baby, which he thought was the best choice. The second choice was to be used as a Guinea Pig and go to Pikesville to see if the doctor could save the baby by moving it along the tube doing several sections.

The hospital and the doctor agreed that this procedure would cost us nothing. Our only expense would be the cost of travel. At the bottom of the letter, he gave us two appointment dates. He asked us to send back that portion of the letter checking which date suits us best. We looked at the dates and chose the one closest to Jurius' time off and mailed the letter back. The return letter from Dr. Allen came back to us confirming the appointment.

The day to go to the office for the follow-up appointment, both his parents wanted to come along. That meant we had no one to care for the boys while we were gone. My sickness and weakness made it almost impossible for me to get the boys up and ready to take along. Jurius had to do most of the work while I got the clothes out. During the trip, all the different smells started to make me feel sick. And I could barely sit up in the car. I rode in the front seat. Mr. and Mrs. Miller and the boys were in the back seat. Jurius did the driving since we had to get there in time for the appointment. His dad drove so slowly and we would miss the appointment.

My plans for the boys to stay in the car with their grandpa were to no avail. Everybody wanted to join me. Mrs. Polly always had to see the doctor along with who has the appointment because she wanted to tell the doctor what to do or not to do. Doctor Allen explained to all of us about the procedure, which she didn't understand, for she was so sure I was not expecting. I understood and was not sure any of the others did.

My head was beginning to spin a little, and my stomach felt bloated. Little Mark only wanted me to hold him, so I wanted to hurry and leave. Dr. Allen handed me papers and stated that the doctors in Pikesville would not see me without these papers. I saw that everybody was confused, even Jurius. I decided to explain it in the car on the way home.

"Do you understand?" the doctor asked. "Yes," I answered. "If you need anything else, let me know." "Doctor, there is one thing I need help with, if you will. I am very nauseous all the time and can't keep food down." "Yes, I have some pills ready for you, something to build up that blood count, vitamins that should help you feel better. Have you been vomiting?" he asked. "Yes, two or more times a day." "These pills will help you keep from vomiting. Be sure to tell the doctor in Pikesville."

Every time the doctor mentioned Pikesville, Mrs. Polly would say that's a long way from here. After Jurius took the baby from me and headed for the door, I stood up. "Wait a minute," he said and called for the nurse. "I need to know what your blood pressure is today." The nurse came in and handed me a bag with the pills and proceeded to check my pressure. The doctor ushered everyone out of the dressing room into his office. I saw that the meter reading was lower than the last time. The nurse wrote the numbers down and said to me, "Let me get you a list of things to eat to see if you can get this pressure up before seeing the other doctors."

When Doctor Allen mentioned the Guinea pig procedure; where they would be performing a never before tried experimental process, both of the Millers were against doing it. The doctor said this decision has already been made by Hattie and Jurius. He then walked toward the door and let us out. "See you when you get back; you already have an appointment card." In the car on the way home, I started explaining to Jurius so he could understand what the doctor said about the procedure.

His parents could not hear what I was saying because of the noise of the car. The road was bumpy, which produced a lot of noise. My voice was weak from being sick and tired from the trip. "Jurius, what did she say?" his mother yelled. I turned to my side so that my voice could reach the back of the car. They kept asking the same questions, and I tried to repeat myself until Jurius yelled out. "We will tell you when we get home."

"Thank you, God, for giving us another baby. I know that you will make everything alright. Thank you our Heavenly Father and Savior Jesus Christ." My praying seemed to make the trip easier and more tolerable. I also prayed that God would let Mr. and Mrs. Miller understand and not let them try to discourage us. My faith in God grew as tall as a tree and as high as the mountain. I felt nearer to God. I took the medicine bag from the dashboard and continued praying that God would let the pills be sufficient for what I needed to feel better. He had already given me help with the boys and gave Junior understanding to help me when I was in pain. "Bring me water, diapers, put the diapers in the pail," and Junior did as I said.

One day, I couldn't make it to the kitchen. Junior pulled a chair up to the cabinet and got the peanut butter and Jelly. He brought that to me and went back for the bread. That was how God provided for us when the children were hungry. I can't say it enough that God will always make a way. There is nothing he can't and will not do for his children.

When we were back home, I explained what the doctor said about the procedure to his folks. They were somewhat surprised when I told them that I would have another baby. None of them wanted(us) to go to Pikesville to have the procedure done. They had not heard of tubal pregnancy and were sure something else was wrong with me. Jurius tried to explain about the test and X-rays, but they thought the doctor was fooling us to have us go for some other reason.

"It will just be a waste of trip," Mark said, "we don't need those extra miles. That's a long way to go." "Dad, tell me now if I will be able to drive your car," Jurius said, "maybe I can ask Dolores to let me drive her car. She's always asking if she can help us. Wait until tomorrow. I will have my car checked out."

Jurius' shift was back on for the next three days. He would have no way of knowing what his dad would say. "What about the boys?" his mama asked. Jurius was a bit surprised that she asked. I was not surprised, but I saw the expression on her face when she could not change our minds about going. I also heard a different tone in her voice when she asked about the boys. "We can take them with us," I stated, trying to keep my voice pleasant so as not to let the shaking show.

I knew it was time to pray and to leave. The baby had started to get fussy and I moved toward the car. His daddy said to Jurius, "Go on and take them home and come back so we can talk." We were quiet all the way home since it took just a few minutes to get there. Jurius got out of the car, took Junior out, and opened my door so I could get out. I stepped on the porch to open the house door.

I looked back trying to ask if he would join me in prayer, but before I could talk, he said, "Let us go in and pray." We prayed and helped get the boys settled in. He put away their coats and hats, and for the first time that day, he showed a little emotion for me. "Let me get the medicine so you can take it before I go." I took the medicine, which I really didn't need at the time because I wasn't feeling sick.

I was just tired and needed to rest.

He made all of us a sandwich and grilled cheese. The boys had milk and we had Pepsi. That was the only thing I could keep down. I forced myself to eat the food, hoping and praying that it would give me some strength. He drove back to his family house to find his dad upset because he stayed long at our home. He said he tried to explain to his dad that he had to take care of us.

The children were hungry, and I needed care also. He told me that his dad didn't want to listen and when he used a curse word at him, he started walking back to the house. While we were talking, his sister Dolores and her husband Roy drove up. We both said at the same time. "Thank you, God." We had prayed for help, but we didn't expect it to come so quickly. We also realized that he would still be at his family house if his daddy had not acted up.

God works in mysterious ways and always works wonders.

His sister - the one responsible for us getting married and made all the plans, and as I learned later, told Jurius that he had to get married – got out of the car. She was in the same position that I was in and had to make the same choice before she got married. "Tell me what the doctor said," she queried. Jurius started to tell them, then he stopped and said, "Hattie can tell you better than I can." I explained everything to them, and he told them about his mom and dad trying to discourage us from taking the doctor's advice.

He stated that we needed to start the procedure next week at the hospital in Pikesville. We needed to be there early in the morning. "That's no problem, but the problem is dad doesn't know if I can use his car. In case he doesn't, what about you? Do you think I will be able to use one of your vehicles? Doctor Allen thinks it won't take more than an hour to do the work. Of course, the check-in and everything will take longer.

If the first treatment works, we will need to go back next week."

Uncle Roy spoke up and said, "I don't see why we can't let you use the vehicle. Talking to the dealers. Come straight home from work; you will be home before I need to go." Uncle Roy worked on the base at night and would get home in the morning before Delores had to leave for work. The business was settled. They would bring the car to us the evening before the appointment. It was decided that Jurius would get a key today because he would not be home before Roy had to go to work.

"Thank you, both of you, and you have let God use you to make way for us," Jurius said. "What are you talking about? As much as you helped me, staying with me at night while Uncle Roy was at work, don't you remember driving me to the hospital when our first baby was born? And then driving to the base to let Uncle Roy know. I can't ever repay you for all you have done for our family. Don't make me start talking about it all.

Come on, Uncle Roy, let's go back and check on these old folks over there. Was dad drinking today?" she asked. Jurius replied, "No, he went with us to the doctors. How are you feeling?" he asked me, "is the medicine helping?" "I don't know," I responded, "I'm just letting God do his thing right now and I don't know if he is using the medicine or not."

The trip to Pikesville went well. The doctors were very hopeful that the baby could be saved. The move of the baby went better than they expected. They gave me directions to follow that was almost impossible. Complete bed rest until you return next week. "Lord, what are we to do with two little boys? We need your help, or we don't know what to do." Jurius said, "I will beg my mama to keep them while I'm at work, and I will keep them when I'm off." "How can I make it for three days having to use a bedpan?" Jurius didn't answer me.

And when I glanced at him, I believed he was supportive. I had already prayed. So I just began praising, "Thank you, my heavenly Father. I know you will always make a way, especially when we don't see a way." At that time, I looked up and saw a sign that said Civil City, Left turn. "Make that turn," I said quickly to Jurius. "Why would we go to Civil City?" "To get my sister to come and stay with us.

She is not working now. I think she will be glad to help us. That's what God just told me." "I had not thought about that," Jurius said, "I hope she can come back and get ready quickly because we have to be back in time for Uncle Roy to go to work tonight. I pray that God will let her be at home and that she will be willing to come. And that we get back in time. God, I don't doubt you would help us.

This was your plan from the beginning. Forgive me for that little doubt that gripped my brain."

Ruth came to the door when she heard the car horn blowing. She didn't recognize the car and was very surprised when Jurius got out of the car. "What are you doing here?" she asked. "We've come to get you." "Get me?" "For sure," Jurius said, "we desperately need you." She came through the car window where I was sitting and asked, "Why do you need me?" "I have to be on bed rest for a while, and you can help us with the boys and everything. Can you come with us?" "Yes," she replied, "let me go and pack a bag. Dallas Junior came out of the house, and we talked about our problems. He was willing to help if we still needed help. Junior came and helped.

It was hard for me to stay in bed 24/7, but I had help from my family. The third trip was the last one. All the doctors had to do was test to find that the fetus was in place. Thank God. I don't know who was more excited: Jurius, I or the team of experimental doctors and nurses. They would go down in history as being the first to conduct such a test. The Millers were the first Guinea pig that survived the experiment. The doctors put me on medication that was a muscle relaxer to keep me quiet and relaxed for three months. My brother Dallas Junior and Sue Ruth, the last in my family, who still lived at our home, took turns helping us.

Jurius' mom and dad have finally accepted that we were going to have another baby. Before Mrs. Polly could give in and acknowledge it, she just had to say. "What about the Doctor's report after Junior was born?" "Well, long before that, God let me know that if I asked him anything in the name of his Son Jesus, He would do it. God will keep His promises." "I'll have to agree," she said, "I can see his work for myself." We went back to the hospital at Pikesville for the last time, and I was cleared for light work. No heavy lifting or anything that is stressful.

My brother kept coming to stay with us throughout the pregnancy because Ruth had gone to New York to work. Dad was in the Veterans' Hospital in Salisbury and Miss Cera had gone back to live with her son and his family. Dallas junior was quite lonely as the only work he had done was on the farm, and the season was over, except for cotton picking. He jokingly said, "I could pick from sun up to sun down without taking a break to eat. And still, I couldn't pick fifty pounds. My time is best bet here helping you and the boys."

For sure, I will be able to eat because I love to cook. I would start picking cotton and then hoped the rest of the pregnancy would be better than it was. Until about two months to go, my legs and other extremities started to accumulate fluids. The doctors took me off salt, sugar, and bread. I could eat meat sparingly. I was eating mostly fresh vegetables with a little butter. Oh gosh. What a diet! I quickly got tired of the diet.

There was nothing growing in the garden except greens and okra. The okra was alright. But have you ever had vegetables cooked in water with no salt? I got a bright idea and started eating canned vegetables. I could get a bigger variety, and they tasted better. I had it made. What a good idea, but guess what? The first problem came back. That fluid came rushing back, and I had to go back to fresh vegetables.

One day, Captain Anderson asked Jurius about us and Jurius told him about the problem. He said, "Why don't you get her something better to eat? When you go home today, tell her that you have carrots and cabbage on the menu. That will be a change from eating collard greens every day. He also sent me a couple of cucumbers and a few bananas. "Hallelujah!" I yelled out when I saw the bananas. These were foods that we had not thought about. The season was over for cabbage, cucumbers, and tomatoes. All these were not sold in the local stores near us. We knew God had asked Captain Anderson to bless us this day. When I thought about how God make ways when you see no way, tears of joy came to my cheeks.

The banana was the first I ate. Even though I had already had a series of collard greens, I still ate some of the cabbage and carrots. As soon as I finished eating, I wrote a note to Captain Anderson to tell him how much I appreciated what he had done. "God will bless you and your family," I wrote. "Thank you for allowing God to use you. I will always cherish your act of kindness and good deeds forever." I put my note in an envelope and gave it to Jurius. The next morning, I reminded him not to forget the note. "How can I forget?" he said. "I stayed awake most of the night, thanking God for the energy and praying for him and you."

When Jurius got to work the next day, everybody was telling him about what he had missed. As soon as he had finished his work the previous day, he was told that he could leave a little earlier to get some food. The second shift checked in, and Captain Anderson called all of them together and told them that they had done such a tremendous job. He recommended that they'd all get a higher rating and some would get a step up. "Sorry, I missed the good news, but going home to my family was good enough for me. I've not seen such happiness on their faces in a while. Nothing could have been better for me," he said to his co-workers.

I was happy to get the variety of vegetables. It made my meals easier to deal with when I had no desire to eat in the first place. Happiness compared to unhappiness is good news. Throughout the days, I would ensure to eat whatever I was supposed to so that God's will be done. He cannot take back His word, and He never lies. My eyes lit up, and I smiled when I saw the different vegetables, but I surely knew that God made a way.

As a little girl, I learned that God can and will use whoever will allow him to let His will be done. Captain Anderson allowed God to use him when he sold Jurius the car and again when he sent the vegetables. His generosity let us know that there are some people who will let God use them.

We went to Centerville, where we could get a variety of fresh vegetables. We bought enough to last a while. We got apples, oranges, bananas, cabbage, spinach, cucumbers, carrots, and whatever the store had that I could eat raw. My blood pressure improved, and I was not retaining fluids anymore.

Time passed for my due date, and nothing happened. My birthday would be in a couple of weeks. I was hoping the baby would be born before then so I could have dinner like I was craving; some real food with fried chicken and a pineapple cake. We went to Silver City to get Dallas Junior to come and stay with us and be with the children when we had to go to the hospital. Doctor Allen had already made preparations for my visit to the hospital so that we wouldn't have any trouble being admitted.

He didn't tell us, but I think he knew there would be some complications with the delivery. A few months earlier, Junior had surgery in his chin, which was an emergency. We were already waiting for Christopher to turn two years old so he could have a hernia repaired. You might think that this was a lot of problems for a young. However, Jurius and I knew what to do and had already turned over these problems to an almighty hand who knows exactly what to do.

Doctor Allen had already assured us that he would take care of all this and we would have nothing to worry about. Mrs. Polly said to me one day when we met at the mailbox at the main road, "Did you want all these children to bring all these problems?" She laughed and acted as if it was a joke. I was wondering why she asked me this when she had more problems? She had several miscarriages and a couple of stillbirths.

One of her babies even died within a month after putting to bed. I was looking at her when she asked me the question, and I started laughing. I had no intention of mocking her. "It was the Holy Spirit who helped you with your problems when you had them during your childbearing years, and you had nine living children." She stopped laughing.

I turned to walk away but stopped and said to her, "The same God that helped you through all of that is my helper too. If no one else cares about me, He loves and cares. He has already solved my problem, and if by chance there are any more, he will take care of it." I didn't just learn how to trust God and depend on Him, I also know who he is and what he can do. He never failed me yet. We can do nothing on our own without God's help. Thank you God. I got two hours, and I had to turn toward the door. Looking back, I said, "Mrs. Polly, I love you, and God bless you." She waved the hand that held the mail and said something I couldn't understand.

This was a weekend off, and we will be coming home in about an hour. I had planned to go to Centerville to get my special birthday food. I wanted to take Dallas Junior and the children with us so they could get out of the house for a while. When Jurius got home, he had other plans which didn't include us. I gave him a list of things I wanted and decided that I needed to stay home since my due date was passed.

Dallas Junior asked me, "What will we do if you go into labor without any way to get to the hospital?" I smiled and said that it's not going to happen, and if by chance it does happen, my help is always near. "God will make a way. He would take care of me."

My birthday came, and I had my dinner as I had planned. Jurius did most of the cooking, and I made my pineapple cake with icing on top. We waited for Jurius to get home, which was later than I needed to eat. I couldn't eat as much as I thought because I had gotten used to eating a smaller amount. I ate a big piece of cake since I had not had anything sweet except apples for a long time, which seemed like forever. I was almost sure that the baby would come that night because I had done more work than usual and still felt good except for a little discomfort from all the food I ate. To my surprise, morning came, and I was ready to go.

Jurius took Dallas to catch the bus to go home. He needed to get his garden ready. It was time to plant the garden. Daddy always planted potatoes, onions, peas, and salad greens around Valentine's Day. He would only stay two days and come back. Jurius was off-duty and wouldn't report back until the baby came. Friday came, and no baby. I felt well enough to cook dinner, but I was not really craving dinner. I wanted some breakfast food like I had not had for a long time. I made scrambled eggs, sausage, and grits. I was still feeling well. I bathed the boys, got them in bed, and read them a book. I got sleepy reading to them, so I hurried took my bath. Jurius had gone to the church for a meeting and would be back shortly.

"God is our refuge and strength, a very
present help in trouble."
Psalm 46:1

# CHAPTER 12

# Another baby's ordeal

Before I went to bed, I went to the front door and could see that the meeting was over. Some cars were leaving. I got in bed and fell asleep. I don't think I finished my prayers which I had started doing on the bed. It was hard to get on my knees and harder to get up. I awoke and felt like I had slept all night. I realized that Jurius was not in bed. I also discovered that I had peed on the bed.

I got up as quickly as I could and threw back the covers. I was surprised to see blood instead of pee. I tried to wake Junior and had no success. He was sleeping like a solid rock. I moved to the side of the bed, got my feet to the floor, and started praying for God to send help.

I got to the door holding the bed sheet between my legs and started yelling for help. There were some people still at the church, and I could hear them talking and laughing. They could not hear me. In just that instant, I saw Jurius' car coming my way. I went back to the bed and felt something move under the sheet I was holding between my legs. I dared not look because I thought it was the baby. Jurius came in laughing and telling me about the conversation he had with his pastor. I yelled, "Help!" He rushed into the bedroom to find me drenched in blood. He almost fainted and was speechless for a while. "Get the boys in the car!" I yelled, "and get a blanket to wrap up. We don't have time to get dressed."

All this time, I was feeling something moving under the sheet. I grabbed my coat and said, "Get the boys' jacket. Hurry as fast as you can." All this time, Jurius has not said a word. He was just following my instructions. "Get my bag and bag for the baby." "Over there," he handed me the bag, but I could not take it because I had to use both hands to hold the sheet and whatever it was there. He helped me get toward the car carrying me down the steps.

He wrapped me in the blanket and ran around the car to get in but couldn't find the keys. I said, "I know everything will be fine. I knew you were here and taking care of things." He went back into the house to look for the keys. He came back and started the car, and we were on the way to New Hope.

I did not think about how long it would take us to get there. Also, the ride was not bad at all and quicker than I expected. I was feeling sleepy, but I dared not because I didn't know if I was holding onto my baby or not. "Thank you, Lord," I said, "thank you for making everything alright." Jurius ran into the emergency room, and in a flash, two men came running out with the gurney.

They opened the door, which I was leaning on all the way so as not to put all my weight on my hips. They put me on the gurney and into the hospital very quickly. They were calling for special help as they went because I was losing a lot of blood. What else they said I didn't understand. My prayers of thanksgiving and praise kept my mind busy. A doctor came in and quickly instructed, "Call Doctor Allen. She needs to have surgery.

She needs at least two units of blood." I heard one of the attendants talking to Jurius, saying, "You need to find someone. Two people to donate blood." When he came back, I asked him, "What about our baby?" "The baby is fine," he said. "What was that in the sheet?" I asked. "That is your after birth. It came first," he said, "you will need to be operated upon to have the baby."

Doctor Allen entered the room and started issuing instructions, calling for nurses to do this and that. "Put in an I.V. Get a unit of blood. Call for Doctor Cooper to help." I had never heard Doctor Allen so agitated. It made me think how serious this must be. They hooked me up to all kinds of machines. They told me I will have to turn on my side and bring my knees up to my chin. When he said that, everybody started to laugh. "What's so funny?" I asked the Doctor. He repeated the instructions. "What?" One of the nurses replied, "He knows you can't do it but will help you."

I had to be in that position for the surgery. They started the surgery at I continued. I started praying. The nurse that gave me anesthesia was monitoring my blood pressure and reporting numbers to the doctors. She would bow down and put her ear to my mouth to hear what I was saying. One of the doctors asked her what I was saying. She asked me what I was saying. I told her I was praying. She repeated to them, and they didn't take it seriously.

They laughed and talked as if they were eating dinner or having a conversation after dinner. All this time, my eyes were closed. I wanted to see what they were doing. When I opened my eyes, I saw a lot of blood. It looked like they had killed a pig and was doing what my dad did when he opened up the pig to take out the insides. I saw this from the big round mirror over the bed. I yelled, "You all need to stop playing around and laughing.

You need to be praying.

Serious looks returned on their faces. I closed my eyes and continued to pray. When I opened my eyes again, they had put a sheet or something between my face, and then I couldn't see the mirror or them. All I could hear was a voice, one or two words. I couldn't hear what they said. A few minutes later, I heard a baby crying, and a few more minutes, someone said, "You have a baby girl," handing me a little bundle of blankets, and when I took it, she was a beautiful girl. It was seven pounds and two ounces and baldheaded like the boys. The doctors made a big fuss over it; seeing black babies with no hair. This was a first for all of them.

They moved me to a room in the maternity ward. There were six beds and all were full. Allen had two other patients in the ward. He visited him before he left the hospital. I was in a lot of pain, and when he came over to my bed before leaving the room, he said, "I ordered you something for pain. The nurse knows when you need it. She will bring you the medicine in a few minutes." He walked toward the doctor, looked back, and smiled broadly. He said, "I'm still praying for you." He always said that every time he saw me there. And I'll always say, "Thank you, doctor."

Throughout the night, I was very restless and in a lot of pain. I would ring my bell, and the nurse would say it's not time for the medicine yet. "You can only have it every four hours." I could not turn over and had to stay in the same position all night. The next morning, the nurse woke me up just as I was resting well without any pain. "I will have to get your breast ready for the baby," she said.

And in a little while, another nurse brought the baby. I had never had any problems nursing before, but now it seemed as if the baby was biting, and I knew she didn't have teeth. Everything hurt from my head to my toes. It felt like I hurt so badly I could not think to pray, but thinking about prayer made me feel a little better. I thought about my last conversation with Mrs. Polly when she asked me why I wanted to have a baby when we were having problems.

My answer reminded me that God had already worked everything out. We will not put more on you than you can bear. This is nothing compared to what Jesus went through on the cross. A nurse came and took the baby back to the nursery.

Doctor Allen walked into the room. My bed was closer to the door than his other patients, so he attended to me first. He threw the bed covers back with just one swish. Next, he started pressing on my stomach, which made me want to yell. In walked two nurses, almost running. Before I was discharged from the hospital, I learned that everybody working at the hospital had to be on their best behavior when Doctor Allen was around, they were mostly afraid of that smile. He was spreading his lips as the saying goes "grinning from ear to ear". He is good to work with, but he wants everything done on time and in order.

He helped me to get off the bed. After I was standing on the floor, he went to one of his other patients and there were already two nurses getting them up. The woman was getting chewed out for not getting out of bed, and she was yelling. Doctor Allen just walked over and helped the nurses, not saying a word. They got her up and walked her around the bed as I was doing. It hurt like never before, but I sucked it up, remembering my baby girl and me. I asked God for the babies. The pain was worth it knowing that God heard and answered my prayer.

"Do you want to go around again?" one of the nurses asked me. "Yes," I said, knowing that the more I moved, the less pain I would have. Doctor Allen came over and said to the nurses, "This is enough for now. I'll leave directions at the desk before leaving." According to the nurses, we're to walk around the bed every two hours. There was not much time for me to rest or sleep while I had to have the baby every few hours for the first three days and nights. I kept moving around the bed as much as I could.

By the second day, I barely felt any pain. And I could get a little snooze while I had the baby in bed. When the doctor visited the third morning, I was sitting on the side of the bed combing my hair, which I had not done in three days. I didn't think about hair or anything else. I was focusing on my body and the boys at home with Jurius. I was worried if he was cooking food for them or just giving them sandwiches and soft drinks. He had not been cooking since he was working in the mess hall at the Naval Hospital. I've been thinking about how he loves to stay busy with his interest in building, gardening, hunting, etc.

The negative thoughts left my mind in a flash as I began to think about his positive aspects. They will be alright even if they get hungry or cold. Jurius came to the hospital with the boys. They couldn't come into the room, so I went out into the waiting room to see them. That was the first time I have seen them since coming to the hospital. Christopher had already forgotten me. He was crying and wouldn't come to me. I know I looked different from what he was used to seeing. My hair was not the same, I was wearing the hospital garb, and my weight was a lot different.

He held onto Jurius with all his might. Junior tried to tell him I was his mama, but he would not accept this. Willis came to visit me. He's one of the men who donated blood on the day of surgery. He teased me that I, for sure, would be an alcoholic. "From now on, let me tell you the best one to buy." He brought Dallas Junior to help arrange our house. I was happy to know that he will be back with the boys. All my concerns have been taken away. He would cook and take care of the boys while Jurius went back to work. It is not good to use all your annual leave in case of an emergency. I didn't expect to see him until the weekend.

Dr. Allen came just before visiting hours were over. He had not seen Jurius since the baby was born. He updated him about how the surgery went. He told him all the dos and don'ts. Jurius tried to talk with him about the medical bill, but he just waved him off and said, "I'll see you all in four weeks. I'll give you some more directions when she's discharged. Don't forget to bring clothes for her." He smiled. So many men forgot that most of my pain was gone, unlike some of the mothers.

Some of the women would say to me, "You're younger," and others would say, "You're tough." I said, "God looked after me when I was in need. He sent his Son Jesus into the world to save the world, and Jesus humbly, came and willingly suffered and wore our sins and pains in his body on the cross. He was bruised for our transgression, and with his stripes, we are healed. Every moment I could, these scriptures would be on my lips, including words of praise and thanksgiving.

This is why I was able to move without hurting and able to take care of my baby. When the women who gave birth before me still couldn't do it, the doctors would not discharge them until they could do those things.

After a week, I was discharged. Christopher still didn't recognize me. It took him a few days of being in a familiar place and hearing my voice, especially when I read to them at bedtime. Junior repeated his prayers at the mean Christopher. He couldn't say all the words, but he remembered. He remembered them as closely as he could when he crawled on the bed one morning from his crib. I knew he was aware of who I was. The boys were happy about their little sister but didn't understand why she was so little and couldn't do anything but cry and sleep. "She will be getting bigger and doing more things soon," I told them.

Jurius found us a bigger house which we desperately needed. There was not enough room for another crib in our bedroom and no room in the living room, which was already overcrowded. Dallas was sleeping on Uncle Corey's bed when he was there until Uncle Corey found out that we were using his bed. He decided to move back in. The biggest challenge with that was we had to supply food for him, and no arrangements were made for it. He just helped himself to whatever he wanted, or cooked whatever he wanted. Yes, it was time to make a move.

The house Jurius found was not in good condition, but it was all we could find in that neighborhood. Jurius and Dallas Junior went to see if they could do enough repairs to make it livable. They patched the roof and stopped all the leaks. They also fixed the floor with the help of his dad. "You need all walls covered," his dad said, "because I can see the sky from anywhere I look, and some of these windows would need to be replaced." When Jurius told me what needed to be done, I simply said, "Lord, please help us.

We have already overspent and still need to do the move." One advantage of the house was that it had electricity. I could already imagine not having to cook with a wood stove. While my thoughts were lifted in excitement, a big bright idea came to me. I praised God for sending the idea to me. There was a big cardboard box that they wanted to throw away at the furniture store where Jurius worked. The walls had been covered with newspapers, which was not even sufficient.

And I knew that cardboard would be much better than newspaper.

When I mentioned this the next morning before the men went to work, nobody thought it was a good idea. Then it hit Jurius like a boom shot.

"Yes, I know what she is saying. I think it might work." "Might," I said, "it will work just like sheetrock those boxes. Is as big as a piece of sheetrock. You can break them down at the scene and fold them to put them in the car. Mr. Mark decided to go along and drive his car, which was bigger. By this time, I was strong enough that I could help with putting up the walls. Dallas Junior had to go home to check on his plants and tend to his garden.

The boys got dressed, and I got the baby ready and packed a lunch. I was waiting with the boys when the men returned with the first load of cardboards. I took a chair from the kitchen so I could sit down when I needed to care for the baby, not realizing that I could not stand but for a short time. Also, my baby was not as strong as I hoped she would be.

Mr. Mark and I stayed at the new house while Jurius went for more cardboard. When he got back, his dad had used all the first load on the walls in the living room. This enabled us to know how much more we needed. The house looked better and clean, with the walls finished in just one room. There was a large bedroom, a small room, and a kitchen. Mr. Mark suggested that the ceiling be covered also. It will make the house warmer and also look better. He also thought we could paint the cardboards and make them look like sheetrock.

Money was a problem for us. We were trying to pay doctor's bills, and we still saved some for the car. "I'll get one gallon," Mr. Mark said, "That should be enough to cover this room, and you can take care of the other rooms later." That was what we did. When Jurius came back with the third load, we decided to get a beige color. Maybe that would blend in with the cardboard and look good. All I could do to help was hold the boards in place while he nailed them in place. The second room was finished, and we had enough materials.

Jurius was to go to the light company to have the lights turned on. While we waited for Jurius to come and help with the overhead work, Mr. Mark was trying to get the water pump started. We need some new parts. He stated the pump; it has not been used in a long time. I had decided to go home on the next trip. It had already been a long day for the boys and me. We depended and trusted in God, and He was with us all the way.

We were highly lifted when the day was over and thanked God how he sent someone to help us when we needed help. Mr. Mark had been distant from us after we didn't take his advice about trying to save the baby. Now here she is, a pretty and healthy baby girl. We never stopped our contact with the family but noticed a big difference with them.

God has a way of making things alright if we just give him a chance to do what he needs to do. All of my babies were good sleepers and were not any trouble when I worked. I would have to wake them to eat. Mr. Mark mentioned the fact that I had not seen the baby all day. He took a peek under the blanket and covered her face. "Oh, I see curiosity in her," he said. We had no problem with her name. No one dare to challenge me. I named her the name I used with one of my girl dolls when I was a young girl - Josephine.

The work on the house went well, and I started packing for the move. Jurius, his dad, and one of the men who lived near the new house were trying to fix the ceiling. Even though the house looked ragged and rundown, the inside looked really good, and the paint made it look clean and bright. The men were almost finished with the ceiling, and the man who lived nearby was working on sealing the windows to make them stable and to keep out the wind. The glass panes needed to be washed, but that could wait until we were in the house. When we talked about putting up the drapes, Jurius said, "I will, I need to wash the windows first to make them sanitary for the baby."

All the men pitched in, and they had that job finished in a few hours. We used the rods from the farmhouse to fix the windows in this house and we didn't have to buy new ones. There was a big surprise when next I walked into the house. The rooms were finished, the drapes were at the windows, the ceilings were painted, and the linoleum was on the floor. We had enough furniture from the farmhouse and the ones we had to furnish the house.

All our neighbors and church members welcomed us and were happy to help us move in. They offered for us to come and eat with them while we got a cook stove set up in the kitchen. Our electric stove was still in Mr. Mark's barn because we used a quarry stove at the current house. We prayed that the stove would still work and the rats had not chewed the wires. There was no way to test it yet. Our furniture was moved to the house, but not before all was checked for snakes and other reptiles.

In winter, the couch and stuffed chairs were good places for some animals to keep warm while hibernating. Until spring, the furniture was put outside and sprayed with pest control and left outside in the cold overnight to rid it of the pests and the scent of the spray. It was a joy for us to at last have another house of our own. Jurius promised that the next time we moved, it would be our own home.

**Our fourth baby**

We cleaned Corey's house and made sure everything was better than we found it when we moved in. We left him food and more cooking utensils than he had before. We also left bedspreads, curtains, and cleaning items. But to our surprise, he moved back to Susie's house as we moved out. We were so busy moving and getting the yard and grounds ready for the children to play outside and a place tilled for a garden that nobody - not even me - paid any intention to me. Baby Josephine started to spit up the milk after eating. That was a sure sign for me that I was pregnant. When I told Jurius that I needed to buy milk for the baby, he never suspected as I did, so I didn't say anything. This was another one of my secrets that I didn't want to share with anyone. I didn't tell anyone my suspicions, not realizing that this was God's promise to us and nobody or nothing could jeopardize it.

I kept the secret until one day when I was thinking about what I was doing to the baby for sure. We both needed vitamins and doctor's care. I couldn't wait until Jurius got home to tell him what I suspected. As soon as he got a day off from work, we made our way to New Hope to see Doctor Allen.

After the examination, it was confirmed and no longer a suspicion. He said, "If we can get you through this one, there will be no more risk and taking chances, there will be no more." I said with assurance and as positive as one can be, "God only promised us four, and I'm sure he will keep his promise." "Well, I don't know about God keeping his promise, but I'm going to make sure that you will be around to raise the kids.

Your life is in jeopardy every time you get pregnant. And these miracles that go through you are not an assurance that you will survive. I would never forgive myself, knowing what I know and let you keep risking your life. Be thankful for the ones you have." "Doctor, I am thankful for the ones I have, but God will not take back his words," I said.

"Well, God does not have to take back his words. He put me into your life and gave me knowledge and understanding to use my wisdom to make decisions for the people who can't or won't make the right decisions for themselves." All this time, Jurius was standing there listening and not saying anything. "What exactly are you saying, Doctor?" he said. Dr. Allen replied, "If your wife makes it to the end of this pregnancy and the baby, I am not going to take another chance on her life.

We should have sterilized her when we did the Cesarean section at the birth of the last baby. We doctors made a terrible mistake in judgment. We once said at that time it would be impossible to conceive again. Talk about miracles. It was a miracle that she and the baby survived. I just can't chance that miracles will always happen."

"I'll have to think about it," Jurius said. "What you need to think about is that your wife can make it this time. And pray to your God, our God, that He keeps his word and gives your wife a chance to live, even if the baby doesn't make it. If I have anything to do with this, I will save your wife first and the baby next. We pray this is not going to be. She is about three months along and has had no prenatal care. That's a risk for her and the baby." Jurius started to cry, and I wondered why he was crying. What did the doctor say that struck him that hard?

"Well, bring her in next week. I'm going to seek help from one of my coworkers and get his opinion about all these things that we talked about. We need to start prenatal care as soon as possible. Come in the morning next week so we can have more time to work with her. Cheer up. Everything is going to be alright. Drive safely and take care of your beautiful family. See you next week. God bless all of you." "God bless you also," both of us said.

We were very quiet riding home. The only thing we said was when I asked him if he wanted me to drive. He kept sobbing, and I couldn't see his face. He would speed up to the normal driving speed and gradually slow down. I got my driver's license last year. I had gone three or four times and always passed everything, except parallel parking. I would always be examined by this same officer that frightened me more than any other.

He knew he was frightening me and would talk about it. When we got back to the station, I would practice at home with the parking area that Jurius marked off for me. I could park perfectly when I got back from the road drive. I usually shake because the officer would help me make a couple of moves. Calling them out in a spur of the moment. I would always make the right move but not knowing what he would say about them would make me nervous.

I once walked over and asked him to stand where I could not see him. And to my surprise, he walked around to the side of the building. And I parked the car perfectly in the allotted space. That was the first time I saw him with a pleasant look on his face. When we walked inside to get the license, he said, "I had decided that if she didn't make it today, I was going to let her go without parking it right. I'm glad you suggested that I not watch you. Now, I know she can do it. Her driving was perfect. She passes every test I gave her and now I know her parking is perfect."

Also, curiosity wouldn't let me drive when he was in the car. The only time I got to drive was when he was off to work, and I needed to run an errand or needed something from the store. I was the first woman in our community who could drive and had her driver's license. Two of my sisters-in-laws wanted me to teach them to drive. Their husbands said they could not learn but seeing me drive and having to call on me to drive them places; they decided they could learn. Not only did they learn, but I also taught several other women, even those who didn't treat me good, when I first moved into the area. I didn't hesitate to teach them. I taught some younger boys and girls also.

When we got home from the hospital, I prepared dinner and put the children to bed, all very quietly. Even the children were well-behaved, no questions as usual after saying their prayers. They didn't even ask me to read a book; they are beginning to pick up on our problems. We got ready for bed, When Jurius began asking me if I understood what the doctor was saying. What he, the doctor, suggested doing when this baby was born. His voice sounded angry and stern. I didn't answer because I was silently getting in touch with my help; the Holy Spirit could help me say the right thing. It had been a long time since his voice spoke to me as it did tonight.

"Let us pray," I said.

"You pray," he blew it out, raising his voice. "I have already prayed, and I don't like what I heard today."

"I don't like it either," I said. "Precisely, the doctor was speaking mostly about my life."

Those were not words you want to hear coming from anybody. "Did you hear him say that the baby or me might not survive this? Why didn't you say something?"

He yelled, "What could I say?"

I was listening to what the doctor had to say and thinking that I know that God has the last word. He is keeping his promise. That's the reason this baby was conceived in the first place. My worry is not what the doctor said; it's you that I'm worried about. Why are you so angry and upset with me as if I agreed with the doctor? You're not considering anyone but yourself and quickly casting blame on me."

I got out of bed and went into the living room, where I could be alone with God. Sitting there in the dark, my mind went back to the doctor's office. In his exam, the look on his face was serious and confused. He left the exam room without saying anything to me. Usually, he would say get dressed and come into the office. His silence led me to believe he was seeking higher power. I remembered him saying, "I will contact one of my coworkers and get his opinion."

I know he is a believer and has the best he can do in mind for his patience. God will use anyone who will allow him to use them. He needs our hands and feet, also our minds and heart. Who will you give us? Our knowledge and understanding? We are curious, and I need to trust God that he has put all the help we need in our path. Back in bed, I said to Jurius, "Let us trust God. The doctor will do what is best for us. We need to trust God and let his will be done, and that will be the best for us." All he said was goodnight and turned over before I could lean over and kiss him.

I got up, walked all around the bed, and bent over and kissed him several times without saying anything else. This was my way of making a peace pledge. Jurius' shift at work the next day started at 5:00 am, and he was up and ready for work before I woke up. He came over to me and said, 'I'm sorry about all I said and did yesterday. I know that you are not responsible for what the doctor said.

Thank you for understanding." The real truth is I didn't really understand him. I just tried to make the best of a bad situation. The boys and I really enjoyed our time together at the new house. We were planting flowers and vegetables. We separated flowers that were already in the yard. And we found some daylilies growing in the ditch. They had not fully grown yet. We helped them and hoped they would bloom in the spring.

We would also take walks after dinner so that the boys would be tired at bedtime. The walk would make me stronger, and I prayed it would make me healthier. My clothes were tight for the first time. With all my other pregnancies, I wore regular clothes. I lost so much weight from the sickness. By the time I gained back what I lost, it was delivery time. This was just three months and I couldn't fit into anything except my house dress. I talked with Jurius about going shopping for material. However, money was a big problem.

We were struggling and had not paid Doctor Allen anything in nearly two months. I decided I wouldn't talk to Jurius about that again because I didn't want to worry him. I started searching my bag for a couple of dresses that had enough allowance that I could amend. I needed clothes I could wear and assist Mr. Mark to plant corn. Tonight was a weekly bible study and prayer meeting at the church. I needed something that I could wear that wouldn't make me look so big. I got busy and took the gathers out. I made a skirt with one of the dresses. All of this was handsome with long stitches. I wore one of my blouses and let the bottom hang over the skirt. The outfit worked well.

Jurius came and was astonished about the clothes. This was the first time he learned that I could sew. I could stretch our finances by making clothes for the children. Hand down shirts would make both boys a pair of jeans and shirts. The next trip to the Doctor was a big blessing. Jurius sold a pig we had been raising for food and helped with our finances. My brother, Dallas Junior, had given us a sow to breed with. There was a litter, and we had nine pigs. The one we sold was the largest. The money would be paid to Doctor Allen for all the bills he had charged us for surgeries and office business.

We were very proud to have something to pay all the bills. We didn't even know how much we owed him. Maybe today, he would get a receipt and the balance. We took the children out of the car and went into the doctor's office. We were both happy about having money to make a payment. Jurius, who was carrying Josephine, put her on my laps and proceeded to the nurse's desk to pay the bill. He told the nurse what he wanted to do. She opened the drawer, took out a well-used Ledger, and started running her fingers down the book's margin. She came to a place, opened it, and began tracing her fingers across the page several times.

She looked up and said, "It's all paid. You owe nothing." Jurius looked back at me. I jumped from my seat and hurried to the desk. She turned the book so that we could see. She traced the lines again and said it's all been paid. We tried to explain to her all the surgeries and office visits. "Yes," she said, "it's all here, and the dates that it was paid," looking at the transaction as she traced her fingers. It all matched. The bills were paid on the same day the services were rendered. Going back to my seat, I turned and said, "Thank you." She replied, "You are welcome, but I had nothing to do with this."

"Thank you God," was what Jurius and I kept repeating. "It's a mistake. I got to talk to Doctor Allen," Jurius said. The exam room door opened and Dr. Allen and a patient walked out with a document and headed to the desk to give the nurse instructions about the patient. Jurius rushed over to talk to the doctor against my advice. The doctor asked him to wait. I beckoned for Jurius to come and sit near me. He came and we began to talk about what had transpired here today.

"Nobody can make a mistake that many times without noticing it. The bill was marked paid on the same day it was recorded in the book. It didn't look like the nurse's handwriting. It looked more like the doctor's writing." "I didn't pay any attention to that," Jurius said, "I'll go in with you and talk with him then." Each time we were discharged from the hospital, we never got a statement about our bill.

The nurse called for me and Jurius stood up and was telling the boys to stay, he would be back in a short time when the nurse said, "Mr. Miller, you can't go in now. This is for her exam. The doctor is very busy today and won't have time to talk with you. Everything is alright with your bill. You don't owe anything. It's all been paid." The nurse called me, and I approached the desk. She put her hand on my shoulder and led me to the exam room.

"He's hard to convince. Are you as hard as he is?" "No," I said, "I asked God to help us and this is what He did. I can't doubt that this is His way of helping us." I asked her to thank Doctor Allen for allowing God to use him in such a mighty way." "You can thank him yourself while he is doing the exam," she said. "He seemed very busy today; he doesn't want to be bothered. He's never too busy to talk when he's with his patient.

He likes to distract them from what he's doing."

She laughed and said, "He knows what he's doing even when he talks. He is always telling me to multi-task so I can get everything done." She laughed, and so did I as the door opened and Doctor Allen entered the room. "What are you girls laughing about?" he asked. "Do you want me to give you more time?" That big smile came over his face, which I had not seen in a long time. I've got my doctor back as my mind returned to the first day we met six years ago. "Mrs. Miller wants to say something to you," the nurse stated and left the room.

The doctor and I looked at each other, and my words could not come out. "Oh, we want to thank you for taking care of our bill. You know all the money we owed you; thank you for allowing God to use you. You have helped us more than you will ever know." While I talked, he stood there looking at me with that special smile. He then moved over to where I was lying on the bed and reached out and took my right hand and said, "You are welcome, but I didn't do it; my wife did.

We agreed that it should be done. I tell her about you and Jurius every time I treat you or your children. She would say I'm praying for that family. They are going through more than they should be. They are only children themselves. She helped me with my books and she saw that I could pay the hospital bills without any problems, she decided that we could live without the money you owed. Something about the two of you makes me want to be a better husband, father, doctor, Christian, and all-around better person."

My eyes were filled with tears and running down my face. When I wiped away the tears, and he had started the exam, I saw his face had turned a different color, and the smile had disappeared. That serious look was there. He said that everything looked good. He called the nurse to get Jurius and bring the children too since they are well behaved and have good manners. "No wonder God wanted to give them to you."

Jurius and the children came in. He pulled out a chair from the desks for Jurius to sit down, holding the baby. In a flash, he picked up the boys one at a time and put them on the bed. "You can sit up," he told me, "we will leave in a few minutes so you can get dressed." He continued, "Dr. Carr and I have decided that we can give both of you, she and the baby, help with vitamins, pills, and shots.

At first, I wanted to see her every week and then every month. She will also need a blood transfusion to help with the low blood. I will give that to her here at the office starting next week because she can't have iron by mouth. We don't want her blood to get any lower and hopefully raise it to the point with one unit, and then she can keep it up with food. My nurse will give her a list of food to eat to help her and the baby stay healthy.

Another thing is the scar."

He called it another name we don't remember. "The Scar has not had time to heal properly, which could be a problem. I'm watching that closely and will make my decision about that when necessary. I think that's enough for you to think about right now. I'll see you next week, come early in the morning and try not to bring the babies because it will be a long day." He started out of the room, looked back with his big smile and said, "Take them all to lunch with the money you were so eager to give me. Lunch on me today; these babies are hungry." He didn't know that our lunch had already been packed before we left home.

We had no idea that God had already solved our problem. The money we were able to keep from the sale of the pig will help us get milk for the children and maybe some cloth for me to make a few outfits for myself. The children and I started to eat as soon as we got our hands wiped with the wet bath cloth, soap, and alcohol. Junior didn't like the smell of the alcohol, so he grabbed a diaper from the baby's bag and wiped off the scent. I offered Jurius a sandwich, and he refused. "You and the children eat it," he said. "One was made for you. We all have one and a piece of fruit. The baby has one also."

While I was eating, she would get a pinch of mine like we always did since she learned to eat. It was hard training her to take the bottle, so she rather ate. With the money we have, I could get the vitamin the baby and I needed. Maybe there will be enough money for Josephine to get some also. "Jurius, did you have something in mind for the money?" "No, except the vitamins and a fill-up of gas for traveling." "Well, sixty dollars ought to be enough to get what you mentioned and pay daddy for the paint and nails we used.

He needs money for seeds to plant and to pay for help with planting the tobacco. We can figure all this out when we get home," I said, "also, I will tell you what Dr. Allen told me during my examination."

"Do you still have the sandwich and something to drink?" Junior quickly handed him the sandwich, and I handed him the water. "May I drive while you eat?" I asked. "I don't want to stop and change drivers," he said. I got it. He had already unwrapped the sandwich and taken a bite, with the water bottle on the seat beside him. "What's the hurry home?" I asked, "maybe we can get something done with paying off dad and getting the vitamins and milk at the local store.

Dad will want to go to the store and get more seeds, so we can plant tomorrow while I have a day off." I couldn't stop worshipping God and thanking Him for the blessing He gave us today. I decided that I would write Dr. and Mrs. Allen a thank you note and let them know how much they had helped us with all we were facing. The note will be given to the Doctor next week when we go for my next appointment.

I told Jurius about what the Doctor had told me about the paid off bill at dinner that night. He was surprised that his wife, whom we had never met, did such a thing. "Remember my saying, God uses anyone who allows him? A willing heart is all He needs." We paid his dad the money we borrowed for the home repairs, purchased the vitamins for the maternal care, and filled the car with gasoline to last a while.

We went shopping for milk and food to last until Jurius' next payday. There was enough money left for us to pay tithes at church and for me to buy some material for maternity dresses and a few dollars left. I couldn't get the material until Jurius was off from work again because we would have to go to Centerville. We will have the Dr.'s appointment for his three days off, and the other days will be on Saturday and Sunday. There was no time for me to get the materials and make the dress before the appointment. We decided to go to Centerville on Saturday and get the material and make the dresses.

I was looking at the material and figuring out the price of buttons and thread. The clerk said, "We have a sale on maternity dresses. Do you want to look at them?" I thought I could make them cheaper and the materials I had picked out were of a higher grade. The plain style of dress I had in mind wouldn't take but a little while to make. My heart told me to take a look; it would only be a few minutes.

Just a few steps from where I stood, the clerk led the way to a rack with a big red and white sign marked fifty percent off. My eyes widened when he traced the dresses hanging there. "What's the original price?" I asked the clerk. She stated the original price was three to five dollars. "What's your size?" she asked. "Well, I was a size twelve before now, and that was a little large on me." You still need to try on a size twelve; they fit the same as regular clothes," the clerk said.

Picking out two dresses were much the same. There were no decisions to make; Jurius was smiling and saying, "Get the dresses, you'll look really pretty," as Junior was nodding his head. A pair of panty hose would average the cost, and I needed them for Sunday services. We went home feeling good and joyful, and I was perked up and ready to cook dinner. As we passed a drive-in diner that sold fried chicken, Jurius hit the brakes and made a u-turn. Both the boys yelled out, "Are we going to get chicken, daddy?" "If they will take pennies?" he said. I have a few pennies left.

He pulled up to the drive-in window and placed his order without asking us what we wanted. After the waiter left to fill the order, he said, "I should have ordered something to drink, but I didn't know if I had enough money." "If you need some more, I have a few pennies as you called it," I said. He rang the buzzer, and the waiter came back. "What kind of drinks do you have?" he asked. "We have sweet and unsweet tea, orange juice, milk, and canned soda, any flavor. Both the boys yelled, "Can soda!" Can soda for me too!" I said, "I want Pepsi." The boys knew they could only have fruit flavor, so they both chose cherry. That was a new flavor that they had before.

"Tell your dad thanks for the chicken dinner because I was just sitting here thinking what I was going to cook. All I could come up with was ham, eggs, and grits. That's all I have energy left for." While I was still talking, the boys yelled out, "Thank you, dad." It was my time to thank him, and what I did was to reach over and give him a big kiss on the cheek. The boys laughed and covered their eyes. "Thank you, Jurius," I said, "I'll have to do this again." "Kiss him again," one of the boys said. Just for fun, I kissed him again.

The waiter was back and noticed everyone laughing, and she started laughing and asked, "What's going on?" Of course, the boys couldn't wait to yell out, "She kissed him." And the other boy said, "Two times." Jurius said, "Just because we stopped here to get dinner." "I hope you enjoy it," the waiter said. "Wait here a minute," she said, "I'll get you a desert on me to help you celebrate." She left and came back with a piece of cake for each of us. "This is a real celebration," Jurius said, "starting with the 'Big Blessing' from God through Dr. Allen." The week went fast mostly because our family was happy and doing things together. We even played ball with the boys teaching them how to catch and hit the ball.

This week will be our third trip to the doctor's office. So far, my blood was in a normal range, and I was gaining weight which made the doctor happy. That was the reason for the new maternity dresses. I had never gained that much weight with the other pregnancies. Dr. Allen stated that the vitamin shots would make both of us healthy. I wrote to my sisters in New York about the good news and the treatment the doctor was giving me every week. Mae Ann wrote back to say we know all will be well. Just keep the faith, and God will make everything alright.

Together they sent money for all the birthdays they had missed, mine Josephine, and Junior. The boys started naming toys they wanted to buy with their money, but I quickly reminded them of our plans to save to buy a television. They had forgotten about that and quickly changed their minds. The neighbors had been inviting the boys over to watch their television in the afternoons after school, but we only let them go on Saturdays for a little while.

They like to watch cartoons and Superman. Junior turned six in March and will be going to school soon. He has already learned a lot and could be going to second grade. He was really interested in my reading bedtime stories and words on the road signs. He also learned most of his alphabets from the road signs and my reading. He learned to write his name with a little help from me. He could remember very easy and was always trying to teach Christopher.

One more weekly trip to the Doctor's office, and then we only have to go monthly. What a relief that will be for all of us. My housework has been neglected. I didn't want to do anything to cause problems with the baby. Plus, my energy was not the best. I needed to rest the day before the trip and the day after. Washing clothes would take another day. Jurius helped with the washing before all this started, but he could hardly keep up with everything and work.

He had been distancing himself more and more from us and spending more time with his dad on the farm when he had days off. That didn't bother me so much because he loved to work on the farm, and his dad was getting older and needed the help. I could still manage around the house while teaching the boys to do small chores, like taking out the trash and putting dishes in the pan to be washed after eating.

We did miss that Jurius was rarely there for dinner, and I had to make excuses for him. We used to pray to bless the food and then talk about what our day was like during dinner time. I still have the prayer to ask God to bless the food, and we talk about what they would have to tell their dad, but I could hear the sadness in their voices and know how disappointed they would be when we couldn't wait any longer for him to come.

The children would be getting sleepy. I would give them their baths and put on their PJs, all ready for bed after dinner. Sometimes the boys would be so excited to tell him about something special and would not go to sleep. The minute they heard the door open, they would rush out in a flash. Especially the time we found a box turtle in the garden when we were picking green beans.

They were completely sure that this turtle was coming to them. They wanted to keep it. I explained that this is a wild animal and need to stay in their territory where it can survive and take care of itself. They begged so hard for me to let their dad see it. They were so sure he had never seen one like this before. I gave in and decided that they could keep it to show to their dad, and then we would put it back in the garden where we found it.

We got a cardboard box and put the turtle in. The children put in weeds and a rock from around my flower bed. I'm sure the turtle would have survived without all this care, but I let them convince me that he needed some food and water. They were so excited and having so much fun, and no way was I going to ruin that.

The only thing that came to my mind that they eat was insects. I told them. They went hunting for bugs and worms. While they hunted, I hoped they found none. Insects are not my best friends, I tend to go the other way when I see them, especially worms. A jar lid would make a good water container. I got a jar lid from the kitchen, filled it with water, and said to them excitingly, hoping to take their attention away from their hunt, "Who wants to give Mr. Turtle some water?" My plan worked, and they both ran to the box, and I handed the water to the first who got there. I handed the other lid to the other and said, "This is for the food. Maybe he will eat some cornbread, get some from the kitchen Junior." This was the best thing that I had thought about all day. It worked like magic.

Now, Mr. Turtle, as we decided to name him when they wanted to give it a name. He has all he need: food, water, and a home for a little while. The excitement rose even higher for them to show Mr. Turtle to their dad. The door opened, and both of them jumped out of bed carrying the box with Mr. Turtle, yelling, "Daddy, look what we have," holding the box in front of him. He glanced down and said, "Hun-hun," moving aside from the boys.

He went into the kitchen. Seeing the disappointment on the boys' faces, I took the box and said, "He's probably too hungry to watch him right now, you go back to bed, and I will show him after he finishes eating." "It won't be the same," one of the boys said, "we wanted to make him happy about Mr. Turtle. We will have to turn him loose tomorrow."

I was proud of them for wanting to keep their promise to set him free. "Lord, please help all of us, let me be able to encourage Jurius to pay attention to the boys, if not to the turtle. Lord, please don't let this incident scar the boys, for they are getting older and taking notice of these things. Walking to the table where Jurius was eating, I sat down and saw his face. I noticed that something was bothering him.

"Lord, have mercy and fix this situation like only you can." My voice was shaking when I started to talk. "Let me tell you about our afternoon," I began, "the children and I went to the garden to pick beans. We noticed yesterday they were ready to pick. We all looked when Josie started to laugh aloud and point at something in the row ahead of us. There was a tortoise (turtle). It was running toward us. We all got excited because the children had not seen one before.

They asked if it bites, and I said no.

"Chris, the braver one, went closer, and when he did, the tortoise went into his shell. They all laughed because they had not seen that before.

The children were very excited, and I was also happy for them having a real-life experience with one of God's little creatures. They were sure the tortoise were coming to them, so not to disappoint them, I decided to let them show it to you. They thought that you would be as happy and excited as they are. I'm sorry you had a bad day and got home so late that you didn't feel like interacting with them. They know we will have to let it go tomorrow."

"Rejoicing in hope; patient in tribulation;
continuing instant in prayer."
Romans 12:12

# CHAPTER 13

## Jurius grows distant with the family

All this time, I was talking with Jurius, pausing and giving him time to say something; he did not even look up from his plate. He has a habit of leaning over his plate when he eats. Today, he hovered over it, even put his arm on the table around the plate. After a few minutes of silence, I asked, "Will you give the boys a few minutes after you finish eating?" I said, making my voice as sweet as I could and trying not to sound like I was feeling at that time. Finally, I asked bluntly, "Jurius, please talk to me. What's the problem that's making you act this way?" He did not answer and was eating very slowly. "Do you want something to drink?" I said, standing up to get some tea.

I left the kitchen, passing by the boys' room. I stopped to see if they were asleep. They were still waiting. I went back to the kitchen and told him, "The boys are still waiting for you." I went to the bedroom and waited in bed. I heard the chair being pushed back from the table, dishes being put in the dishpan, and footsteps leading my way, then no steps. A burst of laughter from the boys let me know he was in their room.

"Praise God! Thank You for this precious moment," I said. I felt His precious blessing all over me. "God, I knew you could do it, and you did. You never let me down. I trust you, oh Lord and depend on you. You are the only one with love, wisdom, and mighty power who can touch any and every heart and mind. I know you are our Heavenly

Father, our Lord and Savior, our helper and aide, our hope, joy, and peace."

While I was worshipping and lying there prostrate, my hands were raised in the air. He came into the room without making any noise. My eyes came open and I saw him standing there. "You make me feel so sad and helpless when I see you this way," I whispered, "you don't realize how much the boys and I miss you when you're not here, especially when we don't know where you are. I have a feeling of worry that takes my mind to all sorts of places, accidents, hospitals, out of gas, stuck in a ditch, and yes, the devil takes me back to cheating.

When my mind goes there, I remember to call for my Helper and quickly hold on to my faith and trust in our Lord. I want to believe in you and your love for us, but somehow I am very puzzled right now that you seem upset and have nothing to say. Please tell me where you were and what happened to you that makes you take it out on the children and me. Please, please say something, tell me how you feel and don't try to spare my feelings."

The room was silent for a little while, then he spoke with a trembling voice, "I can't tell you." Silence was all over the room. I had a lot to say, but I didn't want to say anything else. More than a few minutes went by, and I was lying there calling on our Helper. Then he said in that shaky, soft voice, barely loud enough for me to hear, "I'm working hard trying to take care of you and the children.

All I do is not enough. I have to have some time to myself. I don't like you questioning me when I come home. I come home to get some rest and can't rest with all these questions." I didn't say anything else, even though there were many things entering my mind that I wanted to say. I'll just ponder these things and pray for the Holy Spirit to give us a better opportunity to discuss his feelings.

From what he said tonight, he doesn't want to be married. If the situation was reversed, how would he feel? Morning came quicker than I needed it to, but I got up and prepared to cook breakfast and have it ready when the children awakened. Up all alone, my mind went back to what Jurius said last night. I tried not to put more into what he said than what he meant. I began to dread seeing him. This was a peaceful time for me, and I want it to stay that way.

Just what did I hear him say in other words? He did not want to be married, that we bother him, that he was not happy with his family? It was not only what he said that triggered this feeling in me, but the way he looked and acted mattered more.

I finished cooking the pancakes, with the egg already beaten and the pan ready to scramble. I sat down a few minutes before calling them and thought so much about having two parents for our children. It seems as if daddy wants to check out. Maybe it's best to divorce if he's not happy so one of us can be happy. Lord, let your will be done in our lives as it is done in Heaven was all I could think, and even spoke out loud.

I opened the bedroom door of the children's room to find that they were already up and getting dressed. They were so quiet that they made me suspect that they knew something was not going well. Any other time they would still be happy about the turtle and make plans to release it. "Breakfast's ready," I called out as I entered our bedroom door. Josie was already awake, also just standing in her crib, looking toward her dad, who pretended to be asleep. However, with my calling out as loud as I did, he heard it and was still lying down. "Breakfast's ready," I pronounced, lowering my voice. "Alright," he said, moving from under the cover.

I picked up Josie and put her on the floor. "You need to stop picking her up," he said, "I was going to get her out." I started to put on her clothes while Jurius put on his. We heard the boys yelling loudly, "He's not here! He's not in the box!" Jurius got to their room before me and tried to calm the boys. "He's got to be somewhere in this room. Come on, let's eat breakfast before it gets cold, and then we will look for it." The voice I heard coming from him pleased me.

"Thank you, Lord, for sending help to us today." I scrambled the eggs while everyone washed their hands and sat on the table. I put some eggs on each plate and looked to see if I had everyone's topping for the pancakes. Some like Aunt Jennie syrup, one like grape jelly, and my favorite is Grandma's Molasses.

We asked God to bless the food and gave Him thanks for what he had provided. It didn't take the boys long to eat, even with one of us continually telling them to slow down and chew. Jurius hurried to eat when he noticed the boys not slowing down so he could help them find Mr. Turtle. Happiness flooded over me to see the relaxed expression on his face. There was no doubt that they would find Mr. Turtle, and we all would make the trip to the garden to release it, watch it run away as it was doing coming toward us.

After moving the bed from the wall, taking all the shoes from the bottom of the closet, looking under the bed, taking the covers off the bed, we were sure he was not in the room. We searched the hall looking behind everything in there. When Chris started taking the toys out of the toy box, he called out, "I found him; he's in our toy box. He wants us to keep him."

I picked up the box we had him in and held it toward Chris who was holding Mr. Turtle with both hands. "He wants to pull his head out of his shell," he said. "Put him in the box, and maybe he will take his head out. He's afraid of all the commotion. He will be alright," I said. While everyone was quietly enjoying the last few minutes with Mr. Turtle, the dishes were being washed and the table cleaned off. I was reminded of how much we are different in our own ways.

The trip to the garden was a sad occasion for the children, but I knew it was best for Mr. Turtle. When I asked Jurius his opinion, he just shrugged his shoulder and said, "What you have already decided is best." His working shift starts today at ten o'clock, and he's already getting ready to leave two hours early. We will have no time to talk about anything, not even about how I'm feeling. He's taking my trust and faith in God and my hope in the whole family lightly. This is a time I believe that both of us need to be honest and true, and there should be no hidden agenda. I believe in being guided by the Holy Spirit, and evidently, this is not the case with my partner.

As God is my helper and aid, I continued to do my best to help him understand and do all I could to keep this family together if it is God's will. My monthly appointment would come up next week, and the doctor will set a date for the birth. He didn't think I would be able to make the nine months. It was three months to go. I was beginning to feel as if I couldn't make it. All my work had to be done sitting down, and I found myself calling the boys to help me even more than the previous week.

I haven't said anything to Jurius because of his attitude. I kept hoping that everything would level out soon. He never asked me how I was feeling or how I was getting along during the day. I tried not to make him uncomfortable or upset. I hoped that we could make things better by not talking about certain things, but I know nothing is solved by silence deep down.

My prayer today was focused on patience and courage along with help for the baby. There had not been much movement in a while. This could be a start for conversation tonight after the children are in bed. My cooking for dinner was as easy as I could make it: hot dogs, slaw, and potato chips. The children loved it, and it was satisfying for me because I like hot dogs. Jurius didn't necessarily like junk food like this for dinner. However, this was all I could manage with the boys' help. He should have seen how happy and proud they were to be able to help. These were the special times that he always missed, things that could lift his spirit sky high.

Nevertheless, I was still trusting that this situation would be made smooth by the amazing love of our Heavenly Father. Jurius came home thirty minutes late, but his facial expression didn't suggest that any problem bothered him. The children were all bathed, PJs on, and ready for bed. They each got a chance to tell him about their most enjoyable experience. Then he ushered the boys to their room. When he returned to the living room, Josie was waiting for him to put her to bed.

This little interaction was better than what had been going on. When all the children were asleep, and he had eaten his dinner without grumbling about the hot dog, I started the much-needed conversation about how I had been feeling physically. "You know I stated I'm not feeling up to par lately. My energy is gone to the poops, and I am having a hard time standing and bending. The boys have been helping me a lot, doing everything they could do to help me." "Why didn't you tell me?" he asked.

"It's been really hard to talk to you for quite a while, and I didn't want to stress you any more than you already are. I'm saying something now because I don't think I can wait until next week to see the doctor." His eyes opened wide, and he stood up. "What are you saying?" he asked. "I'm saying that I tried to get by without your help, but you distanced yourself from the family. It seems as if your problem was more important than the family; it seems that it was my job alone.

The baby has not been moving as much as usual." "What do you think we ought to do?" he asked. "What do you think we ought to do?" I asked. "Think about all you heard tonight and decide. I'll be alright as long as you are alright. When I need to go to the doctor, I will find someone to take me if you're too busy or need time for yourself."

"What are you saying?" he raised his voice. I let all the anger and rage that had built up in me these few weeks come out, and I threw them back in his face. "Do you need to go to the hospital tonight?" he asked. "No, just to the doctor's office when it opens tomorrow." Jurius' work schedule tomorrow morning was five o'clock until two o'clock. Maybe I would be alright until he gets home at two-thirty and we go to the doctor's office at three-thirty.

Somehow, I couldn't wrap my head around the way I was feeling right now. We went to bed, but not one of us slept well. He was up way before time to get to work. He left the house without saying anything, not even a kiss. I heard him drive away and immediately fell asleep.

After what seemed like a few minutes, I awoke to the sound of the car coming in the driveway. He rushed in, saying, "You are not ready?" "What time is it?" I asked. "Eight o'clock, you wanted to be there when the doctor's office opens," he said. "I didn't know you were coming back to take me. You never said anything about your plans when you left. Will you wake up the boys, help them get dressed, and ask your mother to keep the children while we are gone? Before you go, please get Josie out of the crib so I can get her dressed." I tried to rush to the kitchen, but there was a problem, for I could barely put one foot ahead of the other.

The boys came in and asked what to eat for breakfast. "Take the box of cornflakes and put it in this bag and get a jar of peanut butter and a jar of jelly for lunch, and get the jug of milk for the cereal. Junior, please help the others get their food and clean up any mess you all make." By this time, I couldn't stand any longer because, among other things, the baby was kicking right and left, and it really hurt when it kicked. Why aren't Jurius back by now? I wondered.

When I saw the car pass the front window, he rushed in, "Are you all ready to go? Don't forget the diaper," he said, reaching for the bags Junior and Chris were holding. "Go get in the car," he told the boys. Reaching to pick up Josie, he handed me one of the bags. Trying to push myself up from the chair was a huge struggle. He took the baby and bags to the car and came back; I was still seated in the chair. "Come on," he said, and when I reached out my hands for help, he looked surprised and said, "Why didn't you tell me?" He lifted me up out of the chair, took my hand, and led me slowly to the car.

To my great astonishment, both of his parents were in the car. I didn't see any space for me. Mr. Mark was in the back with the boys, and Josie and Mrs. Polly were in the front seat. Knowing how to handle this kind of situation, I stood leaning on the car. Jurius took Josie out and put her in Mr. Mark's lap. He came around the car and led me to the driver's door and helped me squeeze past the steering wheel to the middle of the seat. The self-control that I prayed so much for was working well, and I kept whispering, "I love you Lord, and many Thanks."

The trip seemed to be twice as long, bumpy, and uncomfortable. Breathing deep and slow made me relax. I knew that God would make way for me. The only concern that bothered me was the baby. Maybe the doctor would check things out, give me a different shot, and send me home for complete bed rest, except his appointments, until the end of the period. I couldn't depend on Dallas Junior now because he got married a month ago. All I could think of for help was the boys. They had learned a lot, and maybe this would be God's way to get Jurius' attention to the family. My eyes opened to us being at the doctor's office. "You all stay here," Jurius said, "let me go in and see if the doctor can see her now."

He went in and out in just a minute or two, stating that it would be about twenty minutes. "The nurse said to bring her in, and she would get her ready for the exam." Everyone got out of the car, and there was no need to ask them to stay. Jurius holding me by the arm, led me, barely able to move one foot before the other. "Take her right into that room," the nurse said, pointing at a door.

We entered the room as Doctor Allen was coming through the opposite way. "Don't undress her," he said with a worried expression on his face. I wondered what he meant when he didn't want me to get undressed. The nurse held a gown as she usually did, looking serious. All this began to frighten me. "Lord, I need you; Jesus, I need you to take care of me and fix this problem."

The doctor did not wait for me to get on the bed. While standing there trembling, he came over to me, pulled up my blouse, pulled down my skirt from over my stomach, looked, and rubbed his hand over the sear from the surgery when Josie was born. He then pulled up my skirt and fixed my clothes before looking at me. "Go over to the hospital as fast as you can; I'll meet you there," he said. He rushed back out of the door through which he came into the exam room. Moving slowly but as fast as possible, I went into the main office to find him advising the nurse. He had already told Jurius what to do.

Mrs. Polly was grumbling that she barely sat down and got the children comfortable and now having to get them out to the car again. She had not heard any of the doctor's orders and was talking loudly to Mr. Mark about the trip being a waste. Jurius heard, so did everybody around because Mr. Mark was hard of hearing and she was used to speaking so he could hear. We all shuffled out to the car while the boys complained about being hungry.

When we went to the doctor's office earlier this morning, I hoped that they would stay in the car and give the children the food that we brought with us. We didn't allow them to eat before leaving home because we're trying to get to the doctor's office early. The lack of communication about going to the appointment kept me from having the boys fed and ready on time.

"Mr. Mark, will you please give the bag of food from the back window to Junior, so he can make sandwiches for them?" He reached back and got the bag. "How is he going to make sandwiches in this crowded space?" he asked. "Ask the blessing," I said, "we will when everyone is served. They repeated a short prayer they had all learned from me. I pondered the fact of Junior asking all of us if we wanted one before taking care of himself. A silent thank you was in order for I could see that he and the other children were learning and practicing what they had been taught.

The jug of milk was on the floor, but we had forgotten to bring cups. In fact, when I thought to bring the milk, it was for cereal. We didn't forget the cereal bowls, and Junior suggested that they could drink from the bowls. We were at the hospital getting out of the car when a nurse and an orderly came rushing up to the car with a wheelchair. "Is this Doctor Allen's patient?" she asked. "Yes," I replied. "You need to be very careful, let us assist you in getting out of the car," she said.

Things are more serious than we know, I thought. But God knows just what to do. I knew I'd be alright. They were very careful taking me inside, trying to miss everything that would cause a bump. At times, they would lift up the chair to get over rough surfaces.

As we entered the door of the hospital, two more nurses were standing there, ready to take me to the operation room. When my family heard what they said, they made a big fuss. I couldn't understand all they were saying because they were all talking simultaneously. Dr. Allen came running out from one of the nurses' station where he was prepping the nurses on what to do. He said, "This is an emergency and another miracle that you got here when you did this morning.

Another miracle is the operation room is free. Usually, we doctors have to schedule a time and stick to it. You know, only God performs miracles," looking at Mrs. Polly when he said that. She had just said to the doctor that a baby never lives at six months; it has to be seven months.

"We are not worried about the baby," he said, "it's the young mother and father that we are thinking about," he said, looking at her. "Mrs. Polly, leave it to God, He knows what to do, and I'm going to do what he tells me to do. Take her on," speaking to the nurses. To Jurius, he said, "Wait in this room with your family," pointing at the waiting room door. I was wheeled to the operation room, where my memory took me back to just over eighteen months ago when this same situation was before us. God worked it out then, and I know He will do it again.

All worries and fear disappeared from me. God took away all my worries and fears, and gave me complete peace. I didn't have any doubt in my mind about what Dr. Allen and his associates could do after what we heard him say this morning about miracles and God. With my eyes closed in meditation, I heard the nurse say, "Mrs. Miller, are you alright?" "Yes," I replied, opening my eyes to see the doctor holding what looked like a six-inch needle.

Even this didn't frighten me or make me nervous. "Do you remember me?" he asked. Before I could answer, he continued, "I remember you," he laughed, "telling us to pray; you taught all of us some bedside manners." How can I ever forget you telling me to pull my knees to my chin?" "Oh yes, you know what needs to happen this time, don't you? We are waiting for Dr. Allen's assistant, and then we will start. How are you feeling?" he asked.

"Like I want it to be over with," I replied.

He looked at his watch and said, "We have a calming med this time, but it seems as if you will be alright without it." I noticed then that he had a pole standing nearby with a face mask on it. "We will start this when the doctors are ready." All at once, I could hear Mrs. Polly's voice echoing in my mind, "Six-month babies never live," repeatedly when my mind went to what Dr. Allen said, "This is a miracle; only God works miracles." God promised four children, and for sure, Dr. Allen would do the sterilization this time, and now I appreciate his decision.

If nobody else could understand, I surely did. "Mrs. Miller, we are ready," the Dr. announced. Again, before I could say a word, he put the mask over my face, "Just breathe normally. Now, knees to your chin," they all laughed, knowing that I couldn't put my knees to my chin. The laughing didn't bother me this time. God had already taken care of it. Somebody pulled my knees up until the anesthesia doctor said that's good. What a horrible pain when the needle first pierced through the spinal cord. Before I could react to it or say a word, the pain subsided, and it was over. I could feel the doctors straighten out my legs and turn me over as the mask went off my face.

I kept my eyes closed and my mind focused on spiritual things and meditating on the days ahead. The procedure seemed to be taking a longer time than before. Finally, the doctor standing near my head bent over and asked, "Are you alright?" "Why is it taking so long?" "We have to do twice as much work as before," he stated, "Dr. Allen asked what your concern is. Dr. Forgo was the doctor who administered the drug. "Tell her everything is going well, and we are almost finished," Dr.

Allen pronounced. "I hear you," I called out, "I don't need a transmitter right now." "Mrs. Miller," one of the doctors' assistants said. "Yes," I replied, "is it alright for us to laugh? You have made us tickled, and we are afraid to laugh. Remembering the last time you got on us, my hands will be much steadier if I can get this laugh out, you will be much safer." "Go ahead all of you, laugh all you want, just be sure you are not cutting me when you do."

"I've never seen anyone like you," one of the nurses replied, "usually, the patient is afraid and nervous when they are awake, and you are lying there joking and talking with us. Knowing what is being done, I would probably faint to put myself out." "She is not just trusting us," Dr. Forgo said, "she is trusting the Chief Doctor, the one with all knowledge and power." Talking did seem to make the time go by faster, for there was murmuring from the crew that I didn't understand. The second I closed my eyes, there was more commotion and a loud cry of a baby. My eyes flew open, but there was no way for me to see anything. They didn't forget to put the sill between them and me this time.

"Every good gift and every perfect
gift is from above."
James 1:17

# CHAPTER 14

## Our baby girl

Time passed, and everything was just mumbling from the doctors and nurses. "Mrs. Miller, you have a little but fat baby girl," Dr. Allen called out. "We're getting her cleaned up, and then you can see and your family likewise. How is her blood pressure?" he asked Dr. Forgo. "I heard a little excitement in her voice and saw some movements from her arms and head that we had not seen all day. We want to keep her pressure down so there won't be any problems." Dr. Forgo read the pressure numbers to them and got back a reply, "That's good, we are almost finished."

The baby was brought to me with just a receiving blanket wrapped around her. "They have not finished preparing her," Dr. Allen said, moving closer to my head so he could peek at her as I unwrapped the blanket. "Another bald head," I mentioned. "That's to be expected," the doctor stated, "she is premature, you know, and she doesn't have fingernails or toenails, but she is doing good." He took the baby from me and handed her to the nurse. "Give me a minute or two, and I will come in for another check," he said to the nurse softly.

After they cleaned me up, they rolled me past the waiting room where all the family was ooing and awing at the baby. Again, Dr. Allen rushed in and asked the nurse to take the baby back into the nursery. An hour or more went by, and Jurius and the kids had to peek in to see me. I waved to his parents while they stood in the hall in front of the room door. "No more visiting today," the nurse came in and pushed everyone out.

She needed to rest now before the medicine wore off. It's been a hard day for all of us. Jurius rushed back in to get my pocketbook. There was no place to keep it at the hospital. "Get hotdogs or hamburgers for everyone," I told him. There is money in my wallet. I had no suggestions for him about caring for the children and was relieved that he didn't ask.

There were a few things I would have advised him about, but God wouldn't let me think about it. I had started potty training with Josie, and he didn't know anything about how to do it or maybe about getting a little potty chair for her. He was never there to help with this chore. Well, I knew Junior would help him with that. My mind was busy for a while, and I didn't feel the start of the pain. The medicine was wearing off; I could wiggle my toes again, and every time I moved them, it hurt. The babies were brought in for feeding. Every mom got her baby except me. I watched the door every time someone came in or passed by.

Finally, Dr. Allen came in and hurried over to my bed. Sitting on the edge of the bed, he first asked me, "How do you feel?" "I'm hurting now; may I have something to ease the pain?" "I've already placed your order; it should be here in a little while," looking at his watch. Without taking a breath, he continued, "Don't be ashamed. The baby is doing

good. Just that her breathing is not as strong as I would like it to be. I'm going to take her to St. Luke tonight to put her in the incubator. We don't have one here in this hospital. I'll keep my eye on her. She's alright.

Turning over, which hurt a little, I brushed the thought of my hurting away and began calling on God for Mercy for my baby, who had not been named yet. Shortly afterward, two nurses came in, one carrying my baby and the other a bag of things for the baby. "We are going to St. Luke to take the baby to Dr. Allen," they told me. "Dr Allen is not allowed to transport patients to or from the hospital. I'm going to be there all night," one of the nurses said, "and for as long as she has to stay." "Thank both of you for the concern, kindness, and help you are giving my baby." "She is so precious and beautiful," the nurse holding the baby said, "I know she is not named. May I name her?"

I paused for a moment and remembered that we had not picked out a name, not even thought about or discussed one. "The Registrar will be in tomorrow. I will be sure to be there and have my favorite name. This is what my girl would be named if I had one. I've been hoping I could name a special baby someday, and this is the most special one there could ever be." Turning over for the second time, sleep and tiredness overtook me, and I was out for a while.

The noise of the food cart woke me up. The clinking of the stainless steel dishes was nerve-racking. The closer they got, the louder the noise. If only there were earplugs, I could finish my rest and sleep. Hunger was not my problem at this time. It was not a problem for most of the moms, for they were still asleep. A nurse appeared through the doorway and called out, "Mrs. Miller!" "Yes, I answered." She approached my bed with instruments to pump my breasts. "Your baby will not be here tonight, so we will need to save the milk, and you will be more comfortable doing it before you eat."

She started the process with me on my back but decided it would work better if I sat upright. This made part of the instrument rest on my stomach. Not realizing that surgery had been done, she got upset when I yelled from the pain. She continued calling me a baby and other not so nice names until another nurse rushed in and told her, "She's Dr. Allen's patient." That was all she had to say.

They exchanged places, and the second nurse tried to explain to me that the first nurse was having a bad day and didn't realize that I had an operation. She went on to say that if Dr. Allen found out what she had done, she might be fired. She continued to make excuses for her bad behavior. Just as she finished with me and was about to leave, she said to me, "Do you understand what I said to you?" "Oh yes, I understand very well, but you need to make sure all these other moms in here understand. You can be sure I will not tell him, but I'm not sure about the others here." She left the room.

The women in the beds started making comments, like, "Why is she working? We all are having a bad day. She needs to be reported. Dr. Allen doesn't want anyone mistreating his patients." I spoke up and said, "She didn't mistreat me. She didn't know that I had an operation." The complaints continued before I had time to finish what I was going to say. "Wait a minute," I said, raising my voice over theirs, "I've forgiven her and have asked God to forgive her," and the complaints were over. In came the dinner trays and all was extremely quiet.

One of the servers asked, "Why the quietness?" No one responded. Everyone was very quiet during dinner. No one complained about the food, as usual, everything was all right, the orders were filled as requested. All this for the first time since day one of my stay in this ward. Very strange. I wondered if my mentioning God had anything to do with it. Or maybe they all were thinking how stupid I was. Maybe my reaction did surprise them all.

My thinking was - this young black nurse do need some teaching, but the spirit that was moving in this place can do no good. What she needed was to know God and be given a chance to accept him. No one in this room at this time was able and willing to help her. The second nurse who recognized her problem did all she could to help her and even took over her responsibilities. This gave her a second chance.

To God be all the glory, we all would not measure up if we had to stand before the Righteous Judge to give account for our deeds.

The following morning, the weather forecasted snow, and all of us could feel the change, even inside. The cleaning ladies issued blankets to us and asked us to ring the call bell if we needed more. "Thank you and thank God for you," I stated. I had to keep my heart and mind clean, for I didn't know what was going on with my baby.

I needed God, his Son Jesus, the Holy Spirit, and all the Angels to help make my baby well and take care of the whole family. My hurting was the least of my problems because it was getting better, thank God. We were not to get out of bed without a nurse. One of the other moms rang the call buzzer about twenty minutes ago, and no one had come yet. I needed to get to the restroom and couldn't go by myself. However,

I needed help to get up from the bed, and it was more uncomfortable than walking across the hall.

I decided to ring the bell to be obedient and safe. The bell rang for a long time, but nobody came. One of the other moms rang her bell, and no one could get any response. Some of us started ringing at the same time. Finally, in walked one mom's doctor who agreed to take the three of us at a time to the restroom. Everybody was asking what the problem was and why he was the one assisting us.

Some of us agreed to use the bedpan, which made it easier for Dr. Peale. We all could be served quicker that way. Why didn't someone think of what a couple of us did before now? We got up from our bedpans and sat on the edge of the bed. It was more comfortable for me to do it that way instead of trying to lie down and raise up to get on the pan. This was Dr. Peale's idea.

After everyone had been served and back in bed, we waited to hear why the nurses were not answering. Dr. Peale gently stated that there was an emergency. "I'm glad all of you are alright now. He checked out Mrs. Jones, his patient, and told her she was ready to go home. My eyes were so tired and felt heavy from the lack of sleep. I pulled up the covers to my chin, closed my eyes, and went to sleep.

Hearing a soft low voice calling my name sounded like part of the dream I was having. Again, but louder, "Mrs. Miller," my eyes flew open, and behold, Dr. Allen was holding my baby. "Sorry I'm late," he said. "Late?" I repeated, "what time is it?" "Still morning, but I intended to be here so you wouldn't have to worry." "I haven't been worried; I'm catching up on my sleep." "Sleep," he said, "I didn't get much all night. I had to stay with your baby. They didn't want me to use the incubator for her."

He sat on the bed, still holding the baby. I reached for the baby, and he said she's sound asleep. "She slept well. It was me who didn't get any sleep." "I asked, "Who didn't want her in the incubator?" A nurse came in to get the baby and interrupted us. "I need to go," he announced, "there will be patients waiting for me at ten o'clock." A feeling came that he didn't want to talk about what happened at St. Luke, so I didn't ask again.

After he left, I began to think, this is an all-black hospital and St. Luke is an all-white hospital. He said enough when he said "they" didn't want her there. Dr. Allen was the Superintendent of both hospitals, and all the doctors were white. You would think that all the leaders of the hospitals would have love and compassion for all people. The trustees at St. Paul were all whites as well as any other officers. Why doesn't this hospital have an incubator with all the babies being born here? My thoughts had begun to run rampant, and I had to get them under control. My first day after birth went well, better than last time.

This was an entirely different situation, and I know God's grace had a big part in the way everything went. Dr. Allen also deserved credit and appreciation for his part in this from the beginning. He allowed God to direct his decisions and use him to carry out the best plan. Jurius and his parents were not satisfied with Dr. Allen's decision to do sterilization. They thought I should have stopped him from doing it. My feeling about it was that God allowed us to have four beautiful children, not all healthy, but the health problems have been solved without any major hardship or disadvantages.

God has kept his word, and I could still trust Him to continue doing all that we need. My life was in jeopardy, and I trusted God to make the decision. He chose a man and put him in charge of the problem to work it out.

As far as I know, I had no choice. Dr. Allen didn't ask me to make a decision; he told all of us, Jurius and his parents, what condition my body was in and what was best for him to do. He also told us that he should not have risked my life by not doing the sterilization. To take a chance of this kind was like playing Russian Roulette. Just a matter of chancing that the bullet is not in the next slot. We all should be thankful for my family and Jurius' parents, because if God kept his promise and word one time, we need to trust him to keep them again.

It's a great blessing and reward to be able to trust and depend on one who will never disappoint you or let you down. He will never leave you or turn his back on you. I didn't put my faith in Dr. Allen to do what was best for me. Surely, my hope, trust, and faith are in the Lord our God. Jurius felt like Dr. Allen took advantage of us by not giving us a choice. My feeling was and still is that God gave me a chance instead of a choice. My mother, who died because of childbirth, had neither a choice nor a chance.

Every day I open my eyes to a new day, my first words are, 'Thank you, God, for keeping me alive for another day.' I will not let Jurius or anyone make me feel guilty for being alive, and I will continually have peace in my heart and be happy because God has given me that choice to govern my life. Yes, I have unspeakable joy that this sinful world didn't give to me and can't take away. If it is God's will, and I pray that it is, I will raise our children in love, train them up in the way they should go, and pray to God that they will remain in that training. My mind flashes back and remembers my training and teaching, and I thank God for bringing me all this way.

Jurius could have visited this afternoon; he was off from work at two o'clock. I prayed there were no problems hindering him. I was alright but anxious to let him know about the baby and her breathing problem.

The nurses were giving her manual treatment several times a day to strengthen her lungs. Dr. Allen came for his evening visit and apologized for not explaining what happened last night at St. Luke hospital. "You have enough on you already, you don't need anything else to deal with right now. Everything is well; the baby benefitted from the treatment and is doing good. That's all I wanted, and I got that. Another day would have helped, though."

He sat down on the end of the bed as usual. That made me know he had something else to say. "Jurius asked me about what we did during surgery. I told him we had to do an operation to save you and the baby, and both are doing fine. His mother asked about that other part as she put it. I told her that everything went as planned, but that didn't go so well with them. His mother stated that I was playing God and I rushed the baby out.

It's alright if they are upset with me, but you should not have to deal with that. Let me know if I can be of any help to you. By the way, you didn't ask me what we did." "Knowing what you said a while back, explaining what could happen if, by chance, there was another pregnancy, I trusted that you would do what was best for me."

"That's what I did, what is best for you. There will be no more babies. Take care of these children you have and yourself and help Jurius if you can. Don't forget to let me know if you need me." He examined me, and said, "You are healing nicely at this point. Continue your daily walks with the nurse, see you in the morning." Morning came quickly, and there was not much time for me to sleep. The nurses came in every three to four hours with the baby. She would be with me for an hour. Now that some of the pain has subsided, I got more rest while she was with me.

The Registrar for the birth records came, along with Nurse Bridget White, who wants to name the baby. She had already given the name to the Registrar because she might not be here when the Registrar came for the birth record. The Registrar read all she had recorded to me, including the name. That made me give a big sigh, "What's the matter?" the registrar asked disappointedly. "She gave her name," I said excitedly, followed by a burst of laughter. She repeated the name, "Joline Grace Miller. Do you like it?" Bridget asked, moving closer to me? "I have another name, do you want to hear it?" "No! NO! This one is perfect," I told her excitedly. "So it is, which name is yours?" the registrar asked. "Grace," I replied, "that's my middle name also. My other daughter's name is Josephine, and we call her Josie. Joline will not need a shorter name," I said. She's already beginning to look the name; it's already grown on her, so to speak!

Breakfast came, and I was ready for it but guess what? In popped Dr. Allen, who walked over to my tray and took the lid off the plate. There were pancakes, syrup, sausage patties, and scrambled eggs. All this looked good to me. After feeding the baby three times between dinner and breakfast, I don't like to use the word starving, but I was more than hungry. He said to the server, "Take these pancakes away and bring her a big bowl of oatmeal with cinnamon and fruit, leave the eggs and sausage. I've got to check that kitchen and see what they are serving these sick folks. You would think that a dietitian would know not to serve everyone the same." As he was saying that, he was lifting the covers from every plate and putting them back on.

Walking out of the door, he looked back and said, "See you later Mrs. Miller." He didn't take the time to even press on my stomach, and for that, I was satisfied. My stomach was not sore, but pressing on it with the stitches still in it made it hurt like it did the first day. The server quickly picked up my plate and started to put the pancakes in the trash can when the mom on the bed next to mine asked for them.

The server was confused about what to do. "Dr. Allen would not want me giving you this either. He's tough but fair." The mom said, "But I'm not his patient." "You may as well be. All of you will be right from today on. He takes care of everybody here as much as he possibly can," said the nurse.

Before I could finish eating, the nurse brought the baby. She was crying to the top of her lungs. Maybe this will help her breathing, I thought. "She's getting stronger each day," the nurse attendant said, "don't worry about her, she's showing strength with leaps and bounds." "I'm not worrying," I answered. My trust is in God; he never failed me yet.

Dallas Junior was at the house, so I knew the kids were being taken care of. My nights and days kept me busy trying to get some rest and bathing myself and the baby. Yes, all the mothers had to take care of the baby for the last three days. We have to bathe, lotion, comb their hair, and dress them before bedtime. Combing was not a problem for me; it would not consume my time. Joline had no hair; she was bald. This being my fourth baby, I didn't need help from the nurses. I finished fifteen minutes before any other mom. That meant fifteen minutes of extra sleep time. I also learned from my other babies to wrap them tightly and they will sleep better and longer.

Evidently, the nurses didn't realize that they never wrapped my baby the way I did tonight. I expected to get one less feeding than the previous night. Thank you Lord. All these comments I was making was the result of outright tiredness and the need for complete rest without disturbances. All this is the life you pay for bringing a life into the world. Eve brought this about in the Garden of Eden when she disobeyed God's rule not to eat the fruit from the tree of knowledge of good and evil.

We mothers know that this period of being uncomfortable will not last but for a little while. We get an everlasting joy from interacting with them, watching the change, seeing them grow up to be their own person, and developing knowledge and skills. The pain is easily forgotten and all worth more than you ever could realize.

My seven days were up, and I was longing to be home to see the other little folks. Getting some of my brother's home cooking would be a treat also. I started picturing how things there must have gone and all the out-of-place household items. My mind quickly changed. Dallas was there, and he knew I would be coming home today. I could hear him telling children excitedly about it, and all of them rushing around to make sure everything was in place.

While my mind was in a good place and rest had overtaken me, or I overtook the tiredness, Dr. Allen came in taking his usual long steps and looking from bed to bed before casting his eyes my way. With that smile that was not there lately, he said, "Ready to go home?" "Oh yes," I answered with a big smile that I had for a while. The nurse hurried, carrying a bundle of supplies. That was when I remembered that the stitches needed to come out. He had already pulled the curtain around my bed and thrown the covers back. It seemed as if he was trying to get them out by pressing on my stomach. I tried not to yell.

He was talking to the nurse using terms for the instruments that only the nurse knew what he said. He said to me, "Hold on tight, we are going for the last ride." The nurse started a conversation, trying to distract me, I knew. "What did you name the baby, Mrs. Miller?" she asked. Before I answered, I went all around the question, telling her about who named her and then what her name was. To my surprise, Dr. Allen looked at me with astonishment and said, "You let the nurse name my baby! I would have named her if I had known you needed a name."

He took out the last stitch, and it felt like he meant for it to hurt. "We never had a girl," he said, "only two boys. We wanted a girl each time, so we chose a girl's name but never got to use it." I was thankful that things worked out the way they did because Jurius and his parents already thought that I gave Dr. Allen too much authority in making decisions. If he had named the baby by chance, that would have been double trouble for me. "I want you to stay on some vitamins," he said, writing out a prescription, "and come to see me in a month with the baby. If you notice anything that bothers you, come on in."

The nurse gave me her best wishes and said, "I'll bring the baby in soon." Trying not to let my mind get to bad places, I lay there wondering if Jurius would remember to bring clothes. Dallas would remember, I quickly thought. Now is a good time for me to sleep, only there were no sleep anywhere around me. Reaching over to the nightstand to get my bible, my mind went to Psalm 23. This was one of the scriptures we learned when we were very young; I don't have to read that. At this moment, my eyes began to water, and I would not be able to read anything anyway. As usual, when I ask for revelation and understanding before reading God's word, my eyes closed, focusing on who is the creator and maker of all things.

The Lord is my shepherd. I shall not want or worry. He leadeth me beside the still waters. He restoreth my soul. Footsteps caused my eyes to open, and Jurius was coming toward me. My arms went up in the air to hug him. He bent down, and as I tried to rise, the pain reminded me of what I had been through. He came alone and didn't forget to bring me clothes. He pulled the curtain around my bed so I could have some privacy while getting dressed. The first thing I did was cuddle in his arms and get kisses. Then I began telling him about Joline while getting dressed. He didn't know what her name was. He hesitated when I said Joline, but when Grace was voiced, he smiled and was happy.

He fastened my bra, helped me get the slip over my head, and helped me snap the fastener on my dress. All this was unusual; he'd usually watched me struggling to get my clothes on or off and never offered to help. Maybe he has learned what a husband needs to do in appreciation for what a wife or mom goes through. It felt very good and comforting, and it made me want to be close to him and feel his warmth and heart beating.

The baby was in my arms, so I had to keep my distance so as not to put her in harm's way. On the way, he told me he went to the office at the hospital to make arrangements for the hospital bill. The amount was four thousand dollars. The desk clerk told him the only way he could stand for the bill was to pay it all today.

The clerk said the doctor had made an arrangement so she can go home today. I told her I didn't want him to make any arrangement for my wife. The clerk told me that every doctor has to be responsible for their patient's hospital bill, and we will have to pay the doctor. "This is the only way we can operate this hospital. Each doctor has to pay a certain amount, even if they are not able to collect from the family. Your wife will have to stay until you pay the full amount because we can't do business on credit. Your bill will get higher every day she stays. Trust Dr. Allen," she said, "he is a good and fair person to deal with."

Remembering that he dismissed all our previous bills, I reminded Jurius of that. "Yes," he said, "but I don't want him to do that." "You don't have to let him do that," I reminded him. "Just make regular payments and tell him what you just said if it makes you feel less than a man. Maybe he expects you to pay this time. He has other patients he helps, I was told. He helps anybody he can help, even the hospital staff and other doctors.

You should have heard the conservation in the room about what a God-fearing man he is. I know since Josie was born, when I told the doctors who were doing the surgery to stop fooling around and pray, they all got serious. Every time I see Dr. Allen, he says to me, 'I'm still praying.' Dr. Allen didn't pay that bill; God did. He just used him to provide what we needed. I think you ought to thank God for providing, and the Doctor for letting God use him.

To God be the Glory for knowing what we needed and doing what he did.

We needed the money you were going to use and settle the bill to pay your dad, buy groceries, vitamins, gas, dresses for me, and other things. Where would we have gotten that much money from? We just need to trust God and continue to live right so we can have fellowship with him. He did not tell us how he would bless us, but he promised that he would. If this hospital bill was four thousand plus dollars, the amount of the one before must have been around twenty thousand, not counting what Dr. Allen's bill was."

"I never thought about it this way," Jurius said, "it would have taken us many years to pay it off. What God and Dr. Allen did save us a lot of headaches and stress. It took me almost two years to pay for this car, and sometimes there is no money for gas." We both got quiet for a while. Then I started telling him about Joline having to be put in the incubator at the white hospital, causing Dr.

Allen to stay with her all night because the trustees didn't want a black baby there. "The nurse assigned to stay with her before the problem started was afraid to be there alone, Dr. Allen sent her home and he stayed all night. Joline's breathing was very weak, which could have affected her heart if not corrected soon. The treatment was enough, so the nurses at St. Paul's hospital could continue the treatment using the manual machine, which is all that St.

Paul has. Jurius, let us not be so quick to overlook what God and others are doing to make our lives better. He loves us and will do what he knows is best for us."

I told him that I missed all of them and hoped he had come to visit sooner. He did not answer or give any reason for not coming, so I didn't say any more about it. At home, I found the house cleaned and food ready, waiting for us. Dallas came out, followed by the children, all very excited. Chris didn't pay any attention to me. He was eager to see the baby. "She looked different than when we saw her at the hospital," Junior said, "she's pretty now." We were still in the car. I wrapped the blanket back over her head and handed her to Dallas. Jurius came around to my side of the car and helped me out. "Thank you," I jokingly said, "I'm in your debt for this."

We walked up the steps. He was holding me tightly to keep me steady. We made it into the house, and Dallas put the baby on my lap, all the children standing around to get another look at Joline. "Her name is Joline Grace," I told them. Chris said, "Another J? Everybody's a "J" except me and you, mother." He looked at me when he said that. "You do remember me," I said happily. "I've been telling them that you would come home and bring a little baby girl," Dallas said, "and I've been showing them your picture over there," pointing to my picture. "That's mother," Josephine said, pointing to the picture, and then she pointed at me, "that's my mother too."

Chris was quiet. He was just standing there and looking at the baby. "Do you remember me, Chris?" I asked. He said yes, nodding his head and smiling and said, "I saw you on that bed," meaning at the hospital. Will someone bring me some water to drink and the baby diaper bag?" Junior had brought the diaper bag in from the car. He jumped up from his chair and rushed to get it. Jurius was getting warm water from the kettle on the stove. The children gathered around again to see what I would do.

I changed the diaper without letting them see what was inside. "What did she do?" one of them asked. "She used the bathroom in her diaper," was my answer. "Like Josephine does?" Chris asked. "No," Josephine said, "I'm a big girl now." "You are a big girl," Dallas stated, "you don't do that anymore. Do you want to eat now or later?" he asked me. "As soon as I can get the baby in the crib, I'm ready."

Jurius forgot to tell me that Captain Anderson brought more clothes for the boys. Junior began telling me about their new clothes and ran into their bedroom to get the bag and lots of toys. "I had forgotten all about that," Jurius said, "they sent the toys because they are being transferred to duty overseas, and they have to limit what they can ship." Junior was standing there with a shopping bag full of something. "Let me eat, then we will look at all this," I said. Dallas wanted to bring me a plate so I could continue to relax, but I insisted on going to the kitchen and eating at the table with everybody else.

The kitchen was spotless, better than I had seen it in a while. What really made a big difference was the red and white checkered curtains, tablecloth, and a toaster covered with the same design. "Where did you get all this?" I asked. "From the family that sent the children things." Jurius went outside to check on the pigs and came back in, just as Dallas told me about it. "Oh yes," Jurius said, "they gave us mops and brooms, trash cans, dishes, and a few pots and pans.

There might be something we can't remember right now, but it's all here. Let's eat and talk later," he said with a jolly laugh that I had not heard in a while. "Dallas has been trying to fatten us up with his good cooking. See the curtains and tablecloth," he added. "Yes," I replied, "that was the first thing I noticed when I entered the kitchen." Prayer was said to ask God's blessing and thanks for the food.

When I started to serve my plate, Dallas said, "Wait a minute, we have something else to say, Junior," he called out. Junior said a bible verse to my surprise. "Chris," he called, Chris said one also, "Jo," he had started calling her, she didn't speak as plainly as the others, but she said Jesus wept, and to Junior she said, "I told you not to help me," everybody laughed. While we were eating, Dallas said, "Nobody asked me where I got the pork chops." "Where did you get the pork chops?" I asked.

"Jurius, you forgot all about that ice chest we sat on the porch. It was full of frozen food, and that box was full of all the cooking items she didn't throw away: flour, sugar, salt, pepper, tomatoes, ketchup, mustard, eggs, and all the things you keep in the refrigerator and cabinet."

"God, please bless the Andersons," I asked, from the bottom of my heart, "and keep them safe, covered with the Blood of Jesus. I know you must have thanked him?" I asked. "Oh yes," he said, "many many times, he knows we appreciate them. He didn't let any of us know he was leaving until he was ready to walk out the door. Then he called us together and told us. When the group had broken up, he told me to go to my car.

He waited a few minutes and came out where his car was parked behind mine, and we transferred these things from his car to mine. We shook hands, and he got into his car and drove away. I stood and watched him leave and asked God to go with him and keep him and his family safe. When I returned to the mess hall, almost everyone was crying and saying what a good, honest man he was. One person said, 'God sent him here to let us know how we should treat everybody and show love to all.

All the people who would use bad language stopped using them. All the ones who used to get mad quickly stopped. Nobody would let him see them smoking or using tobacco products. He sent a few men home who came to work with hangovers or smelling like alcohol. That didn't happen again. He never argued or fussed with anyone of us, and he would talk privately to us in his office, never raising his voice. 'This is for your own good,' he would say before making a statement," Jurius said.

"I've never met a man like him. He taught us to do our jobs with pride and help the person working beside or with us if we can. 'Together we stand, divided we fall,' he would say to the one who felt he could give a helping hand."

Jurius continued, "I wonder if he could have been an Angel in disguise. He only stayed two years, which was very unusual. Most chiefs of the department stayed four years or longer. I guess we will never know if God sent us an angel."

Dr. Allen usually did very neat work with his surgery, but I noticed that the cut made on my stomach was sinking inward, which caused me some concern. It was still sore and hard to keep clean. My appointment time would be in a few days. Joline would be a month old and doing good. I've had no concern about her. She was gaining weight and growing like a weed. I kept speaking healing into my body and felt that all was well until I compared the two scars.

Dallas left for his home, and Jurius didn't want to ask for time off with the new chief coming soon. They have been managing without a chief so far. All the work Captain Anderson did with the staff had been paying off. With the help of Junior and Chris, we have been doing good. Some of our neighbors have been coming to help with the washing and cooking dinner. My orders were not to lift anything until my next appointment.

That's where the boys helped most. I could sit on the couch and Junior would bring the baby to me. Joline stayed in place on the couch until Jurius got home. He has been better about being around and helping out with bathing the children. I told him about my concern with the scar. He took a look for the first time and didn't like what he saw.

We decided that we would not complain about it to the doctor since it had only been a month and not long enough to heal completely. We would give the doctor time to decide if it needed his attention. I could bear the little soreness. It really had not been a bother until I tried to clean it. Tomorrow would make it one month, and Jurius would be off from work at two o'clock, and we would be ready to go when he got home. We had leftovers from the previous day's dinner, and it's spaghetti, something that all of us loved, and the pasta is something that holds a long time and supplies a lot of milk for the baby.

Jurius laid out clothes and helped all the children with baths, so it would be easier for us to be ready the next day. Thank God for bringing him back from where his mind and thoughts had gone. It felt good for the children and me to have a dad and husband again. He should know how much we appreciated, loved, and missed him because we're showing it to him constantly, and we're thanking the Lord for helping him fulfill his space in our lives.

The doctor's appointment went well. Dr. Allen told me why the scar was like that. I asked him if he would explain to Jurius, and he stopped talking to call Jurius into the exam room. He said, "I thought you would want to know what happened with this scar being different from the previous one. Well, as you know, we had to do some emergency work before time. This was because the scar before did not have time to heal properly, so infection set in, and when medication was not enough to keep away the soreness, we had to remove the entire scar by cutting on both sides to take away all the infection, which could have grown to cause more damage.

We had to make both sides of the stomach meet in order to close up the wound. Over time, when the incision heals, the scar will become smooth again like the other."

Watching the expression on Jurius' face, I could tell that he understood and was satisfied with the doctor's explanation. He didn't feel so left out as he did before. "Do either one of you have any questions or concerns?" he asked. I shook my head no, and Jurius said, "I understand, and thank you for taking care of my wife and baby." They shook hands.

Dr. Allen called out as he approached the door to leave, "See you in six weeks." The children were well behaved while being left in the waiting room alone. "Did we earn a treat today?" Junior asked. "What kind of a treat do you want?" Jurius asked. "to be left here in the doctor's office all night? All three said at one time, "No, we want hotdogs from the hotdog stand, the one with the cart with big wheels and all the balloons." "We'll think about it," he said.

Just before we got to the place where the hotdog stand was, the children said, "Have you thought about it yet, daddy?" He pulled the car over to the side of the road; even I wondered why. He turned around in his seat to face the children in the back of the car.

Glancing at me, he said, "It's near dinner time. What are we going to eat for dinner?" The children all got very quiet, waiting for me to answer.

"Well, they did earn the right to get the hotdogs, and it will be six weeks before we come back for our next appointment. What do you think, Jurius?" The children were still quiet with their hands over their mouths to keep from speaking out. "If anyone wants to have a little snack, we have leftovers, so I still will not have to cook." The voices from the back seats filled the car with, "Yes, yes, yes, thank you." "Oh boy!" Jurius started the car, pulled on the street, and headed for the hotdog stand.

Quietness filled the atmosphere again. That was how well behaved they were, waiting for the adult to take charge." You all can get out," Jurius told them. He opened his door, pulled up the back seat, for this was a two-door car, and I was seated by the other door. As each one stepped to the ground, one of them called out, "Are you getting out, mother?" "No," I answered. "We're not going to bring you anything," Jurius called out. Thank God, I've got back the man who I first met. The one who was always joking, teasing, and carrying on. The boys knew he was joking, and they both agreed with him. Josie being younger, didn't understand the joke, she called out, "Mother, I'll get you one." "Ok," I told her, "just get me mustard and ketchup like yours."

Jurius let each one make their own order and choose their own toppings. When Josie made her order, she asked for two, the man was unsure if he should give her two while the boys only asked for one. When the man looked at Jurius for a decision, she quickly said, "One is for my mother!" "Now I get it," the man said, "you may have two hotdogs. What topping would you like?" "Both with mustard and ketchup," she announced. "Coming up just as you ordered, who's next?" he asked. "I'm the only one left," Jurius explained, "but I want chips and a drink for everybody." The children had already gone to the table on the edge of the sidewalk behind the hotdog cart.

Josie put her hot dog on the table and started toward the car with one for me. The man stopped her to give her a drink and chips for me. "I've got that," Jurius said, "all this is too much for her little hands." With all the food on the table and everyone seated, one of the boys said, "Let us hold hands and ask for the blessing." The hotdog man stopped and bowed his head as they were doing.

Not only did they thank God for the food, but they also thanked God and asked for blessing for the hotdog man. The man replied, "This is so special to me." Many of the people who sat at the table and many more walking away commented, "This is the first time I've been conscious of thanks and blessing being asked for me also."

"Somebody's waiting for you," one of the boys said to the man."

The drive home was very quick and relaxing for all of us. Jurius kept talking to the children, teasing them to keep them awake since it was getting late, and we surely didn't want anyone to take a long nap now and not be able to go to sleep at bedtime. Had they not been laughing and making noise, I would have fallen asleep myself. The baby slept even with the noise. She sleeps most of the time. My concern was not for her or me, it was for the other three not being sleepy if they take a nap in the car now.

They all slept on the way to New Hope and a little while in the doctor's office. I was hoping the drinks being sweet would hype them up enough to keep all of them awake until bedtime.

We got home before the sun went down. Jurius helped me and the baby to get inside while the children stayed outside to help him with feeding the pigs and chickens. That was a really enjoyable chore for them, especially with their dad helping them. What they really enjoyed was spending some quality time with their dad. Nobody wanted anything else to eat but me, so leftovers was sufficient for me. I also got to have a few hours of quality time and glope over being served and treated special again by Jurius. We prayed that would be the way family life would continue unto the end.

My decision had been made for as long as we were married. I would take every opportunity offered to me and make every sacrifice possible to make my whole family happy and at peace. I knew it was God's will for my life, and I prayed Jurius felt the same. I've been hoping for a big change in his life. God has put two special men in his life that could make a big difference in how he thinks and feels about others and himself. And more than men, God has sent his Son to save us and show us how to love and live with each other.

"Do unto others as you would have them do unto you", was one rule that made a difference in me when I was much younger and in high school. This rule reminds me of how God wants us to live with each other in this world and how he has no respect for a selfish person. He loves us all and wants us to have his best and do our best. He will help all of us when we seek his help. Ask and it shall be given, seek and you shall find whatever you need, knock and the door will be open unto you. There is something each of us must do by faith, and surely, God will do his part. I'm a genuine witness that God will always keep his promise and do whatever he says.

Then said I, Here am I; send me."
Isaiah 6:8

# CHAPTER 15

# God calls again

Our four children were proof of that when my body was not developed to have any children. God still works miracles when we need one. He can make the impossible possible and do what no other powers can do. I was praying for Jurius and trusting and depending on God to keep him in the right way and let him be a righteous and true husband and father consumed my mind most of the time. I believed that if I asked God anything in the name of Jesus, he would do it.

While on my knee praying one night when Jurius had not come home from work, and it was getting late, God spoke to me clearly. I thought that someone was in the room. "Get up off your knees," the voice said, "stop aggravating yourself; you have done all you can to help him. Now do what I called you to do, preach my Gospel to every creature you can, and I will be with you. I will never leave you, nor forsake you.

Jurius is in my hand, I got him."

I was already up from my knees and sitting on the bed. My mind started tracing back the second time I heard God's voice telling me to preach. I decided, sitting there on the bed in the dark, that I would tell Jurius about what God had said to me tonight. I asked God if he would give me courage and strength to get his desire across to Jurius and make him listen. He came home a few minutes later with his don't-talk-to-me-I'm-tired face on. Somehow God had done a special job on me, and I was excited. My voice, face, and action showed every bit of it.

I jumped up from the bed and ran toward him with my arms open to throw them around his neck. His expression changed and we stood there hugging tightly. He held me, but loosely. "What is it?" he asked. "God reminded me tonight that he wants me to preach his Gospel." He dropped his arms from around me, and I dropped mine, still had a big smile on my face. Let me say it again, "No wife of mine is going to preach." Still smiling, I said, "Well, I guess you will do what you want to do about me being your wife, but I'm going to preach.

Matter of fact, I've already been preaching, according to the people who hear me teach. If you want to divorce me, you go right ahead and do what you think you are big enough to do, like you did tonight."

He started out of the room, then he turned abruptly and said, "What do you mean I did tonight?" "I mean, you didn't come home when you should. I don't know what kept you from coming, but for sure, God knows. I don't have to know as long as God knows. You will have to answer to him, not me. He is your keeper as well as my keeper. He told me tonight to stop worrying and praying for you. He has you in His hands." He walked out of the room without saying anything.

I crawled in bed, pulled up the covers, and said thank you, God, for being with me tonight. I had already said my prayers and was ready for sleep before the baby woke up for feeding. I was so relaxed and peaceful as never before when we talked as we did tonight. Nothing could have convinced me that God was not in this house right by my side, leading and guiding me. I heard Jurius taking a bath; it was the last remembrance until he got in bed, kissed me on the cheek, and said good night. I turned over and got in his arms, and we both went to sleep.

The baby didn't wake up for her one am feeding, which made me get extra sleep that I truly needed. This had been a long, trying but successful day. We both heard the rooster crowing and knew we had only one hour more to sleep. The children would be up, ready to eat, and start their busy day. Jurius woke up when Joline started crying for her six o'clock feeding. She was just like clockwork.

"I'll cook breakfast," Jurius said, "you can rest a little longer." I was struggling with the fact that Jurius was so blanketed about my preaching when he had been in the church all his life. He had talked a lot about the revival that God had saved him. He remembered who the preacher was, the year, and the day. I can recall how excited he would get when we had these conversations. My experience was almost the same as his. I wondered what happened in his life that made him turn from the person he should be to the person he is.

After God spoke to me the third time, decided that I would obey God because he has never failed me. From my early years when my mother died to this present time, I've never needed him and he wasn't always there. I knew I could trust him and depend on him. He is more than I ever need. Our children will know who he is and learn to pray and worship him as the one who created heaven and earth and all that is in them.

They will know that he is the only true God with all power in heaven and earth in His hand. He is all-wise, all-knowing, and all-present God who rules the world. I wanted our children to know that they have and are living in this world only because of the love of God and his Son Jesus Christ.

I would continue to be a true and faithful wife to my husband as long as I lived, and nothing would keep me from that. I knew that God would help me face the challenge that this cruel world slings my way. God is all-mighty and mightier than all evil we can face. He has already expressed His will to me about Jurius, but I would always do my Master's will to help him know he could trust in God to help him change his evil ways. My love and hope for Jurius would be eternal. I believed that God would keep him in His hand, and not turn him over to a reprobate mind.

Our six-week appointment came, with all of us once again making the trip to New Hope to see Dr. Allen. The baby and I got an A-okay checkup with the doctor giving his approval that all is well. The incision would continue to heal and smoothen out with time. "Jurius, take care of the beautiful family you have. Come and see me if you need me." They shook hands as they usually do, and he patted me on the back and said, "You take care of Jurius. God bless all of you," and he walked to the door, opened it, and held it open until we got into the car.

"There is something strange about Dr. Allen today," Jurius said. "Yes, I noticed it," I answered, "he never said God bless you, for as long as we've been coming here, and there has never been a time when there was not anyone else waiting for him. He is a God-fearing man, we know. Maybe he wanted to say something else to us but just did not know how to say it." We didn't take matters too lightly when both of us could detect the same thing and had the same feeling. "Wonder why he asked you to take care of me?" Jurius asked, "he never said that before either. He always tells me to take care of all of you."

"God has ways to let us pick up on someone else's feelings and problems. We need to pray about it and give it over to our higher power," I explained. "Maybe it was about the bill," Jurius said, "my intention was to tell him that I plan to make regular payments and find out how much the financial bill is. I don't know why it slipped my mind." "We still can write and say that in a letter," I replied. That is exactly what Dr. Allen had in mind also because a letter came in a few days later.

It reads: "How are you folks doing? Hope everything is still going well for you. Enclosed in this letter is your total bill. I know that you would want to know and we forgot to talk about it at your last visit. Please remember that, as always, these numbers are just numbers to me. I have no concern about it. Whatever you choose to do, I will accept, as long as it doesn't hinder you from taking care of your family and their dire need. My wife, children, and me are well taken care of, and I want the same for you, your wife, and your children. Whatever your decision is, I want you to feel good about it. We don't want to take advantage of you in any way."

Sincerely,

Jeremy Allen, MD

The letter was read, and we discussed what it meant. "Do you understand what he is saying?" I asked Jurius. I continued, "My understanding is that he is willing to cancel this debt as he did before, but he wants you to be alright with it." "How do you feel?" he asked.

"Happy! I'm about to shout right now!" He looked at me puzzled, "So you really think we should let him cancel the bill?" he stated. "Why shouldn't we?' I asked. "He told us in plain language that he didn't have any need for the money, that we needed it most. Where are we going to get money to make payments when you are thinking about building a house? We can barely keep up and put food on the table. You didn't question the gift from the Anderson family. Why question this gift? It's all from God. He is the one giving the blessings. We just need to thank Him and Dr. Allen as we did the Andersons. It's as simple as that."

"Alright," he said, "I'll think about it." "We prayed for God to bless and help us, and we trusted that He would. And when He does, you want to give it back to Him because you don't think you are worthy of his goodness. Stop beating up on yourself, swallow your pride, and just shout and give thanks." He answered, "I'm a man, and I don't want to feel less than a man to make someone else glope." "Well, I haven't seen anyone gloping, but I do see you standing here and putting yourself down. You need to sincerely and truly go to God with this problem you are making for yourself. The children and I really need you to do that."

"And whatsoever ye do, do it heartily, as to the Lord, and not unto men."
Colossians 3:23

# CHAPTER 16

## Back to work

Junior started school, and I started work. A new school was built in Centerville, and all the positions needed to be filled. Cooks and janitors were the most needed labor positions. Patricia Bush was hired as the manager of the lunchroom. She lived in our community, and was responsible for hiring all her workers. I contacted her and was hired immediately. Now, I needed a ride and someone to watch the children. Mrs. Polly - bless her sweet heart - had heard about the work and came to our house (for the first time) and offered to keep the children. Two of her daughters had gotten jobs, and she was going to watch whoever needed help. I had no choice but to accept, thanks to her and God.

Finding a ride turned out to be no problem. Jurius had gone to one of our neighbors who lived a few miles away to borrow money. He didn't let me know he needed money badly for something he would not tell me about. Oneil's wife worked at a bank in Centerville and was happy to give a ride to anyone she could help, up to four people. Patricia Bush had already been working as a cook in one of the other schools and filled her car with her two sisters and two others who worked with her. I got a ride with Oneil's wife, who passed by my house to and from work. She agreed to take the children to Mrs. Polly's house on the days that Jurius had to go to work early.

God worked out everything so that it could not be disputed that he had not made this plan from the beginning, including the reason Jurius had to borrow money. My job was scheduled to pay monthly.

In fact, all the schools were state-operated by a monthly schedule. The pay was not very much, but almost as much as Jurius was getting, and he had been working almost four years for the federal government. My thanksgiving went up to God. Everything worked out for us without any hardship or struggle.

Mr. Mark encouraged Jurius to cut the trees on his land and have lumber made for the house. This project was a good decision because the man who owned the sawmill could use Jurius' help whenever he was off from work in exchange for sawing his lumber. Mr. Mark and Jurius started right away cutting trees for the lumber within a few days. Mr. Hudson, the sawmill owner, sent trucks to haul the logs to the mill. The job in the lunchroom was too much for me, with the surgery only being eight months.

All was well except lifting the heavy pots and pans full of food. Mrs. Bush felt that everyone needed to do their share of the work. She didn't say it directly, but I felt that she would let me go as soon as she got a replacement. I had not worked one month yet and needed to be able to keep working.

When we dropped off the children the next morning, I heard Kathy saying to her mom that she had signed up for the lunchroom work and didn't know why they changed her to janitor work. This was the answer to my praying most of the night when I could not sleep for thinking about how such a perfect plan that God had made fell apart so quickly. I walked into the room with my heart pounding with excitement and thanksgiving. I knew God had not let me down. "Good morning everybody," I said very happily and full of excitement! Everyone responded but not with the same enthusiasm as I did. "Kathy, did I hear you say you want to work in the lunchroom?" "That's what I signed up for," she said, "I'll never know why I didn't get picked."

She was always imagining the worst of anything and was going to blame Mrs. Bush when I stopped her to say, "I'll switch jobs with you." Her eyes got big and sparkling, "Can you do that?" she asked. "I'll make the arrangement when I get to work today," I answered. I had to leave in order to get to the highway for my ride. As soon as I got to work, I talked with Mrs. Bush to tell her my plan for switching places with Kathy, who was not happy with her job.

Mrs. Bush said, "I've been trying to find a way to keep you on. You are so easy to work with and a quick and good worker. But for your health and safety, I will let you switch if you can." "May I have a few minutes to talk with the principal?" "Yes, and things like this is another reason I would like you to stay here. Most of my workers do not respect me as being their manager. They just walk out without letting me know."

The principal called me into his office when the secretary told him I was waiting to see him. I stated my problem to him. Afterward, he said the same as Mrs. Bush's. In order to keep your job, I will honor your wish." "Thank you, Mr. Hanks," I said, "I will do my best to do a good job." Going back to the lunchroom to properly thank Mrs. Bush, I met Kathy coming in. "It's done," I said, "we can change right now, come with me to tell Mrs. Bush that Mr. Hanks approved the change.

After all the business had been taken care of, I gave thanksgiving, praise, and adorations to my Heavenly Father, the Creator of this world, the Lover of all mankind, for his goodness, mercy, and grace and for answering my prayers.

Mr. Hanks took me to meet the other janitors. I already knew one of them; she lived in my community and went to our church. The other janitor, a man named Jimmy, said, "I already know you can't lift anything heavy. Don't worry, I will do all your heavy lifting." I walked away with tears in my eyes, thinking how amazing God is. I knew I could always depend on him. He will never forsake or let me down.

The first day, I was assigned my daily workload that Kathy used to do. Jimmy poked his head and called my name as I moved the desks to make the sweeping easier. "You don't have to move every desk," he said, "just the ones with a lot of trash under them. By the way, do you want to switch again?" "Tell me about it," I said. "You can do some of my work, and I will do your classrooms to make it easier for you, but if you don't like it, I will switch back." "Ok, I'll give it a try." He went into a closet, got a push mop, and said, "Just clean all the halls, health room, and offices.

I will help you if I get finished first." It sounded like a lot of work at first, and I was beginning to think that I got a raw deal. Then I heard a voice inside me say, "God will never mislead you. He has used Jimmy to help you."

Trusting God will always pay off. Oletta, my other co-worker, invited me into the room where we could use during break time and refresh if we needed to. She asked me to bring my personal items, whatever I wanted to bring. She showed me what she had and offered to share with me. I thanked her and said, "I don't need anything today and will be prepared tomorrow. I will also bring a snack. The door opened, and Jimmy walked in, bringing three fudge cycles, my favorite.

"I know you girls worked hard this afternoon and will need a pick-you-upper." Laughing, he handed me one. "How much do I owe you?" reaching for my purse. "Nothing," he said. "You already paid for it when you did all that work cleaning the halls. I don't think my leg would've made it to finish today," he had been limping a little, I noticed, but I did not know him well enough to ask about it. "Well, I am glad I could help you out today, and tomorrow too, if you want to seal the deal we made earlier." "It's alright with me," I said, "I think this was better than having to move the desks.

What I forgot to do was the health room." Jimmy said, "You can do that any time of the day tomorrow. It is not a daily chore, just when a child gets sick and have to use it.

My first day of the change was over, and our ride came to pick us up. On the way home, we talked about our day and it made the thirty-minute trip seem like fifteen. Jurius and the children were already home, and dinner was almost ready. I grasped the smell of cabbage and wondered why he decided to make that rather than the canned green beans he usually makes. Canned foods were what they used at the mess hall and in the hospital. Before I could ask why the cabbage, he told me Chris had gone to the garden and brought it to him to cook. He stated that this was the last one and he didn't want it to rot. He said, "I know how to clean it because 'mother' let me help her one day."

"For I know the plans I have for you,
declares the Lord."
Jeremiah 29:11

# CHAPTER 17

# Chris

Chris ran to the house with the others following behind. He was very excited to tell me about the cabbage he found in the garden. Chris was a different kind of child from the others. The others would be playing or swinging in the tyres Jurius had hung from the tree in the backyard. That was their favorite place to be, except Chris. He would be in the garden or field when any one of us was there. He had many questions about the vegetables planted or growing.

"What part do you eat? How do you cook them? Why don't you cook cucumbers? How long will it take them to grow?" Jurius didn't have the patience to answer all his questions. He would tell him to go ask his mother. He wouldn't leave the garden but would remember all his questions at dinner time. He questioned Gene Miller, a cousin to Jurius, about why he comes to take our dad away from the family a lot of the time.

Gene said to him, "Boy, you won't understand if I told you." "Go ahead and tell me and see if I understand." "Boy, you are too smart. I'm going to take you home with me," Gene teased. "Ok, I'll go with you for ten thousand dollars," Chris stated. "A five-year-old doesn't know what ten thousand dollars are," Gene stated! "Just give it to my mother, she will know what it is." At that time, the two men went out the door, Jurius looking back and saying, "I'm leaving the car in case you need it."

Chris came to me and said, "When he gives you the money, I'm coming back home." Then he asked me, "Why is he always coming here to take daddy away, we almost never get to see him?" I replied, "It is only on Fridays when he comes," trying to lessen the obvious or change the subject. "We want our daddy home," he stated. For whatever reason, the mysterious trips that would take almost all night made me think and wonder about it even more. I had not asked questions before to keep peace in the family. Now that my child has become interested in this matter, it is time for me to pray and take notice.

My in-laws made my finding out a bit easier. A few days later, I stopped to pick up the children when Mrs. Polly, her sister Rosie, and Kathy were talking about Rosie's son almost being caught by the highway patrol. They outran him but nearly overturned the car in the chase. They didn't know who was driving, but it was not Gene. He had hired a driver who was an expert in fast driving. "When did all this happen?" I asked. "Last Friday night, they were in Pamlico County." All this information made things clear to me, remembering last Friday was the night Chris questioned Gene about taking his dad away. That was the night Jurius came home nervous, shaking, and wouldn't talk. He just wanted to go to sleep.

I think he realized as I did that Chris' questions meant something. Maybe this is just a warning to them. I said nothing about what I was thinking and heard that evening. I have been waiting for him to start the conversation or outright tell me about what happened. I didn't want to wait too long for something that could be avoided to happen. I thanked God for keeping them safe last Friday night and giving them a chance to change whatever they could. After asking God to help me know how to help him and to give him listening ears, I started rehearsing what I would say.

My help had already come about what I would say. "God send the Holy Spirit to make what I say to Jurius make sense to him. "Please take control, oh Lord!" The children were tired and ready for bed right after dinner. This was good, so they would be sound asleep when Jurius got home. I was tired also because I had not gotten used to working yet. Jurius came, and he came with a big twist of plans to my surprise.

He started verbally attacking me for letting Chris talk to a grown man like he did, and I did not say a word to stop him. "I heard him asking questions to an adult; that was his own concern. What he said was not disrespectful or rude. His questions needed an answer, an answer that you or Gene could have provided. You both refused to answer. You could have told him, if what you were doing or where you were going was legal.

If not, you should not be doing it."

What I said struck a sore spot, and he fired back at me with both barrels. "What did you tell mama and Aunt Rosie at the house the other day?" "I didn't tell them anything because I didn't know anything to tell. You have not told me where you were going or what you were doing. Why do you think I told them something?" "Mama said you were there and joined in the talk with everyone else." "I only asked them a question, that was, when did this happen?

No one mentioned your name. They said they didn't know who the driver was. Was he you?" I asked. "Why would you ask me that?" he said. "Because you came home very late shaking and upset, and would not say anything. Another thing is you get upset whenever the subject is mentioned. You also have been keeping secrets."

"Well, I learned my lesson since Friday night. All I could think about was Chris's questions, and I could actually hear his voice. When we got on the road again, I prayed to thank God for taking care of us and vowed that I would never drive like that again." "So it was you?" I asked. "This is not news," he answered, "you knew all along." "I was not sure, but I felt it was what you were doing. I pray you are serious about that vow you made and don't try to play with God, for your vow was made with him."

"But as for me and my house,
we will serve the Lord."
Joshua 24:15

# CHAPTER 18

## One happy family

For the next few weeks, he was the best husband and father. He came home on time and if he were a few minutes late, he would say as he walked through the door, "I stopped to get gas, or the traffic was extremely bad," and I would know that was true because something was going on at the base. We would go to the bible study and Sunday school and church together as a family should. Gene, his cousin, who he was driving for, stopped doing what he was doing and started attending all the services. He wouldn't come to our house because of Chris. He said, "Little fellow jinxed us. I can't get his voice and questions out of my mind."

The summer went by fast, and it was time to go back to work. Chris also started school. He was so excited about all the boys and girls in his class. He would describe them in detail and tell me their names. If it were a girl, he would say she was pretty. He would show me his classwork, which was all very good. He had learned a lot from Junior, who taught him all he knew when he first started school.

My work helped us to be able to pay all that we owed everybody. We were also able to give Mrs. Polly a stipend. She said she didn't want anything. "Just save for your house," she said. I insisted on her taking it so that she would not have anything negative to say later on. "This is for you taking such good care of them. It's a token of my appreciation, and thanks for all you're doing to help us." I don't have to worry about them while I'm working.

That means a lot to me to know they are safe and in good hands.

I also knew she deserved more than I could give but just wanted to share what I could with her. I realized she had no income except what she got from Mr. Mark, and he only worked in winter after farm season was over. God had already made way for the house, and it would be so according to his will. Jurius' attitude was very good, the family was in harmony, and I believed God was pleased with my work in the ministry.

There is no reason we can't be hopeful and trust God that his will will be done.

Ever since we started cutting the trees for the building, we started thanking God for the completion of the work. I knew we would complete the house because we had given the work to the Master Builder. He is in charge of making all the plans. We only look to him for making all the decisions. He loves that we are trusting and depending on His word.

Work was going well for me and not so bothersome anymore. I'd learned what to do and how to do it and could ease on over it with the help of God and the Holy Spirit. Singing has always been my helper. When working in an area where I won't disturb anybody, I sang just loudly enough that I could hear my words so I could remember them. I sang spiritual hymns that I learned when I was a child and the ones sung in the church choir. The words of the songs lifted my spirit, so work would become a joy. I can also worship God when my spirit is lifted and fellowship as my daddy, siblings, and I did in the farm fields.

The principal gave me another task to lessen the secretary's work. When a child was sick at school, I would call the parent to come for the child. The child would stay with me in the health room until the parent came. The bed linen would have to be changed if the child had a fever and taken to the laundry, a few minutes' walk away. I made the trip back to pick up the laundry when it was ready. The health room was one of my original assignments to keep clean. It was very much in need of cleaning and clearing when I started. The secretary commented that she might want the job back now that she could do her work there in comfort, away from the phone ringing and walk-in disturbances.

While waiting with a child, I would be busy dusting or rearranging to make for a better environment. At the end of the day, there was energy to take home for a continuing task that awaited me. On Jurius' days off, he would make out time to do the cooking and sometimes the laundry and mopping. I always sat down with the boys to look at their school work and make sure their homework was done properly and in order. When there was reading, I listened to them read. Surprisingly, I got a note from the teacher saying that Chris could not read. She didn't write, would not, but could not. Chris had a good start reading after Junior learned because Junior would come home and play school with Chris and Josephine, he being the teacher.

When we studied here every night, he could read his class book and other books we have here at the house. "Chris," I said, after reading the note from his teacher, "Mrs. Smith said you couldn't read! What's going on? Tell me, what happens at school that you can't read?" He smiled very broadly, as usual, and said, "Mother, you know I can read." "Yes Chris," I replied, "I know you can read, but why does Mrs. Smith think you can't read?" That broader smile filled his face as he looked down at the floor.

Lowering his voice to just a whisper, he said, "She's not being fair." "Speak up," I said, "and look at me! Why do you think Mrs. Smith is not being fair?" "Because she lets everybody read, and she helps them. I'm always the last one she calls every day. So I miss all my words so that she can help me," Chris, I replied. I was astonished about what he had just said.

"Do you know what you just said? You said you are mad at her. I am disappointed with you; I can't really believe you did such a thing. I'm surprised that you fooled the teacher. Perhaps that was why she called on you last because she had spent too much time with you. What is really the reason you won't read? You want her time or because you are last?" He was shaking his head side to side for neither.

He came up with one of the strange answers that he had been saying lately, which didn't make sense to us. "I don't need to read," he said, "I don't even need to know how to read. That's all!" He was looking directly into my eyes, with a sorrowful look in his eyes. And that was when he said, "I'm sorry mother, but I didn't want to tell you," he said, fighting back tears. I told him, "It's alright, I know you can read, and you know you can read.

I will write to Mrs. Smith to let her know that for some reason, you prefer not to read, but you are a good reader. If Mrs. Smith wants to hear you read, do your best and please her. Let her know that she is a good teacher." He is always saying to me, 'you're a good mother, the best.' And to Jurius he would say, 'daddy try hard to be a good daddy; I love you.' He would put his arms around his neck or legs if Jurius was standing.

February 28th, a day after celebrating Josephine and my birthdays, which were 25th and 27th. We all had a glorious, happy dinner with balloons, cake, and food of our choice. Chris was anxious to talk about it at school when they had "show and tell." He said in the car on the way to school, "I'm going to still be happy, just as I am now when I tell it, and I'm going to make Mrs. Smith and all the children happy too." Before we left - me and Jurius for work, the boys for school, and the girls to grandma - we all were rushing to go and not be late.

While I was checking to see if all the lights were off and doors locked, Chris came sprinting back into the house straight to his room, yelling, "I forgot something." He only took a few seconds inside, and he came running out. I was standing at the door waiting to close and lock it when he handed me a small jelly jar with money in it, saying, "This is for you, mother." He looked strangely at me and smiled.

"What is this?" I said as we walked to the car, "All my ice cream money," he said, "I didn't buy ice cream when you or daddy gave me money. I wanted to save it for you. You know how we saved for the T.V. last year, now you can save it for the house." Holding the jar in my hand, I showed it to Jurius and told him what Chris had said. I put it in the glove compartment of the car. But could not stop thinking, why did he want to give it to me today especially? So much as running back into the house after being in the car, saying I forgot.

"He healeth the broken in heart, and
bindeth up their wounds."
Psalm 147:3

# CHAPTER 19

# *Bereaved*

Jurius dropped the boys off at school, and I got my ride to work. The day went as usual, and finally, my mind settled on my work and singing. We had almost finished; I had cleaned the two offices and bathroom and was working on my last hall when I looked up to see Mr. Henson, the principal coming my way. I moved my mop and got over to the side of the wall so he could pass. He didn't pass but stopped.

Not looking at me, he said, taking the mop out of my hands and putting his hand on my shoulder - which was the first time - "Leave right now, a car is waiting outside for you." Many questions started flowing out of my mouth as we walked to the back of the school. All he would say was 'I don't know' to all my questions.

I rushed to the waiting room and got my bag and coat. Oletta was standing there looking sad. I questioned her, but all she said was, "I don't know." Mr. Henson was standing there trying to rush me on. What my mind was telling me at this time was they got something wrong. I don't need to go to the hospital. Finally, I went outside toward the car. I stopped because I didn't recognize it. The man in the car got out and started toward me. Then I saw he was one of our neighbors. I asked him who sent him for me. He said, "I went to the base to get Jurius." "He is already there. Is he sick? Hurt?"

We were at the hospital by this time, driving up to the emergency room door. What I thought? I got out of the car, and our neighbor drove away. Walking into the hospital lobby, I didn't see anyone I knew. The desk seemed a long way off, and I could barely walk. I went to the desk and announced myself to the clerk and told her someone had called to come.

The clerk did not know about what I said. Standing there, knowing the neighbor had already left, I was wondering how I would get home. Then I remembered that Jurius was there. I asked the clerk about Jurius, and she didn't know that either. Nobody knew anything: Mr. Henson, Oletta, clerk, nobody knew anything.

I turned abruptly and rushed toward the door. A man's voice said, "She is the child's mother; stop her. The man, the attending doctor, and the clerk called me to come back. I had no intention of going back when nobody had any answers to any of my questions. The doctor caught up with me as I was about to step off the sidewalk. I could not, for some reason, see the step down to the sidewalk. The doctor's voice was loud but not yelling. He called out, "Are you Mrs. Miller?" Wondering why he was calling out for me, I looked around and answered, "Yes, I am." "Come with me; your son is in here," he said as he led me down the hall and into a small room at the end of the emergency area.

He stepped in front of me. As we entered the room, another man and a woman rushed in also. The last man closed the door behind himself. When the doctor stepped aside, he said, "Your son was hit by an automobile this afternoon on his way home from school." He walked a few steps forward and pulled the sheet back that covered the body of a young child, who lay there lifeless and still. To me, he looked asleep. "Is he hurt?" I asked.

The doctor looked at the man standing there and said, "Run, get her husband." A nurse I knew led me or rather pushed me into a chair away from the bed. I just wanted to see which son it was. I never realized how much they looked alike. The room door opened, and I could hear Jurius crying, "Not my boy," over and over again. I started to get up but was very limp.

The doctor started slapping me on the face several times, and the nurse sprayed something up my nose. I could hear a voice say, "Don't let her go to sleep." Something very cold was put on my face and head, and I was put in a wheel chair and rolled out of the room. Several hours passed as I lay there on the bed, not knowing which son was hurt in the accident. Dead did not come to my mind. No one had said the word to me. My subconscious told me, 'he was too still and his eyes were shut; he is not alive.' My memory took me back to the house when he gave me the jar with the money, back to the note from Mrs. Smith and his answer to why he would not read.

"It is Chris," I said out loud. The nurse said, "What did you say?" I said, "My son in the other room's name is Chris." She said, "Let me find out." "No, I'm sure he is Chris." At that time, my subconscious admitted that he knew he would not come back home today. I started to pray and call on Jesus and the Holy Spirit to help me. "Jesus, we need your help. We don't know what to do. Please, send help oh, Lord our God." In walked Jurius and Rev.

Henry, our pastor at the church. Jurius was still crying but not historical like earlier. The halls and waiting room were filled with community friends, both whites and negros. Most were crying or had been crying. Some looked at me - who could not cry - and showed pity or compassion.

How I prayed to cry, for that hurt in my chest was too much for anyone to bear. All I could do was call on Jesus aloud, "Please don't leave us now; we need You." Over and over, I called on the name of Jesus. That was what gave me a little relief from the pain. The doctor called the pastor, Jurius, and some of his family members to say, "She went into shock; you need to watch her closely because she is not crying. She may go into shock again. Here is a prescription for some medicine to help her. The news of her child's death has caused emotional disturbance of mental stability, causing the shock. She still might not have accepted it all."

Yes, I have finally accepted it after my conscious mind took me back through his early childhood and all the unusual and strange things he would say to us or anybody else he talked with. "Oh Lord, please let me cry!" After saying that prayer, the Spirit let me know that

God had kept his promise and given us children. He didn't promise us that he wouldn't take one back. He had given life to him and fitted him for his kingdom. I'm satisfied that he is with God. His spirit is still with us, praying for the best life we can have. I can imagine hearing him say, "Don't cry for me, mother, I'm alright."

Chris was the only child that we had no problem with at birth. Junior was a twenty-four-hour hard breach birth, and the other two have already been narrated in this book. What can we do except trust our almighty and all-wise God? Worship and give glory to his holy name, live and love right so we can be with him in the end. The bible tells us that Chris is not dead; he just transitioned from the earth and entered into God's kingdom. His body went back to the ground from whence it came. His soul and spirit returned to God, our heavenly Father.

Chris lived on earth six years, six months and eighteen days. He was very curious and learned much about a lot of things. He loved gardening and learned about many vegetables and the foods they produced. He loved to eat vegetables because he watched them grow and helped gather the foods from them. He was also very interested in the family welfare and saved his ice cream money to help with the cost of building our house. All who knew loved him and knew he was a special child.

We, mostly myself, thanked God for his gift to us and for trusting us with such a special child. To God be glory for his love, kindness, goodness, and compassion to us and the whole world. Thanks and praises to our Lord and Savior Jesus Chris, for his love and sacrifices for all the world. Thanks to our family and many friends who helped us make it through such a hurtful and trying period in our lives. Many reached out to help us with financial and legal matters.

We love all of you and deeply appreciate your act of kindness and sympathy, especially to the attorney in Morehead City who offered pro bono help with all our legal needs. We prayed for many county and city officers who blocked the attorney from helping us. Our prayers went to the persons who would not let us in his office to talk with us or give us a copy of the autopsy report. We were treated rudely and abusively like we're not humans.

I'm trying to put it in this manner to let you know that none of these rude and ugly actions from our city leaders hurt us. We know Almighty God was with us, and no act of satan could do us any harm.

There were a lot of credible leaders and people of honest status of both races who stood with us to the end through every situation. I pray now that every reader will understand who God is. All authority and power in heaven and earth are in his hand. He loves all his children, especially those called by his name.

Jurius was devastated at this crucial time in our lives. I could have been in the same state of mind as he was, but I refused to let the enemy win over and turn me from all my hope, faith, and trust in our Heavenly Father. He is still in control of our battle, even though we're in a war of deception and delusion. What I knew and tried to help Jurius understand was God didn't kill our son. He allowed him to leave this mean, deceitful world and gave him victory. We will have to stay here and do our most efficient work in helping our children to grow in grace and knowledge of God.

"This is no time to focus all your attention on yourself and your lost. Your entire family also have a deep feeling of loss. What about Junior and the other children who watched that accident take place? What if Junior had been holding his hand and he blames himself for not doing it? Perhaps both of your sons would not be here. Wake up, Jurius, and do your best to do what Chris said to you, as almost his last words to you. 'Try to be a good daddy.' Don't let the enemy destroy your hope and faith in our Lord God and his Son Jesus the Christ. God is right near you, trying to get your attention to the fact that His word said, 'I will be with you unto the end of the earth.'

"Please let go and let God take away all your hurt, pain, misery, and your sense of loss. We have not lost him, he is with our father waiting for us to come one day to be with him again. Let's do our best to live holy, do good and righteous deeds, and be ready for Jesus to come again. The children, your parents, the church, the community, and I all need you. Don't give up on us."

Our pastor, Rev. Humphrey, came every day to work with the children and us. He would take us riding to show us things we had not seen. We made a trip to Columbus City to visit the attorney who offered to help us without charge. We would focus on the sightseeing and were released from our thoughts of pain and sorrow. But only for a few moments because Jurius was not distracted, and the pastor or I didn't know what to do except pray.

We funeralized Chris the following Saturday. The church, with around three hundred seating capacity, was overcrowded with people standing around the walls and every enclosed room and hallway filled. Still, there were many who couldn't see or hear from outside the church. Jurius and I have large families and each of our community members visited, including school children, their parents, and other surrounding areas. There were more than I could even describe. Pastors from all the surrounding churches were more than could fit into the pulpit area. I gave thanks to God for such a beautiful sunny day. No comparison to the day of the accident; it was cloudy and raining most of the day. I was told that the rain had stopped, but the ditch he was knocked into had water in it. God shielded him from the water.

He was buried in the Miller family cemetery near our home. The children and I made many trips there to put on fresh flowers. Some were wildflowers we picked along the way. Jurius said, "I cannot visit this time, I'm fighting too hard to let him go." When the grass began to grow and the debris from the wind needed to be picked up, he was the first to say, "Come let's go clean the cemetery." He went straight to Chris' grave, fell on his knees crying, and gave him up in the Lord's hands.

We dealt with the legal matters and Mr. Ochoa, the driver of the car who hit him. He was a wealthy farmer who owned many houses and lands and had many negro sharecroppers. He owned a beach house on the coast. The road to his beach cottage passed through our community. He was on his way to his home in Roseville. His wife came to visit us along with her daughter. They brought a fruit basket. I believed she was a Christian and wanted to truly express her sympathy to us and let us know she was sorry about what happened. She told us that Mr. Ochoa had been drinking, and she tried to encourage him not to leave that day.

She also said she warned him of the children walking from school. He was driving a little faster than he usually drove and a car was approaching with lights on. He pulled over to avoid hitting the car and ran off the road. He lost control where the school children had crossed and hit four children, one being Chris.

After Mrs. Ochoa visited us, the racial injustice started. We got over it all and have forgiven them for the most part. When the hearing was held, Mr. Ochoa was not present, nor was his name ever mentioned. We were told that he had paid off all the county and city officials to alleviate him from the matter. They put a value on our son's life, as to how much he would be worth when he was grown as if he was a worthless animal.

They got to the judge then, but they will have to stand before the Righteous Judge and account for all their actions one day. The little money we got for the loss of our son was a big disgrace. If I could, I would have given it back to them, laughed in their faces, and walked out. Instead, we prayed that God would have mercy on their souls because no amount of money could give our son back to us.

To live in peace was better for us in those circumstances.

"For we walk by faith, not by sight."
2 Corinthians 5:7

# CHAPTER 20

## Trying to move on

We built the house and used the money for Chris' death to lessen the payments. We didn't build as we planned. At work one day on my break, I picked up a newspaper and there was an ad for home building with only one dollar down. We contacted the company, and they worked out a plan to use all our materials and deduct them from the total cost. This way, the house was finished a lot sooner, and their work was guaranteed. Mr. Pollock, a community member, found we lacked space and offered to sell us three acres near the road in front of where we had cleared the land. We made all of the arrangements and cleared another space where we built the house.

After we made the last payment for the property, Mr. Pollock offered us all the land he owned on that side of the road, totaling sixteen more acres. It was all forest land with the timber being cut already. We got it appraised, and the value was just a little more than the three acres. We jumped at this land with both feet, praise, and thanksgiving, for we know this was an act of God.

Mr. Hellen, the man who owned the sawmill, also owned a bulldozer. We went to see him about clearing the land for farming. We expected to pay for the work, but he offered the same deal for cutting the house's lumber. As the men made plans, Mrs. Hellen, joking with her husband, said, "Why can't Hattie work for me sometimes, in exchange for the clearing?" Mr. Hellen asked, "Hattie, can you wash windows?" I didn't know how to answer because my time was already full, working five days on my job and only Saturdays to do my housework and spend some time with the children.

When I hesitated, she said, "The work will still be here when school is out. Nate just wants to get out of washing windows this spring. You men keep your deal as planned, I will talk with Hattie later."

She didn't forget. A few days after school was out, she came. The children and I were outside planting flowers and raking debris from the Pecan trees, doing a little tidy up to make the place look like somebody lived there. We talked about what she wanted done. The work wasn't a problem, but I wanted to give Mrs. Polly a break from the children for a while. "Well," she said, "if you are willing to help me do what you're doing today, you can also bring the children to help." I knew the children would be happy to be outside with me, no matter where it was.

We discussed a day and time for the job and made it final. My thought was that Jurius would be okay with the plan because Mr. Hellen had always been generous with him working for exchange.

"You can work for her for exchange, but don't involve my children." "Well, the children enjoy being outside with me. She offered for me to bring them when I told her that we needed to give your mother a break." "How much work do you really think these children can actually do?" "They will probably keep me and her from doing as much as we can do. She was polite and kind in asking, and I could not make another excuse.

Why don't we just see what happens? It will be a good reason to visit. You are always telling me how you like working with Nate. Maybe this will be a pleasure for the children and me." "I'm working for the exchange," he said, "you and the children can visit someone, anybody of color, not someone to make you and the children look like slaves out cleaning yards."

"I've already promised to come on a certain day to help her. She will be in the yard with us, and by some chance, if she can't be with us, I will leave. Does Mr. Hellen make you feel like a slave? If so, why are you still working with him?" "No," he replied abruptly, "he is not that kind of person. We get along good. He respects me, and I do same toward him." "Then why do you expect his wife to be any different? Please let us not judge anybody before we give them a chance to prove themselves." "You are right," he said, "go ahead and help her. I'm sorry I saw things the way I did."

We went as planned to help Mrs. Hellen, and she was as nice as could be. She had a big wheel wagon which the children enjoyed working with. When the wagon was emptied after hauling the trash to the field where it was dumped, Junior would let the girls ride back to the yard. Mrs. Hellen went into the house and had some sodas and cookies ready after making the second trip. We all sat on the edge of the porch and took a very long break.

While sitting there on the porch, Mrs. Hellen asked me, "Mrs. Miller, where are you from originally?" I told her where I'm from, and as usual, when you say Civil City, the next question is, where is that? I explained, and she told me her home was in New Hope. She met Mr. Hellen, whose home is in Hallandale, at a junior – senior prom and they hit it off right away. She said, "He told me the next time we met that I would be his wife. I guess it was love at first sight."

We finished the yard work after she served us lunch, which made everybody lazy. We only had a little work to finish, pulling weeds out of the flowers. Junior commented about how more beautiful the flowers were now than before the weeds were pulled out. She decided to give him a few bulbs to plant in our yard. "Come on in, you can wash your hands here," as she washed her hands under the faucet on the porch. We all had just finished washing our hands when she returned from inside. She was holding some money in her hands. "Josephine," she said, "you get paid first. You worked hard, and so did Joline," who didn't do anything except ride in the wagon.

She handed each girl five dollars, "Ooh," Jo said, "a lot of money." "Thank you," both girls said. Junior was standing there with a big smile on his face. As she fumbled through the bills she held in her hand, she finally pulled out a ten-dollar bill and handed it to Junior. "Thank you," he said, smiling even bigger. She handed me a twenty-dollar bill in a flash, saying, "Is this alright?" "This is more than alright," handing the twenty back to her. "No! No!" she said, "I wish I could give you even more, you all worked very hard today, and you did a super job. My yard has not looked this good ever. I'm sure my neighbors will want you to do theirs when I tell them who did it."

We went home and planted the bulbs. "We won't see flowers until next spring," I told Junior. Cooking was easy and quick, partly leftovers, so I only had to fry fish to make the meal. The children were very excited to tell dad about their money at the dinner table. Surprisingly, he was cheerful as they talked about the work and the big wheel wagon. Joline couldn't wait to get a chance to tell about her rides in the wagon. Jo had to talk about her work loading the wagon, and Junior talked about where they piled the trash and how they filled places where water could not stand when it rained. He was very eager to tell how Mrs. Hellen and I could not rake fast enough to keep them busy.

Jurius quietly stated, "I didn't know she was going to pay you for the work. This was to be "exchange" work from what I understood." "Me too," I said, "money was not even mentioned in our talk. She was there in the beginning and asked for "exchange" work with me. I tried to give my money back, but she would not accept it, saying she wished she could give more. The children did good work making play out of it. They never realized it was hard work. She did a good thing encouraging them."

"He shall cover thee with his feathers, and
under his wings shalt thou trust."
Psalm 91:4

# CHAPTER 21

## *Violence erupts*

Summer went by quickly, and it was time to start school and my work. Jurius still grieved about Chris, and school was a great reminder. He started blaming me and saying, if I had not been working, if I had not had the sterilization, we could replace him. Every moment we were alone together, this was my demonic price to pay. I tried to explain that he could not be replaced. Even if we had another son, he would not be Chris.

"The sterilization was to save my life. Would you trade my life for another son?" I asked. Before I could finish talking, the back of his hand reached over and slapped me in the face. It was so instant and unexpected that I didn't know what to do. He jumped up from the bed, and I also did on the opposite side. The lights were not on, and the switch was on his side of the bed. "Turn the lights on," I asked.

"Don't say another damn word to me," he said, "you don't care if Chris is gone, and you don't want another one to replace him.

I started to say something, but he rushed to where I was, holding my face that he had struck. He grabbed my shoulders, shook me roughly, and said, "Shut your dam mouth." He slept on the couch from that night forward and was always late, three or four hours late coming home. He had no communication with me or the children. Worried that his mind had snapped, I spoke to the pastor, thinking he might help him come to his senses. That was to no avail. He beat me for involving someone else in our personal problem. When I say beat, he would go for my head with his fist. Most of the time, I would protect my head with my hands and stood with my face against the wall, praying silently for God to intervene.

God did not stop him from beating me or threatening me, but he took away the hurt and pain and never was there any bruises or scars. God also gave me peace and happiness every day. I could not harbor any kind of ill-feeling or be rude toward him. His late nights and weekends away from the family netted him a baby girl with one of his earlier girlfriends.

She was very happy to flaunt the baby in my face and let me know who the dad was. No matter what he did, he could not break my spirit or trust in God. I could not answer the children's questions of: Where is daddy? This was the most hurtful part of the disgraceful and deceiving sinful scandal.

He finally stopped giving me money for bills and household expenses. "Let the light company cut off the lights," he said when I told him the bill was due and I didn't have enough money to pay. The lights were cut off, and the sad thing about that was that he didn't care. I prayed to God for help, and he sent me to the company to ask for help. I was told they would need the light's charges plus a cut off fee paid before reconnection. I continued trusting God and thanking him for showing me what to do. I didn't feel disappointed. I stood there away from the main desk, whispering, "Thank you, God, for sending me here."

"May I help you Miss?" I heard a voice. "Yes," I said, turning to face him. "Come this way," he said, leading me into his office. I told him my name, "I'm here because my electricity was cut off. I didn't have enough money to pay all the bills, and I couldn't get enough before the deadline." He opened the file cabinet drawer and took out our folder. "Look, this is the first time you've been late. Usually, we will excuse the first month's non-payments and give you time to catch up." That word "excuse" sounded like what God does with us much of the time.

"How much do you have, Mrs. Miller? Can you pay that amount today?" "Yes, I can pay that amount now." "Let me call the workers before they leave work and have them go out and turn on your electricity." Tears of joy, happiness, and thanks flowed down my cheeks. He turned around as I wiped away my tears, handing him the money. He never reached out to take; instead, he seemed to be thinking. "Mrs. Miller, you are excused for the entire month's amount. You might need this money for something else soon." "Thank you very much. And God bless you." "You are very welcome," he answered, "and God bless you and your family." God has already blessed us in such a wonderful way, and I gave him praise and thanksgiving for being our God and Heavenly Father.

When I went to pick up the children from his parents' house, they had already gone home. "Jurius picked them up earlier today," Mrs. Polly told me. The electricity was on, and Jurius wanted to know where I got the money. "I didn't," was all I could say before his fist went to my head. Trying to shield my head and face caused me to fall to the floor. He kicked me in the side and back several times, demanding that I get up using curse words. The children ran into the house, but he heard them coming and stopped before they could get in. Thank God he did, for I didn't want the children to see what he was doing.

I was still on the floor, and they asked, "Why are you on the floor?" "I fell." They ran to tell their dad I had fallen to the floor. They wondered why he didn't help me get up. "That's alright," I told them, "I'm not hurt." God had blocked every punch and kick. He drove off and didn't come back until late at night, accusing me of selling my body to pay for the electric bill. "Go to the company and find out how they got turned back on, you don't have to believe what I told you."

The beating didn't stop for years, and this was between the two of us for years. Our children lived through this for years, they had known since they were in elementary school, maybe before. I thought they only found out when they were teenagers. By that time, he had no communication with them. I was able - with the help of God - to buy a car. This gave us some independence, all our children were very skillful in athletics.

Junior played all sports; Josie and Joline were cheerleaders and in the band from middle school thru high school. The car made it easier for me to pick them up after practice in the afternoons and get them back and forth after games. Not only did I pick up my children but a lot of neighborhood sports players. One young man was with us so much that many people thought he was my son. People still ask me about him as being my son.

I would come home from work and make the trip to school to pick up Joline and whoever needed a ride. I'd go home and start dinner, leave Joline to watch it while I go back to school and get Josie and her group of friends. I'd bring them home, finish dinner, wash a load of clothes, or do some kind of housework, go back to school to get Junior and other sports players from our community and take everybody home. My last trip would get me home by seven o'clock. The girls would have finished homework. After dinner, Junior would have time to do his homework before bedtime.

I have to confess; I could not do all that I did without God's loving-kindness and help. He is always supplying strength and power to keep me strong. He is also always encouraging me to continue doing all I can do to help make this world a better place. I got a better job after segregation ended. Our county school officers hired me to ride one of the buses that transported the elementary children to school. Also, during school hours, I worked as a teacher's aide or assistant.

After working for a few months, our jobs changed according to our qualifications. I sometimes worked as a mentor during recess and lunch at the high school. A job suited just for me. The high school students, especially the boys, had started smoking during break, which was against the rules of the school. Some of the people said I had the right personality to work with young people. I knew I had plenty of experiences living with Jurius these many years.

Plus, my children were teen and preteens.

Another helper in my favor was practicing the golden rule: Do unto others as you would have them do unto you. My smile always played a big part when I had to approach someone. Teaching and preaching taught me to convince anyone that I am right and they are wrong. Another big helper was my debate team. Yes, and don't forget the everlasting strong authority and power from our Heavenly Father on High. He taught me well with all the challenges I went through.

He taught me that "if anybody can do it, I can too." I'm never giving up; I will try for as much time as it takes. I will pull and pull until the rope breaks. Then I will get another rope and pull until my enemy or obstacle gives in, falls or get out of my way.

Despite what God has given me, our marriage also made me stronger and more determined. Only death do we part. Punches and beating can't hurt me or make me leave or give up because I have a helper who takes the hurt away. He was kicking my side and back with blows that should've knocked me down and broken ribs and backbones, but God's power stepped in and protected me. Never was there a black eye, bruise, scrape, scratch, or any mark on my body. I didn't go through any soreness or pain. Humanly, I should have gone to the emergency room; instead, I was up the next morning cooking breakfast and getting ready for work, me and God.

Jurius would always leave the house after the beatings. When he came back, he would look at me strangely and wonder how I was able to stand up and smile. He pulled up my clothes several times to see the bruises but saw none. I wondered why he didn't give up and stop trying to torment the children and me. He would also beat them after they got old enough, but God protected them as he did me. He finally started threatening to blow off my God damn head while beating me. I never raised my hands to fight back. I would pray silently, but it would make him madder to hear me call on the Lord or ask him for help.

One weekend, Josie came home and heard him threaten me with his .45 pistol in hand. We didn't know that she called for help from the county Sheriff's office. They arrived shortly, two of them. Josie had gone to her aunt next door because she was very frightened of what was going on. A knock came at the door, the officers announced themselves and stated that someone had called them about a disturbance at this house. He answered, "No disturbance here." They asked to see me, and I came out to the door, not crying nor had been crying.

That was another way God proved himself to me. I could not cry or get angry during these episodes. When the beating started, he would beat until he was tired, trying to make me cry. When I could say something to him, I would say I feel sorry for you, and I would try to encourage him to get help. So often, I would explain to him that what he was doing was not natural for a man who claimed to love his family.

We always told him we loved him.

After the sheriff officers left the house, he made me get into the car with him and drove to a wooded area, about five miles from our house. There were no houses in that area, and the sun was going down. It was a path that a farmer used to get to his fields. It was very narrow with trees on both sides. There was no way anyone could see or hear anything for about one and a half miles.

He took this path almost to the end. He got out of the car and told me to get into the driver's seat. He took the keys when he got out, so I had no way of driving. When we left the house with his demands to get into the car, I didn't remember to get my purse. His plan would have backfired and sold him out. He planned to make it look as if I had driven myself there and committed suicide.

He pulled out the pistol from his pocket, got in the car on my right side, put the nose of the gun to my right temple and pulled the trigger. The gun clicked; he pulled it again; the same thing happened.

He jumped out of the car and opened the gun to see what happened. He thought I had taken out his bullets. He realized that bullets were still in the gun, but one jammed in the barrel. Desperate, he cursed and did all he could do but could not unjam the gun. He came to my side of the car opened the door. I felt he was going out of the woods, but instead, he put his hands around my neck and started choking me. I tried to loosen his hands until all my strength was gone.

A voice said to me, "Go limp." I didn't know how to go limp, but my whole body lost control in a second. I heard him walking away from the car, assuming he had killed me. I raised my head from the steering wheel and could not keep from coughing. A few seconds later, I heard a car door open and felt my limp body being pulled from one side to another, from under the driver's seat to the other side of the car. He started the car and backed out of the path because there was no place to turn around. He drove to his mistress' house and demanded that I get in the back seat.

His mistress came immediately out of the house as if she knew he was coming. Weakness had overtaken me, and I could not get out of the car into the back seat. She got in, and he drove to an abandoned resort a little ways from her house. They got out of the car and walked to the area of the house where I could see. He raised the already detached screen from the window, picked her up, put her in, and he climbed in.

Many things went through my mind, like: "set the place on fire", or "get something and knock them out as they departed the place", maybe "get out and hide", or "get to my sisters in New York". But all I did was sit there and pray.

They came out of the house hugging, laughing, and acting as if I was not in plain view of them. They got in the car and stopped talking. He started the engine and drove back to her family's house. She lived with her mother, brother, and two sisters. I forgot to mention that she was only sixteen years old and Jurius took her away from her mother, all for what money he could give them. In a few weeks, Fredia was pregnant. What a big mess this was! Jurius was involved with mother and daughter. I will never understand why mother Joann Andrews didn't know that they were up to something illegal when her daughter was leaving home with him.

Maybe some of you might be thinking, why didn't I do something about this problem? Well, I did all I knew to do. I loved him, cuddled, and encouraged sexual gratification every night, sick or well, no matter when he demanded. I talked and offered to help him get medical mental counseling. I prayed and encouraged him to connect with the family more, attend the children's sports, and get involved in their school activities. Whenever he came to school sports, he always left home alone and would not ride with the family.

He would bring the children of Joann Andrews, and of course, Fredia, the young lady that he got involved with, while he was also involved with her mother. I didn't give up on him for two reasons, first because of the children, and second, because God told me he had him in his hands. There is a third; also, God always takes care of me and my belief in the vows I took at our marriage.

I stood there shaking and frightened, not sure when the Holy Spirit opened my understanding of the seriousness of what we were doing. This is a lifetime, very real situation, not a thing to take lightly or misunderstand. My consciousness was awakened to the fact that there would be no turning back on going forward together. We made these vows "till death do we part." My vows were made to God, not man. My belief was, 'if I do what I can to make things right and good, do all I can, my extremity is God's beginning.' His source of power and authority is sufficient to meet all my needs. There is "nothing" too hard for God, nothing impossible; he is God of impossible. He lay low in Zion to hear his children pray, call.

There was nothing I didn't try. There was nothing I didn't do. There was no way I'd give up on him or the family. I was willing and able to wait on God and his timing. My thoughts were, why don't Jurius give up? He has seen what God has done. He kept the children and me in perfect peace amid this war. He kept us safe from harm. No weapon formed against us would prosper or do us any harm, for we are covered with the blood of Jesus.

'Why stay in this dangerous situation?' is a question I hear often? Where will we go? Where will we hide? Where can we run to? Nowhere, but to God and his son Jesus Christ. There is no safety anywhere else. We can run to the rocks, no hiding place there. To the mountain, to the valley, to the rivers, from city to city, place to place, we can find no covering secure enough, no mountain high enough, no valley low enough, no rocks stable enough, no rivers wide or deep enough, no city protected enough.

We were standing steadfast, waiting on the Salvation of God. We would stand on the promises of God. What he promised would never fail. He will never change or take back what he said. He is Holy and never lies or cheats. He loves us and always will. He has no respect for a person. I was a little nobody until he made me somebody - his child. He's my Heavenly Father and loves me, knows all about me, and provides all that I need, physically, financially, spiritually, emotionally, and mentally.

Why should I run even if there were some place safe to run? God is all I need, and there is nothing or no one who can provide for me the way my Father can. Everything in this world belongs to him, and he provides for his children whatsoever they need. I feel safe amid torment and harassment.

When Jurius first became abusive and harassing, yes, I was afraid for myself and the children. When he was at work or away from us, I was happy and at peace. The moment his car would drive up, the big minix (manx) silver-grey cat would first detect the car's sound and run as fast as she could to hide. Fear would creep into my spirit, and I tried very hard to keep from showing it when somebody was around, especially the children. Fear is the devil's work, and I realized soon that I could not live that way. He soon healed my spirit and mind of that demonic threat once I got in touch with God and pleaded my case to him. My protection from God allowed me to be in an undisturbed state of mind.

Nevertheless, I was willing to do anything that would help bring him to a state of mind that would allow his life to be free from violent agitations, jealousy, self-pesters, sexual addiction, selflessness, no self-respect, confusion, no self-worth, great emotional disturbance, and all the problems he was living with that no one detected. The most critical of all, he didn't know there was anything wrong with him. He refused my help, and no one else offered any help. No one else saw what the children and I saw. He could change his actions in the twinkling of an eye.

"I have fought a good fight, I have finished
my course, I have kept the faith."
2 Timothy 4:7

# CHAPTER 22

## *Jurius gets called*

Two of our children went to college after high school, and the other got married. I thanked God they were out of this annoyance. He always put on his best behavior when they come for visits, but they were used to his hypercritical acts. One day, he came home from helping the pastor and a few of the neighboring men repair the church after a hurricane. He was not as excited as he should have been, or maybe he was like me when I got the news, scared and not wanting to believe it.

God had called him to preach! Yes, I was beyond shocked because he had not made any change in his behavior. I know that God can do anything he wants if it's His will. Besides shock, I was a bit confused and disappointed that he didn't want to tell me the experience that led to him hearing from God.

The pastor and leader of his class at church were there when he made his confession of hearing from God. After much counseling and meeting with the class leader and the pastor, a date was set for an initiative sermon. The presiding elder of our district and most leading pastors would be in attendance. I could see the nervousness every day and would pray for him. He stopped going out at night and stopped the harassing and beating me, for which my praise and thanksgiving was often made. There was a great change that only God could do. I offered to read the Bible for him since his reading was poor and gave him Bible books that were easy to read, but he refused my offer. All I was left to do was be happy, excited, encouraged, and pray.

To receive any of these blessings, he needs to be in complete fellowship with God and his Son Jesus Christ. He needed to confess all of his sins to God and, with faith in his heart, believe that God raised Jesus from the dead. Faith cometh by hearing and hearing by the word of God. God wanted him to preach His word. He needed to know the word and apply it to his heart. He needed to live right, love everybody, and believe in Jesus Christ. I will never try to judge or make him what God wants him to be. I left that part to God a long time ago.

I'm not writing these quotes in this book to help Jurius. He has long passed from earth to eternity. I'll be glad if I can help just one person to be saved. I'll be fulfilled for the time I spent writing, praying for the Holy Spirit to give me wisdom, knowledge, understanding, and truth to please God in this task he assigned to me. My life will be completely fulfilled and not in vain. Let me pause my writing to say I never stopped loving Jurius.

Even today, my mind travels back, sometimes I talk about the good times to my family, and again, I will testify of the hardships and struggles that only God could have brought me through. Let me say again, I never gave up on him and God. Knowing God as I did, I believed he would give him another chance to complete his journey and fit his soul for his kingdom.

There is much more of my life story coming later, but I need to continue telling you about my journey with Jurius. Shortly after he began his local preaching ministry, which included first year study, I was led by the Holy Spirit to publicly announce my call to preach. He had no problem with the announcement this time. He needed me by his side. We worked together for forty-two years. We spent most of this time working side by side with each other.

We each had our separate positions and were specialists in the respective jobs. My job was hearing from God and outlining the message for whatever God wanted to say to the congregation. This was taught to Jurius for him to preach. He was a very great preacher as far as his presentation went. People loved to hear him, and many came for salvation and prayer. His prayers were equally spirit-filled and rewarding.

My ministering was sometimes challenging when I was called to serve another church and could not work with him. God always stepped in and made ways. The Holy Spirit worked in unusual ways and provided power and wonders to both congregations. Forty-two years seemed like just yesterday, and God keeps supplying what we need. We never got tired, our energy never ran out, and our spirit never lost its power. There was a prayer meeting Wednesday night, member meeting and quarterly meeting Friday night, and visiting whenever needed. We also had Sunday school, morning service, and afternoon service. We equally had fellowships with other churches and district conference meetings every Saturday. We never felt tired in any way.

Nobody told us that the way would be easy. I don't believe he brought us this far to leave us. Jurius was pastor of only three churches, and no church wanted to see us leave. Every church was badly in need of repair, which got done with no hardship to the few older members who struggled to live on a fixed income. Remember, God specializes in things thought impossible. He can do what no other power on earth can do. My heart still hurts when I think of how hard Jurius struggled with sex addiction and would not get help. He would always say, "God will take care of this matter." We prayed and prayed to "no avail". All I could do was depend and trust God, for he has never failed me yet.

There are things we can't understand with our human minds and we wonder why our prayers are not answered. Why does God seem to be far away? Why are we in a war that seems to last forever? Just don't forget! Remember that God is always waiting for you to come unto him, all you that are burdened and heavy laden. The battle is not yours; it belongs to God. All along this journey, my spirit was always full of hope. I had witnessed his mighty power and love. We just need to hold on to his unchanging hand.

Jurius was diagnosed with several sexual diseases. The doctor would not tell me how long he could have harbored them. I had to be tested because we were active almost every night. To God be the Glory, the doctor didn't believe it was possible for me not to be infected. He sent me to a special clinic in the hospital for more tests, and for sure, my tests came back negative. He had to go through a series of treatments.

The doctor later realized that the diseases were contracted recently, which means that he never got over sexual addiction. Readers, besides salvation, you need to be honest with yourself and with God. Obey his words, love and live according to God's word as is in the Holy Bible. Ask for wisdom daily and be sincere and truthful. You cannot fool God or lie to him, and please don't try or play with him. He is mighty, honest, and true to his word. He's a righteous and holy God. He cannot dwell in the midst of sin. We all have choices to make. God will not force anyone to make a decision. When you are completely serious and sure of what you want from him, he will give you the aid and strength to help you. When you take one step in the right direction, God will make two. I never shall forget what he has done for me.

"For I will restore health unto thee, and I
will heal thee of thy wounds."
Jeremiah 30:17

# CHAPTER 23

## *My trip to the ER*

had an allergic reaction one day when I was thirty-five years old. In the county where we lived, there was no telephone service. The only way to get to a doctor was by car. I was getting weaker by the minute. My daughter, who was fifteen years old and could drive, started driving me to the doctor or emergency room at the nearest hospital. She was nervous; it was her first time driving on the highway and she was gradually slowing down. I took the driver's seat, and with high beam lights flashing, we made it to a little town in Morrisville.

I passed out after stopping the truck on the road in front of the fire station and rescue squad. They transferred me to the squad vehicle and started on the way to New Hope emergency hospital. On the way, they discovered I had expired, no sign of life. During that time, I was flying in the air and met many angels also flying toward me, reaching for my hand and I reaching out to them. As one would not be able to catch my hand passing by, another one would fly closer, reaching for my hand.

I saw a city in the beautiful blue sky with sparkling bright lights. The lights were so bright that I could only get a glance at a time. Angels were still reaching for me and I was reaching for them. All at once, I saw a male angel dressed in all white; his wings were also white. The female angels were different, beautiful pastel colors on each other, but no one was like another. The male was flying so fast, and the wind from flying was so strong that it caused the other angels to drift away from me.

At that moment, I heard the paramedic say, "We got her back." Then he called my name. I answered weakly with barely any voice.

The two attendants talked about my condition, blood pressure, pulse, etc. We got to the hospital and was checked out by several doctors. They verified that I had expired for some time and was amazed that I was back to life. The allergy built up fluid and swelling around my heart which caused the heart to choke. This is what I was told. When I asked what I was doing when I felt ill and before that, there was nothing strange or that I had not been in contact with many times before. Paramedics came a couple of times to check on me to see if I was still doing good. They were surprised that I came back to life.

I'm sure there was nothing that I did or could do to make this happen. "Mrs. Miller, I'm happy for you. Take care, and God bless you," the doctor said. My hospital visits were very long. Someone later told me what happened. I went into a coma, and the doctor that was treating me was not my regular doctor and was not interested in my condition. The cafeteria staff brought food, left it, and picked it up when they brought another tray.

I thank God for he had favor on me and sent Dr. Allen to his patient room next door to mine. He glanced up to see my name on the wall tag. Surprised, he went in to find me unconscious with mucus coming from my mouth. He took the time to find out who the attending doctor was and made a transfer of doctors. No one had called him when I was admitted. Even Jurius should have made the change.

My condition was in a critical state. I didn't know what was going on or barely knew I was in the hospital. Dr. Allen ordered tests and x-rays to determine what was causing my critical condition. I had been in the hospital two days and nothing had been done toward treatment. Jurius came as soon as our daughter told him. All this I was told, I don't remember seeing him at my bedside. Dr. Allen was very upset that he was not in my room as sick as I was.

And angry that he didn't call for him when he first got to the hospital. "I can understand you being at work when she got sick and you didn't find out until later. What did you think when you came and saw her condition? Were you concerned when you couldn't wake her? Seeing her food trays being left out of her reach, even if she was awake, not opened at all? Did you call for a nurse and question her about the condition you saw her in?

Did you ask about medicine, tests, or even what her problem is?

"Well, Jurius, I have ordered tests, x-rays, and a culture of what is in her stomach. This will be done early tomorrow morning. You might not be able to get here before she is taken in for tests, but I certainly expect you to be here when the tests are done. I will need to discuss our findings with you and make more plans for further exams and treatments." "What time will she be going for tests tomorrow morning?" Jurius asked. "I can't say," Dr. Allen answered, "the group that will be doing the tests had scheduled appointments, and I haven't asked what time. Get here as soon as you can because she needs you now. She will know that you are here, even in her unconscious state."

Jurius has ways of not responding to anyone who tries to help him see his mistakes. He was right to think that I would not know if he was there or not. It was certain he could do nothing toward my recovery. But there surely was a lot he could have done for himself. Being there could have caused him to focus on the fact that this is his wife. The one he loves and promised to take care of, comfort, honor, keep in sickness and in health, and forsake all others.

He could have gone to the chapel and asked God for mercy and grace to help him be a better husband and help me through my trials. He could have asked our Heavenly Father, Lord God Almighty, to send angels or whatever help he wills to send help to the both of us. Whenever you desire to help someone and take your attention off yourself, it will give you peace that you're able to do something to help. At this time in Jurius' life, he was still hung up on replacing Chris. He was angry at me that I couldn't bear another baby. He has already tried to have a replacement with three other women, and he only got girls. And now he was trying with one of his co-workers, and I believed that's what's taking all of his attention.

On the way to the hospital, my helper came to let me know I was alright. When the voice of God said to me, "You drive," I knew all was well, for he is the Creator of Heaven and Earth, the Maker of man, who breathed into his nostrils, the breath of life, and man became a living soul. This Holy God, I know, was in the plan from the beginning. When his will and plan is in progress, we can rest assured that all is well.

I don't try to know the mind of God, but I'm sure he was trying to get Jurius' attention to what he was about to do. He used Dr. Allen to wake him to his responsibility. The devil didn't want to let him go, so he closed his mind to not comprehend what God wanted him to know.

The tests and x-rays came, and a discussion was made for my treatment. My stomach was flushed off of whatever caused the green mucus. My vital signs were all better, and my heart was beating stronger. The fever was still hanging around. Dr. Allen ordered an I.V. to supply fluids to replace all I had lost. "This will take several days," he explained to Jurius. Jurius explained his schedule to the doctor without any remorse or concern for me. His main excuse was the girls at home and going to school. Next, he mentioned his job and the importance of him being there. Dr. Allen walked away, not giving him a chance to make another excuse.

He went to the nurse's desk and inquired about available nurses, one with lots of patience, love, knowledge, and caring. A recommendation was made, and he picked up the phone to call. He hired nursing services scheduled around the clock. This was not for one of his family members. This was for one of God's little children. He was trying to make a difference between wrong and right. God everlasting, God omnipotent, omnipresent, omniscient, called on Dr. Allen to use his skills, knowledge, and blessing that God had already blessed him with to help me.

Please understand that God uses whoever He pleases to do whatever is His will. He doesn't have to use anyone; he can do what no other power on earth can do. He can speak, and miracles will be performed. He can speak, healing heart trouble, cancer, and any other sickness will be healed. He chooses to use humans to give his believers more faith and power in man's ability to use the knowledge and understanding that God has granted to them.

God does not interact with everyone, only those who have continuing fellowship with him, who try to keep his commandments, law and statutes, who love him and all humankind.

God is always close to those who recognize Jesus as born of a virgin, the Son of God, the Savior of the world, who was killed for our transgression, hung on the cross, was buried, rose from the dead, walked among men, ascended back to the Father, sits on the right hand of the Father and makes intercession for the world. He will come again to receive his children unto himself.

After three more days, God woke me up from my sleep. The nurse was happy and astonished to have looked away for a few minutes to look back at me and find that my eyes were opened. She declared there was a smile on my face. I didn't know it, but I can agree with her because smiling is what I do most of the time. Smiling goes along with peace, joy, happiness, and contentment. I had no pain or sickness but found that there was no voice; I could not talk.

The nurse had many questions for me, and all I could do was shake or nod my head. This continued until the next day when Jurius was off from work. He came as quickly as he could, bringing our girls with him. When the room door opened, I opened my eyes, looking toward the door, and a big gasp and oooh came out of my mouth. The nurse was completely thrilled and aroused. She rushed to me, took both my hands and lifted them upward as she had been doing to give me strength. She never looked around to see Jurius and the girls standing there. She had not seen them during her work shift.

Finally, I released one of my hands and pointed toward them. She looked around and apologized for her emotions and joyfulness. Helen, my nurse, explained to them that she heard a sound from my mouth and that was the first noise that came from me since I got there. She also explained that today was the first time my eyes were opened. My mind, heart, spirit, and soul were thanking God for what he has done for me. My visit with the girls was very enjoyable and educational.

Even though I could not talk, I jotted down a few questions with the help of Helen. My hands were not strong enough to manage the pen. Jurius was somewhat quiet and wanted out, but the girls had a lot to tell me about. They had been trying to keep my schedule without me.

They wanted to ask me about cooking certain foods, and they wanted to tell me something they didn't want their dad to hear. Helen wrote for me after I very quietly whispered in her ear, "Write it."

Jurius was anxious to leave. I beckoned for them to give me another hug, as I said to each girl, "Write me a note and mail it." Helen quickly gave one of the girls a letterhead page with the address of this hospital. I was saddened to see them leave with great hurt on their faces. Helen and I held hands and prayed for a safe trip back home and that Jurius would pay more attention to his daughters. She begged God to please help all of us and give us mercy, grace, and peace.

I knew we didn't have to beg God, just sincerely ask him in faith, but I could not speak. So I asked God to forgive me for the begging and felt relief in my heart that he did. The nurses exchanged stations, and Geraldine would work during the night. The two nurses were sharing joy and laughter over seeing me awake. Dr. Allen was passing by to visit his other patient. He heard all the commotion and decided to stop here first.

He joined with the others, saying thank you, God, with no shame of who heard him.

By this time, Helen and Geraldine were weeping when some of the nurses on duty at the desk rushed in to join the others. My celebration was only made by raising one arm to God and silently praising Him as I had been doing since I opened my eyes and saw another beautiful day. Dr. Allen was so happy he reached over and lightly hugged me, stating that this was not ethical. I know, but this is my reward for all the prayers I sent up to God today and every day.

"Girls," he announced, "this is just the beginning, just watch God work." He pulled his stethoscope and began to listen to the sounds of my organs. "Okay girls," talking to the nurses that had gathered in the room to share the wonderful information of what God had done in my body. "Go back to work. I have work to do here. Tell the news to others if you want to continue celebrating."

The unconscious state I had been in for more than a few days - I really didn't know how many - left me wondering how serious my illness had been and how concerned everybody must have been. I had been in outer darkness or long dreamless nights. I needed to think about what I could remember. At that moment, Dr. Allen grunted very loudly as he listened from the back. He turned me on my back, listened from the chest, and began nodding his head as if what he heard was better. Maybe I shouldn't think of anything so soon; just continue to praise and thank God for what he has done thus far.

I couldn't think about Jurius, the girls, or about my being here, except my heart would start pounding. How sick am I? My heart started beating very fast again. I could not talk or call for help and couldn't reach the button to call. Fear, fear! It's Fear! What am I afraid of? Heart pounding again, I started to call on the name of Jesus in my mind, over and over. I just echoed Jesus! Sleep must have overtaken me. I woke up to hear my name, "Hattie, Dr. Allen wants me to give you some medicine. I will put it into the I.V. This will help you relax." "Thank you Jesus," was echoed again and again until I closed my eyes again and slept through the night.

The next morning, the nurse wanted to see if I could drink something. My mouth had been very dry. She had been mopping it with a small sponge with warm water every half hour or when she saw my lips dry. My mouth and throat were mighty sore. Nurse Cathy said it was from them pumping my stomach. I could see and hear better every day. My thoughts began to open up as each nurse prayed with me and read God's word from the holy bible. Not only did they read the Bible, but they also explained what they read. Memories of my reading to Jurius and our children at bedtime and at our Sunday morning altar flashed through my mind.

Eventually, my mind caught up with the spirit, and I could say in my mind the "word" before they pronounced it. Little by little, my body got stronger, and my mind, memory, and understanding gradually improved. I had a daily talk with the Ever-Present One, who never left me alone. I thanked Him for His goodness and the angels that ministered to me when everyone had gone to sleep at night or was busy with their daily chores. I learned through difficult experiences that we could completely rely on and trust Jesus. I didn't simply hope that nothing could separate me from the love of God. All through my youth, as far back as I can remember, my trust in Jehovah God almighty has been a comfort and sustainer to me.

I never doubted God. Just remembering his Love, faithfulness, goodness, mercy, grace, and promises was enough for me. Why I couldn't speak, walk, eat, or help myself didn't bother me. God never makes a mistake. He can never disappoint anyone who trusts in him. All of my life, no matter what I had to face, God has never failed me. Whenever my petition was made, God brought me out of all my troubles. Now I feel in my spirit that he wants me to worship and give Him the highest praise with thanksgiving from the depths of my soul.

My mind was focused on the one and true Almighty, Everlasting, Only Potentate, All-Wise, Eternal, Sovereign, King of Glory, Holy One of Israel, All-Powerful, Ever Present, All-Knowing, Wise God, and Our Heavenly Father. You are the source of my life. Glory, adoration, and praises to your most Holy efficient name. All power in heaven and earth is in your mighty hand. You can kill and make alive. There is nothing you can't do.

"Oh Lord of Host," I spoke the first words aloud. I had not spoken in a long time. I began to praise Him with a shout of, "Alleluia! Alleluia! Halleluiah! Halleluiah!" Then my eyes opened, for I always reached my Lord and Master, the Savior of the world, with closed eyes, humbled heart, and determined to get in touch with him. Nurse Helen was with me. She quickly took out the I.V., for the spirit of the living God was taking control of my entire body.

Who knows the mind of God, how He works in mysterious ways, the wonders to perform? Just keep your mind in Christ Jesus; He knows what to do. God's mind is higher than ours, as high as the heavens are above the earth. Don't try to guess what he is thinking; just know His word and apply it to your heart. His word is as powerful as a two-edged sword, cutting sin on the right and left.

The letter from Josie and Joline was given to me by one of the office clerks. Thank God my life had been renewed, so I could read it myself. Maybe there would be something in it that was personal; I would not want anybody to know. The letter read:

Mother, we need help; we miss you very much and are praying for you daily. Our peers and teachers also, to know how much a lot of people love and have best wishes for you, makes it easier for us to face the day.

We don't see much of daddy, and when he comes home, we are already asleep. He leaves in the morning before we awake or rushes out after we are up. It is hard for us to get breakfast and get ready before the bus arrives. We missed the bus for two days in a row because we overslept. We hope you are getting better and will soon be coming home. We love you and will continue to pray for your recovery.

I called out to nurse Geraldine, who had given me some privacy, to read my letter. She rushed over, willing to meet my needs. "Would you please get me paper, pen, and an envelope so that I can write to my daughters?" "Oh yes," she replied, "I have all this in my briefcase. I've been doing some writing myself." She picked up the briefcase, opened it and smiled. She said, "I have a pad, especially for your girls," handing me a pink one. Here is a pen and envelope to match the paper. A big smile spread across my face when I asked, "Do you happen to have a pink stamp?"

We both got a big blessing because we could see my life coming quickly to fulfillment. Breakfast was ushered in and disrupted our joyfulness. "Will I be able to eat?? I asked Geraldine. "Well, there's nothing to eat," she said, opening the plate's lid. "Do you think you can drink using a straw?" she asked. "I surely will try because my middle names are, never give up." It was a hot beef broth, ugh! The smell. "What's wrong?" she asked. "That smell has already spooked me. It's been a while since I've smelled food, and beef is not one of my favorite foods." I reached to get the straw while holding my nose with the other hand. Geraldine began laughing again. For me, this was very serious. It was prayer time for breakfast and for help from above.

Still holding my nose, she put the bowl of broth closer, holding it away from my nose but near the side of my face. Boldly and determined, even if my throat is sore, I will drink this hot broth, trusting that what I asked in prayer will be performed by my faith. The taste was better than the smell, even if it didn't have salt or pepper in it. The second swallow was better than the first. The hand that held my nose automatically lost it and reached for the bowl from the nurse.

"Go sit down," I told her, "you have labored with me enough. Let me do what I can for myself." She let go of the bowl; smiling, she said, "Now I know for sure that your prayer has been answered. We have a mighty God." While I was unconscious, the nurses spent a lot of time massaging my whole body from head to toes. They did all that was within their powers to make me comfortable. They did not tell me that, but other workers and Dr.

Allen wanted me to know how much I'm loved.

My letter was written with help in mind for Josie and Joline. That was the first thing they wrote in their letter to me. I think they were hoping and praying that I would speak to their dad about helping them. At least to give them money for breakfast at school and wake them up in the mornings. They did not know that their dad was so involved in his determination to "replace Chris" and even I could not "reach him to talk. What is meant by "reach him" is that his body is there, but his mind and spirit are tied up and consumed with his problems and person. He hears and doesn't hear or intends to do what he wants to do. I trusted God to help me write what would be helpful for the girls.

I started the letter by saying that:

Daddy is quite busy these days and has more on his mind than he can handle. Just love him and pray for him; please don't forget to tell him that when you get a chance to see him. Look in our bedroom, get the clock radio, and put it in your room on the nightstand on Josie's side of the bed. It is set for six o'clock, look at the face of the clock you will see how each button operates.

As soon as the alarm sounds, get out of bed, both of you. This will give you time to eat breakfast and get ready for the bus in time. Go to the cafeteria, speak to the manager, and tell her I will send the monthly check for lunch when I'm out of the hospital. Please know there is nothing anyone can do for you that our Heavenly Father will do. Continue to ask him in faith, believing that it will be done, and all will be well for you.

Remember, you know how to take care of yourselves; just make up your minds to do what you know. Continue to study and do your homework with the same schedule as if I'm there. With God, you can do all things. Take care of each other and remember you are best friends. Don't forget your bedtime schedule, just as if I'm in the house.

I dropped the pen on the table across the bed and handed the letter to the nurse. She looked up and saw me giving the letter to her and said jokingly, "Did you forget you can talk now?" "No energy," I told her it took all my energy to write the letter. "I need more broth." Just as I said, we could hear the food cart coming our way. "It is not only broth you need," she said, "you need to rest.

This has been a very busy day for you. You worked right through your rest time." I took a few deep breaths and said, "Bless that letter, Lord, let it be sufficient to give our girls the help they so desperately need. Thank you for the mind and strength to write it. Let it go in the precious name of Jesus, carrying the power of the Holy Spirit."

I closed my eyes, still listening to the food cart coming, and sleep overtook me. After eating lunch, I slept all afternoon until Helen called me to eat dinner. I went back to sleep until Dr. Allen made his rounds. "Do you think you can get up on your feet?" he asked. "If you think I can," I replied. "Well, let's try. We will give you some help," he stated. The nurse reached for my bathrobe. "No need to fuss about that," the doctor said, "she will use all her energy getting it on. This will be just a few minutes, a first start." My strength had not returned as I hoped and prayed for. "You will have to work to build your strength up," the doctor stated, "and that will take time."

Before he barely finished talking, I asked, "How much time?" "Can't tell," he answered, "let's not get involved in time; I'm so happy to see this much progress. You are doing wonderful, don't try to rush it. Helen wants to stay a little longer, she likes you." I was standing with one on each side, trying to move my foot. I tried the right foot and then the other one. My balance was very bad; it took all the two of them could do to hold me up, and my back and legs began to hurt.

They helped on to the bed, and what a relaxing feeling that was. Dr. Allen was looking at me and smiling from ear to ear, and said, "You did good." "I did good?" was my question. "I need to pay both of you double pay for as hard as you worked to keep me from falling." "You heard what she said, Helen, don't let her forget that," he said, laughing. "Tomorrow morning," talking to the nurse, "get help and try this again.

Time how long she stands." With those long steps, he reached the door, opened it, looked back and smiled. "Take care, and God bless you both," he said.

Without either of us knowing, a crew of physical therapists arrived at the room the next morning. "Mrs. Miller?" "Yes," I answered. "Dr. Allen wants us to work with you today." It was early, and the nurse was still in the bed. "Excuse me," she said, "I had no knowledge of this, and I need to get a decent sleep." "You are all right," one of them replied, "we are going to take Mrs. Miller as she is. We will be out of your way in a jiffy." They transferred me to their bed and rolled me to the physical therapy area, where more patients were being treated. The therapy was very rewarding. They worked on my legs to loosen them up. All my joints had become very stiff.

Breakfast had been served when I got to the room. Instead of hot broth, there was cold broth. The nurse offered to get me a hot one, but I tried a sip, and it tasted alright. Maybe because my body was hot from the workout. Dr. Allen had good news when he came. He would release me to go home as soon as I could walk without help. He was unusually satisfied with the treatment today. "Work out every day this week and move on your own as you feel like."

Jurius came but without the girls. "I came from work to here," he said, but I knew he took a side step. His shift was at two o'clock, and he got here at four. I asked him to bring the girls the next time he could come. At this time, I was excitedly happy with lots of news to share. He didn't seem so happy, and I could tell something was bothering him. He did come over right away and gave me a kiss.

This was the first time he had seen me since I couldn't talk. I was anxious to tell him about the physical therapy, my eating, and the news about going home. He wasn't looking at me. He was staring at the wall up high. As soon as he turned to see me, I stretched out my arms to hug him. He moved quickly toward me to get my hug. "Do you have something you want to tell me about?"

I asked. When he didn't answer, I said, "Have you noticed I can talk now?" He smiled and said, "I would have to be deaf to not notice."

I began to tell him all my good news. He never looked at me the whole time I talked. He was staring at a magazine on my bed. "What about you having three nurses?" he said sternly. "What about it?" I said. "How can you afford to have three private nurses watching you night and day?" "How could I not afford them when my condition was in such a critical state that I didn't know I was in this world?" Dinner interrupted the conversation.

Nurse Helen came in to help me. She paused and said to Jurius, "Maybe you want to help her." He stepped aside and beckoned for her to do it. "You go ahead," he stated, "this is what you are hired for, isn't it?" "Oh yes," she replied in a joyful tone. "Your wife is a pleasure to work with, even when she didn't know we were here."

She put the tray over my bed near me so I could easily reach it, adjusted my bed, unwrapped my silverware and poured the milk in a glass. She asked her blessing for the meal and I asked mine. Jurius looked a bit astonished and said, "She even asked for your blessing?" "Yes," I stated happily, "aren't you praying for me also?" "Tell me," he said sternly, "who's going to pay for all this service?" "Payment is not one of my concerns right now," I answered.

"With all the help from above, I am trying to recover from this drastic sickness. Don't you worry, I will pay it all if I have to. My job has promised me continued work, and I have an insurance policy. You know about that. Why stand there talking about paying bills when you haven't asked me how I feel? You make me feel worthless to you. Is that what you think of me? You rather let me die than pay for my recovery."

Helen heard my voice and came rushing in to calm me. "Mr. Miller," she called out loudly, "please don't upset your wife. She has made a remarkable improvement lately. Please don't cause her to have a setback." He was moving slowly toward the door. "You don't have to leave; she is so happy you are here." She rushed past him and out the door. He stood near the door away from me, put his hand in his pocket, took out some money, and returned to the bed and handed it to me.

"I don't need money, I need my husband." "There is no place here for me to keep it. Just give the girls some, and please see if they need any personal items. I know it will help you to talk about whatever is bothering you. You know you can tell me anything; I will pray with you about it so you can release that stress you are suffering with. If you can't talk with me, please pray and tell God about it.

He knows how to solve every problem. Please, Jurius, I need you." "You got me," he stated. "I need to go so I can check on the girls." "Give them a kiss for me," I said, "and tell them I'm getting better and hope to see them soon." Holding my arms open and out, he came and gave me a tight squeeze. "I love you," I said "I love you too," was his reply. "Drive carefully and take care of yourself and the girls."

## Finally discharged

I was discharged after three days on Saturday. Jurius' early day off would be Sunday. How to get him the word was a problem for me. Mail would not reach him in time. I asked Dr. Allen if it was possible to use the hospital's phone to call the hospital base when Jurius was back on duty. I knew it would be long-distance and I was willing to pay the charge. "I'll check on that," he said, smiling, "and you can just stay until he decides to come again. But then you will have to go home in that gown you're wearing. He will not know to bring you clothes." "She has the clothes she wore here," Helen said, "that problem is solved." "Let me check on that call," Dr. Allen said and exited the room.

He returned a while later and said the hospital couldn't let patients use the phone, but their doctors could. I don't know why I didn't think of that before. "I called and got a Captain Anderson," he said, "he wrote everything down and promised to send for you as soon as Jurius got to work. He seems to know you but didn't know you were in the hospital." "I didn't give him any information. Jurius needed to do that." Captain Anderson was a very good God-fearing man. I had known him for several years and his relationship as Jurius' supervisor from earlier on in his base job. I don't understand why he didn't let him know about me. He didn't even tell me he was back. I pray things are well between them."

He came for me, bringing the girls. The office told me he had to sign release papers before I could leave. This was not the same hospital I was in many times before. A hospital was built after integration so that all people could be admitted. The separate hospital had been closed down; their rules were much different than the other. He signed the release papers and didn't mention anything about the bill. The papers the hospital gave him to release me had all the information on them.

He handed them to me, and I started to read them. When I came to the page where the cost of everything was itemized, "Wow! I couldn't believe these figures and for twenty-two days!" To me, I could only know about one week. I was told that I had been there a long time but didn't know it was twenty-two days, close to a month. No wonder the girls were missing me.

I began wondering about the other two weeks. Where was I? This experience was not like any other ones that I had before. For sure, I was in safety, in God's Almighty hand. He kept me confined in his presence until he was ready to release me back to this world. Thank you, God, for keeping me safe and bringing me back to my family and friends. The ride home was long and quiet, even though Jurius was rushing to get back to work.

"Dr. Allen said he talked to Captain Anderson when he called to let you know I had been discharged. Is this the same Captain that was there before?" "Yes," he answered, "this is his third time; the second time was two years after his first transfer. He came back and found everybody in the same working position as when he left. He moved everyone up that deserved to be moved." Jurius was still a Mess Attendant, first step. He got the biggest move to cook assistant, for that job was opened because of another move. "You deserve this place," Capt. Anderson stated. "You've been doing the job but not having a position."

This time, Jurius had been made a Cook. This pay grade caused his salary to double what he had been getting. I could not believe that with all the excitement about his first promotion, even if I was unconscious, he didn't tell me about this great news as soon as I could hear. He didn't even remember to tell me about the Captain being transferred back. "Oh Lord my God my Helper, please bring Jurius back to his right mind. Please lift the burden that he is carrying. Oh, our Heavenly Father, Your word says you would not put more on us than we could bear," I prayed. The Holy Spirit spoke to me, saying, "I did not put this on him; he put it on himself. He is as far from me as the east is from the west."

"OH, LORD!" I cried out loud, and everyone in the car wanted to know what was wrong with me. "There's nothing wrong with me. It's what the spirit of God just told me. I cried because the Spirit told me that Jurius was as far from God as the east is from the west." "What!" Jurius spoke up. "What are you talking about?" "I'm talking about what God told me in answer to my prayer. I prayed for God to help you bear your burden and what God's word said about it.

This was God's reply through the Holy Spirit." "He is as far from me as the east is from the west. I don't believe that," Jurius said. "Believe it or not, you know there is something in your life that is not right with God or with your family."

"You can never talk to us about anything, except something negative and upsetting." "You are always angry and ready to blame someone else for your feelings. You don't take responsibility for your own actions. You are not willing to share your problems with the people who love and care about your welfare. You rather suffer in silence and make others miserable than coming to God and your family for help. Remember, God knows all about you, and He loves you, but He will not help you until you get your heart, mind, and soul right with him.

You need to acknowledge your faults, confess your sins, not to me or anyone else, but to God our Heavenly Father. You will find that you will be released from all that heavy load you have been carrying around the moment you do. There will be a smile on your face, something I have not seen for a long time.

"Please listen to what the Spirit is saying to you through my voice. You are not your own; you belong to Jesus, and he paid the price for you on the cross. All because of love. Jurius, remember I'm your wife, the rib from your side. We are one and when you hurt, I hurt. What I go through, you should also go through. We are more than just a man and a woman. We are husband and wife that God joined together until death do we part.

I'm here always, willing to listen, share and do whatever is necessary to make you, this marriage, and this family what God would have it to be. Give yourself a chance to live again and be happy. Give all this extra baggage over to the one who knows what to do with it. It is more than you can carry. For one thing, if you try to keep secrets about something that you should share, you will always hurt yourself more than necessary.

"Trust God and the ones who can give you the best support. I know that person is me, your wife. I already know a lot about your secret life. I'm just waiting for you to come forth and make the first move. I'm waiting until you are ready to share with me." He yelled out, "What do you know?" My reply was, "I've already said too much with the girls listening. Maybe they have heard something that will help them in the future. What I know is between me and my Lord and Savior Jesus

Christ, until you are ready to come forth and talk. "I mean talk." Not yelling out of control or casting blame at each other.

"I recommend that we both get serious about this, or I should say you get serious, for I've already taken this matter as seriously as possible. We need to "Fast and Pray." The word said that some things could only come by fasting and praying. Please agree with me about this. I need my husband, and the children need their dad." "You got me, and the children have me," he said. "Think hard and long about what you have been doing and where you have been outside work. How much time have you spent with us in the last six months or even longer?"

We got home and went into the house, and each went our separate ways, in different rooms. I straight to bed, the children doing homework, and Jurius to the bathroom. What about dinner? I wondered. My mind and spirit had been caught up with trying to help Jurius; I didn't notice the time or think of dinner. I should not have to think about that anyway. That should have been planned before now. I will not spend another minute thinking about dinner. Let me give thanksgiving for my being home once again, for the healing of my body, for a safe trip, and for all of us having our right mind. There is more blessing than I can really name or give thanks for throughout the night.

My prayer time began, and all at once, my hunger disappeared. That's just like my God Almighty. All we need is to come unto him, all you that are weary, and he will give you rest. When we got home, the telephone company had finished putting down the wires to our house. All we needed to do was buy a telephone. The crew that put the jacks inside the house had done their job before I went into the hospital.

I had decided to get a phone after the next pay period, but things that happened kept me from that. I will ask Jurius to buy one since my weakness will not permit me to do anything for a few days. With a phone, I'll be able to call my workplace to let them know that I'm out of the hospital, but I need to be released for work by my Doctor.

There were so many "thank you" notes to be returned. Maybe I can take some of the stress off Jurius to make him feel needed. From what I know about his troubles, this will definitely put more problems on him. The young sixteen-year-old, who was having his baby, has been put out of the house by her mother. He has rented an apartment for her. This is where he spends a lot of his time when he is away from home.

Providing for her, with all she needs, has taken most of his salary. This is one reason he didn't tell me about his promotion and the raise in salary. Maybe it is the reason he didn't want me to know that Captain Anderson is back at the base. ( this doesn't add up, I wasn't there maybe this was Clamisa and Lynn, and maybe this was the Tyrance girl)(a little confusing, maybe go back over details)

We can't hide anything from God. We can agonize trying to keep secrets, pretend to be who we are not, but we can't fool God or his children. He has ways to speak to his children that nobody can hinder. I was trying to protect the children from being hurt, but I have an idea that they know more of what he is doing than what he thinks. School children can find out news that nobody else can. The girls and I still pray together, but they don't say anything or question me about their dad.

Junior was away in school at Chapel Hill. He came every weekend while I was in the hospital. Soon the games will start, and weekends will be taken up with football games. Dr. Allen sent another letter. This time, he addressed and sent it in my name. This caused me to wonder even before the letter was opened. What did he know about what was going on in our family? This has never happened before. Usually, the letters were always addressed to Mr. and Mrs. I slowly opened the envelope and took out the letter. It read:

Mrs. Miller,

Your bill, including the hospital charges, has already been taken care of and paid in full. Those were the words that were always used, paid in full. You have enough to take care of without trying to pay this account. The bill for the nurses' service belongs to me. I had no intention of you paying for that. Please believe me when I say my service has been and still is for the best I can do for others. I will be retiring soon and will need to see you in my office before the end of this month.

Please make an appointment at your convenience to let me know if you can come. I need to make sure you are well enough to go back to work this school year and recommend a doctor for your family. Take care of Jurius and the children. I can depend on you.

God Bless, Dr. Allen.

I immediately prayed, "Thank you, oh Lord God, our Heavenly Father. I worship, praise, adore, and love you for all your mighty acts to your believing children. Thank you for how much you have blessed our family through one of your special servants, who is willing to trust you to continue to provide for him. Continue, oh Lord, to take care of him and his loved ones, and keep him strong and in your will. Give him and his family good health and provide all they need. Oh God, let him prosper in all his ways and keep him humble and kind doing your will for your glory."

Jurius got the telephone, and now I could call instead of writing a letter. He had been home for three nights on time from work. I could not rest in peace to think that this pregnant child was in the apartment alone, expecting anytime. So I mustered up courage; no, God gave me enough courage to ask him about her. He was surprised that I knew after I said she should not be in the apartment alone. "How do you know?" he replied.

"It is not important how I know, but it is important that she is taken care of." His eyes got bigger, and I saw relief in them. "She's in the hospital," he stated. "She had the baby?" I raised my voice, for I was surprised that he had been coming home from work and was not checking on her and his baby.

I expressed my feeling to him, and he dropped his head and said, "I've been going on my lunch break. This meant he had been going during work hours because his lunch is only thirty minutes, and that's not enough time to get there and back, let alone having time to check on them. "Is the baby a boy or girl?" Still looking at the floor, he answered, "A girl." What came out of my mouth was very much a surprise to me.

I had no intention of making this statement. I didn't want to hurt him any more than he was already hurting. "Don't you know by now that you can't replace 'Chris?' How many lives and homes are you willing to ruin or destroy, trying to do something impossible for you to do? 'Chris' was 'Chris' and he is living in heaven now and would not come back here if he could. Go ahead and accept this fact right now, so you can get right with God and stop blaming me and ruining and destroying yourself and others."

"I can't accept it," he said, "I have tried." "Just make up your mind to know that God gave him to us for a short time, and then he decided to take him back to himself. If you decide that you can't help yourself and let someone who can help do it, you will better understand how to turn Chris' loss into a gift and live your life in acceptance of reality, and not make-believe. You are trying to play God, and you can't do that. You will always fail and not be happy with a fulfilled life. I believe if 'Chris' was here now, he would say, 'daddy let me rest in peace. I'm alright. Don't that sound like something he would say? Four girls, isn't that enough to prove that you can't do the impossible?"

We prayed, and he felt a little better. His face showed some relief, and his voice also did. I prayed that now I knew, he would stop being miserable and making all of us the same. I will soon remind him that he has others to provide for other than his illegitimate families. He will need to share his responsibilities with all of us. Joline, Josie, and I, had no financial support from him long ago. We have been surviving on my salary and the girls' summer jobs for school clothes.

"With God all things are possible."
Matthew 19:26

# CHAPTER 24

## Junior's scholarship and Fredia's case

Junior has a full football scholarship with a monthly stipend that he has made to be sufficient for him. Glory and thanks to God our Father, who has been gracious and merciful unto us and has provided for us according to our needs. In high school, we traveled with the team for every game. Integration had just started, and some people had not fully accepted it. He was the only negro on the team and being the star player; everybody was not going to like that. They called us racial names and threatened us, but his teammates' parents supported us.

At first, we were the only ones attending the games. When the other parents in our community, who had children attending the high school found out about what was happening, they started going to the games. Soon the news traveled to all the schools in the district league to let the fans and parents know that Smartsbay would protect all of their players, parents, and fans. More and more citizens from Smartsbay school started attending the games. Even the off duty law officers would gather around Junior and us to escort us to our bus and car.

You got it right; my prayers never ceased, asking God to help the enemies get themselves in control and to protect everyone. "Oh Lord our God, don't let there be a riot, no shooting or killing, no disturbance among the schools. Please make everyone here civilized and calm." The schools we played had always won against Smartsbay; now, Smartsbay is winning against them. Some of the players would try to hurt Junior to get him out of the game. They never did, for he was protected with the blood of Jesus. He always asked for help from above, and he always knew we were praying for him.

One player tried to hurt Junior but ended up hurting himself; he had to be taken out of the game. Many lessons were learned by those who needed to learn. One lesson was you can't do wrong and get by. Two cars wrecked, both trying to chase our car, not knowing that our car was already surrounded for protection by other drivers and by Almighty God's protecting angels. One man in the wrecked car lost his life. This incident spread all across the district, which caused an awakening that they needed to accept the things they could not change, change the things they needed to change, and ask God for the wisdom to know the difference.

Josie also was one minority cheerleader and was accepted by all Smartsbay, but was not accepted at first by other schools. Our county was the first to integrate schools, and later, all the schools had to do the same. It was better for all, in a certain way, when all the schools in the state obeyed the rules. Jurius was at every game and very protective of all of us. He made many friends: husbands of all the ladies I worked with and all the teachers, janitors, and staff. His personality changed, and he could laugh, tease, and joke again. However, this did not last very long.

The hospital would not release Fredia until the bill was paid. This was our county hospital, not the one that I was in. They all had the same rules, except they did not hold the doctor responsible for the payment. The hospital called her mother, and she got social service involved. She didn't have the money, neither did Jurius because he had the apartment and utilities, plus food to pay for. Now he needed to buy clothes for the baby and pay the doctor's bill.

Social service discovered that Jurius was a married man, so they wanted me to come with Jurius for an investigation. One smart thing he did was keep the letters and drawings she sent to him before he got involved with her. Because she was underage, he could be charged with child abuse or rape of a minor. This was a scary situation, and he could be sent to jail. When the social worker said that, he tried to explain how he became involved, but they didn't believe him.

He claimed he was studying at her mother's house, which is his original reason for going to her house regularly. He said when he would get in his car to go home, Fredia would be there hiding until he was away from their house; she would fondle him and beg him to be with her, as he was with her mama. He knew that she knew about them and felt he had no choice, or she would tell me and everybody else, she threatened him.

He reached into his inside coat pocket and took out some letters and drawings of male and female genital parts. These drawings were very well demonstrated. There was no way someone could make a mistake of what it was. The diagrams were placed exactly where she intended them to be and what she wanted them to demonstrate.

The social workers - one man and two women - all examined and read the letters. They were not sure that she had done it. I remembered my niece saying that she had asked her to get the address of where Jurius worked. She wanted to send him a letter; these letters were addressed to him at work. They decided to do a handwriting match. Phrases were picked out from the letter to include his name, city, and state. It took a few days, but they were sure she had written the letters and addressed them to him when we met again.

God was with him, and surely he was in God's hands that day. This kept him from prison time. I was there to hear first-hand what my cheating husband had been doing. If I had not already known, it would've weakened me. All this was old news to me; I had already known about three others.

The first one was a surprise when a child walked up to me and asked me where my husband was. "Who are you?" I asked. "I'm his daughter," she stated, "and I have not seen him in a long time, and I need some shoes." I replied, "Where is your mother?" "She's over there," pointing at a car parked a few yards away, with the motor running and the lights on because it was night. "Can you give me the money?" she asked. "I'm not your mother, so will you go and tell her I would like to talk with her? I don't do business with children." She went to the car, and I watched her go to the other side of the car, got in, and they drove away.

The social workers looked at me during their investigation without asking me anything. My face had half a smile, half of what I usually have. They accessed his salary and decided he should pay a small child support, a lot less than he had been giving. My faith and trust in God have sustained me many times, but today surpassed them all. I could hear God's voice, "Stop agonizing over him. Stop those continual prayers for him! I got him. He's IN MY HANDS." Whenever I started thinking about his situations and problems, these words would come to me. I wanted to do something because I still loved him no matter what he did. Thank God he still loved him also, and I know he loves me too.

He finally broke up with her and her mother. He realized she had been courting another young man around her age. This man did not want him to have anything to do with her or the baby. He had to give up because he tried to get visiting rights and was told the child support had cleared him of all rights. "Let her go," he was told, "we are taking care of your baby. Mr. Miller, you have a beautiful wife and family, go home, take care of them, and enjoy what you have." I knew child support could not take away his rights; it gives him rights.

Just as before, I smiled and said nothing. As far as I know, he did not see her until she was old enough to make her own choices. By then, he was a little wary because she was always demanding, committing crime, and going to jail. He would get her out, and she called again to get her out of jail. This went on for as long as he lived. After his death, her mother called to get her out of jail.

I could not trust her to meet the court demand, and I didn't have the money to make a cash bond. I had to say, "Sorry, God bless all of you."

"And we know that all things work
together for good to them that love God."
Romans 8:28

# CHAPTER 25

# Job transfer and other medical ordeals

Following Junior's first year of college, I applied to transfer working at the base during the summer. The bus counselor/teacher's assistant job in the state was coming to a close. The job lasted for six years. There had been no problems on the buses between races; all the children adjusted well with the change. I was hired at one of the elementary schools located in the area where the officers lived. It was considered the best of the three elementary schools on the base. Of course, I consulted God before I applied and expected Him to give me the best. God helped me do my best in every area I worked in. Every grade level, every class, every teacher, every department, no matter what task.

Teaching was my specialty, the whole class, or one-on-one, small groups, testing or whatever was assigned to me. Supervising recess or lunch with large groups was no problem for me. I enjoyed interacting with the children. That's what I did with my children at home. Also with the children at the church and community, on holidays, such as Easter and Christmas. The responsibility of planning activities was most of the time given to me. With the help of Jesus and the Holy Spirit, which I knew I could depend on, the activities were always entertaining, educational, and glorifying God.

Never did I have any problems with discipline. Young people, even those in the schools where I worked, always gave me the respect to obey the rules given. Parents of children in our community trusted their children to go to the beach with me, though they knew that I could not swim, nor their children at first. But they knew the respect that their children had for me. Children who did not attend church or Sunday school were welcome to go along. The fellowship, love, and God's Spirit encouraged most of them to join our church, Sunday school, and youth choir.

When you live your life for God and intend to do his will, walk in his ways, and keep his commandments, your light will shine, and someone will see your good works and want to change their ways. There is no doubt in my mind that if your eyes are 'evil,' you will see 'evil,' if your eyes are 'good and right,' you will see 'good and right.' Children live what they learn. When they learn better, they will do better. Thanks and praise to God for teaching me how to teach my children, even though they sometimes went astray. When they got older, their teaching did not depart from them.

The devil, Satan, or whatever you call that liar, cheater, stealer, deceiver, has power over you, but God the Father, God the Son, God the Holy Spirit, has more power, love, and caring for you than anyone. God loves us so much, he sent his only begotten son, Jesus Christ, to the sinful world to save the whole world from sin. Jesus loves us so much. He left his place in heaven, came to earth as a baby, was born of a virgin, sacrificed his life, showed us how to live and love each other, and taught us how and about his might and power.

He proved to us he is the Son of God. He was beaten by cruel men who tried to make him deny who he was, made him carry his cross up a hill while still beating him, and he never fought back or complained. Falling on his knees when he could not go any further, they compelled a man from another country to help him carry the cross.

I was told that the cross was made from a dogwood tree, which was cut down for that purpose a little while before it was made into the cross. The cross was heavy because there was no time for it to dry out. He took my sins and your sins, and the whole world's sins, in his body and hung on the cross. They nailed his hands and feet with spikes, put a crown of thorns on his head, and mocked him because he said he is the Son of God, King of the Jews. He suffered watching his mother and brother being helpless. He still remembered to help his mother, asking his brother to care for her. Because of him, our sins have been paid for.

We owe Jesus for giving his life for us, that we can have life to its fullest eternally with the Father our God. While hanging on the cross, God separated Himself from Jesus because he cannot be in the midst of sin. If we do not accept him as Savior and ask for forgiveness of sins, his mission on earth is in vain. The only way to God is through Jesus Christ, our Savior.

I am so glad I totally surrendered myself to him at an early age. I heard his word preached when I was six years old and decided there was no other help for me. I was a motherless child and didn't know how I was going to make this journey. God's word said that God would provide all that I needed, with faith and hope. I grasped with all my strength and power and was determined to keep faith in God.

The preacher said he would be a mother for the motherless and a father for the fatherless; he would supply everything you need. My dad and older siblings taught me what my needs and wants are. This preaching and teaching have brought me this far by faith, God's grace, mercy, and love, and because of Jesus, the Holy Spirit, and a big supply of angels, I've made it alright.

God had brought me through many death experiences, especially when He saved my soul. That is an experience that I will always be happy about and never forget. You read one of the death ordeals earlier in this book. There are three more medical events that God has brought me through. The second is when I had a hysterectomy in my early fifties. I was working at the school on the base and had the summer off from work. The doctor said I would be alright if I waited until the summer, even though I was in some pain and bleeding lightly.

Jurius took me to the hospital the evening before the procedure was to be done the next day. We were put in a room with another patient, who had the same doctor as I did, for the same surgery as I was scheduled for.

After the nurses got us ready, we wondered which one of us would go first. We made jokes about why each one of us should go first. "I'm older, I should go first," I said jokingly. "That's the reason I should be first," she said, "I don't have as much patience as you." We were laughing when we heard the surgical cart coming near the door. They paused outside the door, and we both said at the same time, "I wish they would come in." Guess what? They were telling Jurius about who was scheduled. He would have to get breakfast before, and he could visit me afterward. Jurius peeked his head in the door and said, "I'll see you later. I'll be praying for you, love you."

The end of the cart rolled into the room, and immediately my roommate yelled out, "Please take me first." One of the nurses said, "Sorry, but the schedule has already been made. Mrs. Miller is ready to be taken now, don't worry, your time will be very soon. Enjoy this time and be happy, for after the work is over, you won't be able to do anything for a while. Her family came in to stay with her so she would not be alone and get nervous. The doctors were ready and waiting. They transferred me onto the surgical bed. They did what was expected, nothing new except the anesthesiologist asked me to count backward, starting with ten. Before I could get very far, my voice began to get slow and heavy, and sleep came just that fast.

How long it had been, I have no recollection. I heard "cold blue," "cold blue," then sleep came quickly again. After what seemed like an eternity, I heard the doctors say, "Close her up, go ahead and give her a normal closure." I heard them talk some more but could not understand what they said. Then I heard one of them say something about anesthesia, and this is a reaction from it. I also her the words, her husband, I thought I heard the words, lost her demise.

I was trying to say something to tell them I was not dead, that I was alive when darkness covered everything. And next, I saw angels carrying me to a beautiful place. I was partly flying, with an angel on each side holding me up. When we got closer to the bright lights, I could no longer see because the lights had blinded me.

The angels let me go, and I started to slip backward toward the same direction that we had come. I was struggling to fly, but I could not. I continued to slip backward and tried to hold onto everything I passed. Reaching and grabbing, trying not to fall, I heard voices again, and this time, I heard as I landed on the ground, with a big thud. In reality, it was the doctors doing all they could to bring me back.

Right after I landed on the ground, a voice said, "She's back; we got her." I could not open my eyes or move any part of my body even though I was subconsciously trying with all my might. My roommate had been back to the room after she was able to leave the recovery room. Finally, the doctors told my husband that she is in recovery, and that was true. All they should've said to him before was there were some complications; we will let you know soon. Thank God they didn't have to tell him what really happened. They never told any of us about what really happened.

The next time I needed surgery, I told my doctor about me being allergic to anesthesia. "Who told you that?" he asked. "No one," I replied. When I told him how I knew and what I heard during my surgery, he immediately checked my records and saw that what I told him was true. He contacted someone to talk with them about my problem. This was when I had already been scheduled and prepped at the hospital. The doctor told me he was afraid to do the surgery for the reasons he had just discussed.

This procedure was for my eye, which had already lost sight. "I just finished a patient whose eye was not as bad as yours, and it took me more than two hours, which is why I'm late coming to you." I got in touch with my never-failing helper, who was already with me. I could feel his presence when Dr. Plough was talking with me. He turned to leave, and I called him, he turned quickly, and I said, "Relax Dr., everything here will be alright, you got this." He smiled and said, "Usually, I'm telling the patient what you just told me. All this is very unusual. If you're okay, I will also be.

The anesthesiologist decided to give me a small amount at a time. About five minutes into the procedure, I could hear them talking only because the medicine was wearing off. "I can hear you talking," I said. "You are not supposed to hear," Dr. Plough stated. A few seconds and I was out. Then I heard several voices saying, "You finished already," coming from the other attendants. Then I heard, "Thank you, God, for coming," from the Dr., knowing what I had already experienced before, I started praising also. The Doctor quickly finished washing up and rushed out of the room.

"Can you see?" the nurse asked me. "Yes," I replied, "but everything is fuzzy." "Can you see light?" she asked again. "Yes," I said, "I can see you but not clearly." The Doctor came back and said it only took twenty minutes, "Oh my, what a miracle, only our God can do things like this." When he went out, he went to tell my son and daughters because he had briefed them about the condition of the eye and the complication in correcting the problem.

"It took a long time for her to come and see me. The lost time caused the eye to worsen," he stated. My son Junior was also astonished by what had just taken place right before our eyes. "If Dr. Plough had not rushed out when he did, we would have gone to get something to eat." I was set to find entertainment for two hours. I will have to agree that God was in this all the way. I reclaimed my sight.

But I'm so happy that God had already made plans for all of us and carried them out in his own time.

We got home before the time the surgery would have taken, ordinarily. We even stopped at the drug store to get the medicine the doctor prescribed. My eye was completely healed in a few weeks and was as good as the other one. Thank God he was in the plan from the beginning. When I woke up one early morning to prepare for a doctor's appointment in New Hope, my left eye was partially closed, and there was a gluey substance all around the eyelid. Grabbing the hand mirror I keep beside my bed; I took a look at the eye. I saw what I had seen many years ago when I was a child. The eye was neither red nor pink, so I went to the bathroom and cleaned it as I washed my face.

On the way to my appointment, I had traveled approximately halfway, when suddenly I heard a pop from the eye, a bright light flashed from it, and my head began trembling. I pulled to the side of the road and prayed for God to help me. All the symptoms went away, I didn't know if I should call 911 from my cell phone, but I decided to go on because I felt as good as before. In retrospect, I should have told my doctor about it. I never thought about what happened until my eyes became blurry. I called my doctor, and he recommended me to a specialist after he was told what happened and when. He made the appointment for me himself while I was on the phone. The appointment was scheduled for the next day.

When I woke the next day, there was big snow covering everything: the trees, ground, and roads, letting me know that it was more than I could drive through. I called the doctor to let him know I could not make the trip. He told me, "It's a very small amount of snow here, the roads are clean, come as soon as you can." The snow lasted for two days. The temperature dropped, and the snow froze, making it difficult for the highway department to clean the roads. In cases like this, they always clean the roads used for the most emergencies, the streets in larger cities and towns first. Where I live is one of the last to be cleaned. By the time they get to our roads, they are already passable.

Let me remind you of the passage in the Bible where Mary and Martha's brother Lazarus was sick. His sisters sent for Jesus, and before he came, Lazarus died. When Jesus heard that Lazarus was sick, he said, the sickness is not unto death, but for the glory of God. I know, as Jesus did on that day, that all the problem I was having getting help was to let some unbeliever know who God is and what he can do. This doctor in New Hope made an appointment for me in Raleigh. The first available time was three days away, giving Jurius Junior time to come and drive me to the doctor. Josie met us at the hospital on that day.

More problems followed us. The anesthetist found out that I was allergic to sleeping drugs and would not take my word. He went to my records to find out this was true. He also did some research to get advice on what to do. All this was done while Dr. Plough was delayed in his work with a prior patient. God had it all worked out from the beginning. The problem with my eye was a broken blood vessel in the back of the eye. This condition caused me not to see out of that eye. Thank God for giving man wisdom and knowledge to understand the body and have courage when needed. Thank God he never sleeps and is always near, waiting to hear our call for help.

My license for foster care was up for renewal. All my work on the application had been done, except the fire department had to come and do their inspection. They would give me a date and then call and change it.

The morning I got to the hospital in Raleigh, a call came from the social service child care department. The call was shocking and knocked me off my feet! My caseworker had visited me the day before and promised she would make sure the fire inspection would get done if I had to stay in the hospital. She took the applications I had already had approved with her, and the call came to let me know she had passed away that same night. The whole department was upset, and nobody thought to take care of her work.

Regretfully, all the work I had done on my recertification was wasted. My application did not get in on time. This meant that all the schooling and class training had to be done over again. My family and I decided that I had done enough. To take the classwork required me to drive twenty miles one way, at night, and with my surgery just being done, there were problems with my night vision.

My time spent for sixteen years, with eighty-seven lovable children and teens, had already satisfied my mind. Spending ten years with children aged zero to eighteen years was rewarding and my heart's desire was fulfilled. This work placed me on a 24/7 schedule. Sometimes they only stayed overnight or just long enough to give the caseworker time to find a home. Eighty-seven does not add the children who came more than once. Some of the toddlers could not function in other homes. They would be sent back to me until a family member could be found to provide for them. The same with some teens who wanted to stay. They would not get along with other families, so they could be sent back.

Every teen who stayed long enough left my home with lifetime skills to be able to take care of themselves. They would come expecting to be waited on and treated like a queen or king, not knowing there were chores they had to do. Cooking was the most valuable thing for them to know. Some of them were happy to learn and were a joy to teach. Others rebelled and didn't want to do anything; they were the least of my problems. God had already given me his plan. If you want to eat, you cook. When there was more than one teen, they would take turns cooking, but everyone was in the kitchen watching. It finally became fun and enjoyable.

Most of the teens are placed in foster care because parents wait too long to try to train and discipline them. The children get by with being cute and funny. The parents enjoy this until it is no longer enjoyable. By that time, the little ones are no longer little ones and begin to rebel and fight back, determined to have their way. I prayed and hoped that all my kindness and consistent ways let them know who was in charge.

Most of them were happy to have a caring and loving authority figure in their lives. It's easier to let the proper adult take the responsibility. I pray whoever reads this will take these few remarks and add them to what God will give you. Be determined to be the best parent you can be. Your child deserves that. No material thing can take the place of your teaching and love. If you love them, don't try to give them everything, even if you can.

They will appreciate it more if they earn what they get. No work, no pay, you and them will be happier for that.

A spoiled child will become a spoiled adult. Train them up in the way they should go, and when they are old, they will not depart from it. After I worked in education for thirty-seven years, my years spent in child care gave me more joy and pleasure than words can express. God's gifts and talents he gave to me were put to good use and I'm satisfied.

"Blessed is every one that feareth the
Lord; that walketh in his ways."
Psalm 128:1–2

# CHAPTER 26

## Fiftieth anniversary

We celebrated our fiftieth wedding anniversary in the year 2000. This was held on the day before the Miller family reunion. The family could attend both celebrations in one trip. We had a big turnout, and a big anniversary. All three of our children, sixteen of our seventeen grandchildren were bridesmaids and groomsmen, eight each, our two daughters were maids of honor. My brother escorted me down the aisle. My three granddaughters-in-law were managing the book for the gifts and serving at the concession table. Friends from both our jobs were highly in attendance. The festivities were very enjoyable for not only our family and guests but also guests of the Grande Marriott Hotel.

Some commented that they had not seen such a celebration before. They had never witnessed a bell ringer in a wedding before. The hotel stated that this was the largest group of all time. Family and friends came from all over the United States. Jurius was a very proud man, and this was the start of a new era for him. His behavior improved a lot. No outward jealousy, hitting, or bouts of angry fits. He could talk and hold a conversation with me, and we could agree to disagree.

I never heard as many, "I'm sorry or forgive me please." I prayed that God would help him in all the ways that he needed help and that this would be for as long as we lived. We both had retired from work, and all the children were out of the house. We spent a lot of time together, and it was as if we didn't know each other, even though we lived in the same house. We were like newlyweds.

Maybe he really heard these vows this time and was willing to abide by them. He wanted me to go with him everywhere we went. We had to agree on which of these trips were necessary and which could be solved by other means. He was like he didn't trust himself, I had to let him know I trusted him, and he would have to trust himself or we both would be miserable.

Just call on the name of Jesus and be honest with him, ask him to help you get over the feeling of guilt and shame. Ask for strength and courage to make the right choice. I felt like I could not help him do what he needed by following him around because there would be times when I couldn't be there. What will he do then? I know that when God turns you around, you will have no desire to turn back. That is what he needed, a complete turnaround from God. He will have to work that out himself, get serious enough and be determined to make it work.

I remembered he was in God's hands. All of our help comes from the Lord, all of our needs he will supply. He promised and will keep his promise. It's not hard to live in harmony, peace, and love. God's word is our road map, our GPS, but we must use it or we will get lost. You must set your mind on where you want to go and be determined to follow directions. Is that not what you use your GPS for? You turn it on, put in an address, and read the road map shown on your screen or listen to the spoken direction. If you don't decide that you want to go to Heaven, you will not make plans and efforts. You will lose your way and go someplace you don't want to go.

Pay attention to your road map, the holy bible and the voice of God's appointed servants. You can find one near where you live, in the church, a place where the faithful children of God assemble regularly. If you can't find what you need, ask somebody. Ask and it shall be given, seek and you shall find, knock and it shall be open unto you. If you're lost in a place where you don't know where you are, and you see signs that say "wrong way," you can turn around.

You can go to the other side of the road and call on God to send help before you get too far in the wrong direction. I know that God will send help. I don't know what kind of help, way, or how long, but I do know he will send help; he never fails me.

Sometimes I keep calling, over and over again, not because I don't think he didn't hear me, but because I know he wants me to be sure I need his help. Sometimes he tells me to wait, just to see if I trust him enough to wait. Sometimes he wants me to ask for patience. Other times he wants me to be sure that I trust him to lead me, and I will follow. Help is here; we don't need to wait too long to seek him. God sent his only begotten Son, Jesus, to this world to save humanity. When his mission was accomplished, he ascended back to his Father, and God sent another helper, the Holy Spirit, to be with us forever.

When someone accepts Jesus Christ as Savior, he will give you the Holy Spirit, to be with you, lead, guide, teach, strengthen, and help you stay in the path of righteousness. To God be all the glory, there is no need to be lost. If any man, woman, boy or girl sins, you have an advocate, Jesus Christ the Righteous One. He is the propitiation for our sin, and not just for you and I, but for the whole world's sins.

You can confess your sins to God and repent, which is to be sorry for your sins, intending not to do the same again. God will forgive all and make you a new creature. I was lost in sin; Jesus saved me, took away my sorrows, gave me peace and joy like I never had before, and gave me love for my enemies. He made me free from these worldly goods. He took away my heart of evil and gave me a new heart of love and compassion.

He gave me a new mind and desire to help someone who needs my help. He also gave me a determination to stay on this battlefield for my Lord.

Jesus gave me the will to know his word when I was six years old. My enemies thought it was amusing that my mother had died just four months earlier. Thank God for my family knowing God the Father, God the Son, and God the Holy Spirit. They took us to church and taught us that this is the house of God. I didn't know much about God, but I was anxious to see him and know more about him.

I listened attentively to what the preacher said. I knew the preacher was not God because he had been at our home for dinner. To my surprise, the preacher said God is a spirit. He is everywhere at the same time. He knows all about everything all over the whole world. He knows how many hairs are on your head. He knows your heart and knows when you are wrong or right. You can't hide; he knows where you are.

He is love, he is Almighty, he is faithful, he is merciful, he is gracious, he is our God.

There is none like him. He is King of King's, Lord of Lord, the Lilly of the Valley, the Bright and Morning Star. He is the way when there is no way. He is a wonderful counselor; he is everything to me. These are some of the messages that stuck with me as a child. When I walked into the church, I was always reminded that this is God's house, and he is here even though I can't see him, his word is being spoken.

Usually, my siblings and I would sit side-by-side on a pew. When one of them wanted to whisper something to me, I would hunch them with my elbow during the sermon. My older sibling who was watching us younger ones to keep us from disturbing the service, saw me hunching and beckoned for me to sit beside her. This was like throwing the rabbit into the briar patch.

When I could not read the word, I could hear the word: radio, television, CDs, tapes, etc., of the whole Bible. There is no excuse for not knowing God's word. God has equipped me for the task he had planned for my life, starting at six years. I never turned from him, and he never turned from me. Yes, I strayed from him, I did things he was not pleased with, but he just whipped me and brought me back.

**Family reunion and other tribulations**

Two years after our anniversary and family reunion, it was time for another reunion. This reunion was held in New Hope, and the Shelton Hotel was large enough to hold the reunion. There would not be a large gathering as before. The sponsor asked all the family members who celebrated marriage, graduation, birth, etc., to represent by wearing the gown, wedding dress and tux, and bringing the baby along with birth announcements. Jurius had already gone ahead to help set up the auditorium for the meeting.

Packing and putting everything in the car was a little much for me. When I told him about it, he agreed but continued to say, "I already have the tux, rest a while and slow down. I know you can do it." If I rested or slowed down, I would not get there in time. In a few minutes, a car pulled up. I thought it was a hindrance and by the time we greeted, there would be no way we could make it in time.

A voice spoke to me, and I did exactly what it said. "Run to the car, get two of them to help you finish putting your dress and bags into the car. Ask one of them to drive while you relax. You can meet and greet when you get there." No one came into the house except the two who helped me. I locked the door, and off we went. We got there thirty minutes before time, and I grabbed one grand-girl to help me get dressed.

Unlike I was thinking, I had not been told that the whole McCabe family from Detroit was there, sixty people in all. They could not attend the last reunion and had not seen our wedding. There was a cousin who married, and only a few family members were able to attend. Many high school graduates and a few college graduates were there.

We paraded down the aisle and across the stage and greeted more than you could ever imagine. When the D.J. came and was getting ready for the opening of the festivities, I found Jurius and asked him to take me to our hotel. This hotel was not large enough to accommodate everyone, but their banquet room was large enough. I took a hot shower, hoping that it would relax me and that I could be ready for tomorrow's activities. Jurius brought in my belongings, saw me in the shower and went back to the gathering. I got ready for bed in a short time and had no problem falling asleep.

Jurius came back after about two hours and found me asleep but could not wake me. He stated that he didn't want to think that I was dead, but there was no sign of life. He called the hospital desk to get emergency help, and they came in a short time. The hotel was close to the hospital, and the rescue team would not say that dreadful word that Jurius said he didn't want to think about. He said they worked very hard to get my pulse and heartbeat. They finally gave up and decided to take me to the hospital.

I don't remember anything, and I didn't hear any voices or noises. All I knew was I went to sleep and didn't have any dreams. The next thing I recall, I was in the emergency room. The paramedic said they got a pulse shortly before we got to the hospital. They continued checking on me because they had never seen such a recovery as this; the dead brought back to life. I stayed in the emergency all day, with several tests and blood work being done. There were also x-rays and other procedures, trying to find a reason for the strange episode.

At first, my temperature was very high when the paramedics checked. But the blood pressure later became normal and the pulse rate good. The doctors decided to put me in a room to be watched overnight. The next morning, after more tests were made, and all of them positive, the doctor decided that maybe some tests got mixed up. So they put me in another part of the hospital, away from the heart ward.

I was scheduled on Monday to be released on Wednesday. The heart doctor decided he wanted to do another test to see what happened to me. My primary doctor had already witnessed what had happened to me one more time. I agreed with Dr. Monroe, the primary care doctor, when he said, "We know what happened, don't we, Hattie?" Dr. Edison called my children and explained his reasons for another test. "There could be a hidden blood clot that will move while she's at home and could cause a stroke or heart attack." My children took Dr. Edison's advice and tried to convince me.

After Jurius agreed with them, knowing what had happened three times before, he stated this could be a different case. I gave in after much prayer and fasting. The test was scheduled for Wednesday, the day I should be discharged to go home. The next day, I was very anxious to get the test done and over with. I could not eat or drink anything until after it was over. It was getting late in the afternoon, and finally, they came to get me from the room. My family was waiting as well, and when I was wheeled from the room, they went for food.

The test, they were told, would be about an hour, was finished and I was brought back to the room. The doctor told my family I should stay on my back one hour before moving; my legs had to stay straight. I was partially awake but couldn't sleep in the same position. Usually, I lay on my side, with my legs bent a little at the knees. That was the position I wanted to be in. It took both my daughters and a nurse to keep me on my back. The hour was finally up, and the nurse checked me to ensure everything was okay. My family left the hospital, except Jurius. He planned to stay all night with me. Jurius always slept whenever he was sitting and waiting more than five minutes.

He was sleeping when the nurse came in to bring me some food. I had not eaten anything all day. When she tried to wake me, she could not. Then she noticed that my arms and face were much larger than usual. She contacted the doctor and other staff members there. They tried to find a pulse, and found none. They used the machine that would jolt the heart to start it beating again, but that didn't work. Jurius would not leave the room. He watched them doing all they could to get a heartbeat or pulse; nothing worked. The nurse tried to find a pulse on my feet, still nothing.

Jurius called the children, but they had not gotten home; there were no cell phones, or they didn't have one. He had to wait until they were home to tell them to return to the hospital. The doctor advised him not to tell them the news until they were back. After the children were back, the doctor pronounced me dead. He wanted Jurius to tell him what mortician he wanted. He would not say who to call. He stated, "I'm calling God and his son Jesus. They are the only ones I need."

Again, I tried to get to that beautiful city, with strong, bright lights and angels flying all around me, but could not get to me. Reaching out my hands to them, they didn't seem to see me. I struggled for a long time and finally gave up and began to go backward until I could no longer see the city's lights, and then all the angels were gone. I woke up in the bed, with everything on the bed very wet.

That was my first remembrance. Then I realized I was wetting the bed. I checked for the call remote and could not find it. I decided to go to the restroom. I never noticed Jurius still sleeping in a chair next to the head of my bed. He was out of my view. Water ran from me. I had no control of it, so much until I felt it touching my hip. I reached back and flushed the toilet, which brought a nurse running in to find me out of bed and in the restroom.

This nurse had just come on duty and had been briefed on all the conditions but was told I was waiting to be transferred to a morgue.

Jurius was aroused by all the commotion from the nurse and me. He jumped up and thanked and praised God for doing it again. God was glorified. When Dr. Edison found out what had happened, he confessed that nobody could do this thing except an all-powerful God. He stated, "I know what you and Dr. Monroe know now. It's amazing what our God can do if we would only believe and trust in him. This is an experience I will never forget, and I will be telling this always.

Can't wait to tell my family. I know they will not believe at first, but I will make them believe. Mr. Miller, I'm so glad you would not let me send your wife away last night. You keep your faith in your God and continue to call on him when you need him."

I went home the next day. Some of my strength left me, but I didn't complain because I knew this was all God's plan for my life. I will always trust him and never doubt because we are in complete fellowship and know each other very well. The greatest power available to us is faith, the force by which you can move mountains. You can, if you believe you can. I totally surrendered myself to God and prayed every day that God would use me in any way he wills. There has never been any question about why I have gone through these sicknesses and problems. I count it all joy and blessing to be used by God to help somebody who needs help. For instance, Dr. Edison, who didn't really believe in God's miracles, finally saw and believed.

The small price I paid to help save a soul is nothing compared to what Jesus Christ paid for our sins. Dr. Edison depended on his knowledge, skills, devices, tests, and medicines. He never once thought about where he got his knowledge, understanding, and wisdom. He was a very great physician and had done well in his field of medicine. God wanted him to recognize where all the power came from and realize that he had not saved a life. He was only being used as an instrument to perform the duty God had entrusted in him.

Let us be very careful to give honor to whom honor is due. I've heard unbelievers give thanks to God for his mighty works on all occasions where God worked miracles in my life and in others. God will wait on us and give us opportunities to realize who we are and whose we are. He will send help to us as he sent me to Dr. Edison.

Let's look back a few days when I was ready to enjoy families and see some I had not seen in a long time. The family reunion happens every two years. God knew the doctor needed to be awakened from his 'self mentality' of accepting praise and glory for what he thought he had done. I'm so glad that God knew he could use me, and missing the family reunion would not bother me. He knew that I was willing to give all I could for kingdom building. I had already been "tried and tested." Nothing could stand in the way of God's plan that day. Nobody could stop the progress of this doctor knowing who God is and what he can and will do.

The doctor stated, "I can't wait to get home to tell my family about this great miracle. They will not believe, but I will make them believe." He was willing to make sure that his family first - then all others that he came into contact with - would know that we have a mighty powerful God who can do all things, even awake the dead. I could have been sued and charged with wrongful death, but God saw my needs beyond my faults. My life as I knew it would have vanished, all my material property gone, and my family destroyed. But somebody prayed for me when I didn't know they were praying.

God made the uttermost impossible possible. He gave "new life" to all who witnessed this 'great ordeal.' "Mrs. Miller and her family already knew God and his love and miraculous acts. Mr. Miller did not give up on God; he said, 'you call whom you want, but I'm calling on God.' The way he said it, I thought this man was in his grief and needed more time with his deceased spouse. But then I heard something in my spirit say, 'he has confidence in what God had done five days ago. He's a witness of who God is. He knows.'"

Can you see the plan God had for Dr. Edison? He was known as the best heart doctor in New Hope. He had done some extraordinary work with heart patients. The emergency room doctor on duty could not handle this case, so they called in Dr. Edison, all in the plan of God. God had to do serious business with him that day and for a few more days. He had to take responsibility for his decision. He was good at what he did and very good at convincing others and giving advice. He agonized overnight, thinking about what could happen, not once knowing or thinking about who was in charge.

When a problem or trouble comes about in my life and family, my first thought is "God," please let this be your first thought. God, our Heavenly Father, is all we will ever need; he is never failing and always near. He will never leave or forsake you; just live by faith and do his blessed will. He's a wall of fire about you, and nothing in this world can harm you. Today, I'm a living witness for he stopped a .45 caliber bullet from going through my head. He stopped it in the pistol, between the chamber and the barrel; no man could unjam or get it out. This pistol was "cursed" forever. It was no good for shooting anymore, forever.

Read your Bible, ask the Master for understanding through the power of the Holy Ghost, and know his will for your life. Keep his law and commandments, and love everybody. You might think you can't love everybody? I know you can't, but I know that you can with God. How did I live with a man, for fifty-six years, who took advantage of me, and our marriage relationship? Who thought it was not wrong to take his anger and jealousy out on me by beating, hitting with his fist, and kicking with leather shoes when I was down.

Never was I hurt, bruised or scarred, no soreness, no pain while he was hitting me with boxing punches to my head and body. He was a man who was over two-hundred-fifty pounds, with lots of muscles and no fat. Since boyhood, he had done manual work on the farm and cut and carried firewood to heat the home.

I never raised my hands to fight back. I would use them to cover and try to protect my face, especially my eyes. I never cried, yelled, screamed, or said anything. My mind was completely on praying to my Lord God Almighty for mercy and grace for us. He would go as long as he could, and when he finished, he would be sweating and out of breath, barely able to speak. I could get up if I was down, walk past him and say excuse me without losing a breath. He would stay angry for more than a few days, not talking, puffy and frowning on his face. I'd be smiling, speaking when he comes in, and telling him about my day, which was always good. I'd tell him about the children and the mail that needed his attention.

Who do you think could do this without a living and almighty, amazing, loving, all-powerful, ever-present God, who holds the whole world in his hands, always listening to hear his children call in prayer? He knows just what to do to rescue his humble little ones from Satan. Sometimes, I felt like my life was always struggling for material things. Jurius was using his money for his pleasures, not remembering how he got it and that his salary was twice mine.

He left all the household responsibilities for me. He only took care of the cars at first. When he decided I made a sufficient amount to take care of my own car, he refused to help me with tires, oil change, maintenance or anything. I was driving a small Toyota, and he was driving a big Cadillac, which he wanted to trade to get a later model after he finished paying it off. I begged him to add more room to the house when the children were at home instead of trading cars, but he refused.

A short time later, his church needed a person to go to a county-wide summer camp to be an escort for the young people from the church. None of the able-bodied members could go, so he asked me if I wanted to do it. Six young people were going, and I would have to transport them to the camp for a week. My small Toyota would not be enough. I had to drive the Cadillac to get everybody there. We had a very enjoyable and educational week.

I was an escort to six teenagers. They were very nice girls. When the night session was over at ten o'clock, they were not ready to slow down and go to bed. They had not had any interaction with the boys. I was very tired because I was on my feet all day and doing the activities we were expected to do.

I finally convinced some of them that we needed to shower tonight, for there may have been ticks. Three of the girls helped me get the other three girls to understand that this was a week's project and we needed to follow the schedule or miss some of the activities. Finally, all were in bed, and the lights were out. But one girl couldn't sleep in the dark. She was encouraged to use her flashlight under the covers so no one else would be disturbed. All was quiet. Another girl came to my bunk and wanted to sleep with me because she had been sleeping with her mother. Another girl was afraid to sleep alone, so this problem was solved quickly.

We all went to sleep and the morning came very fast. So did the week. We attended the closing ceremony and packed up for home. We had to go to the church, where the evening service was finishing. It was Jurius' birthday, and they wanted to celebrate with him. He was scheduled to be in another meeting at six o'clock, and I was driving home alone and wanted to get home as early as possible, before dark. He decided that I should not stay; we would talk tonight about all that had taken place. I listened to one of the tapes I made of a group who entertained us with songs on the way home. I was very surprised that there was not much traffic on the highway.

Jurius called, "I'm at the meeting; where are you?" I described the area to him, and he said I was making good time. A few miles later, coming to a slight curve in the road, I noticed a car approaching the curve just before I reached it. The car crossed the center line, and I watched to see if it would go back to the other side. Instead, it came further across the line toward my car. I switched my car to the right to miss him hitting me head-on. I hit a mailbox, lost control, and ran into a ditch.

I heard a voice say, "Don't hit your brakes; you will turn over. I took my foot off the accelerator, but it seemed that the car was speeding up. My prayer was silent, "Lord help please, drive me." While the car was in the ditch, leaning to my right, it seemed that the left wheels were not touching the ground. In a twinkling of an eye, the car came out of the ditch, running at the same speed; it felt like I was driving on the highway. It came out on the right side and into a light pole, which was the last pole on that side of the highway. The lines crossed over to the left side. What a mystery! But God was in control.

Several cars that were passing by stopped, which was another unusual fact. From no cars to one car, the one that ran me off the road, to several stopped ones, and many others passing by. The first car stopped, and a man yelled, "I've called the patrol and rescue squad." I was a bit dazed and decided I must get out of the car. There was a sizzling sound and smoke coming from the engine. I looked out of the side window and saw a man standing there. He opened the door and answered me when I stated I must get out. I was very weak and leaned on the car. He asked, "Are you alright?" "I'm very weak," I said. "You will be alright," he said.

I closed my eyes for a second, and when I opened them, he had disappeared. I looked for him to see where he had gone and could not find anywhere he could have gone. People were trying to get to where I was but couldn't because of the wide and deep ditch. They had to go back to a driveway about fifty yards. I looked for a car that he could have driven, but there was no car in sight. This was before any of the other cars arrived.

The rescue squad came and, with the car's condition, insisted on taking me to the hospital. We left before the state patrol arrived. At the emergency room, they made several x-rays, checked my blood pressure, and found my blood pressure was a little high, and everything else was okay, except seat belt bruises. I was sitting on the side of the bed when the state patrol came in. Jurius was shocked to see me sitting up on the bed. They said with the condition of my car; they didn't expect to see me alive.

Jurius was on the way home from the meeting and came up to the place where the accident was and discovered that it was his car I was driving. He, too, was amazed to know I was not killed in the accident.

The patrol told him of another mystery when he got to the hospital. "The car left the ditch and jumped over two driveways about one hundred feet apart. The cement drain pipes would have done more damage, and there would be no way she would have survived that jolt," he said. "I can't believe what I saw. You are one lucky woman," another of the rescue squad said.

My mind would not leave the man that was standing by my car. I asked after my thanks and praise was done. "Lord, who was the man that opened the door and said I should get out?" A voice spoke back and said, "He is your Guardian Angel." "My Guardian Angel?" I spoke aloud. The attendant in the squad stated, "That must be true. Yes, you have a Guardian Angel. That's why you have survived."

"Bless the Lord, oh my soul, and many thanks for protecting me this day. Thank you, Almighty God, my Heavenly Father, for your love, kindness, and goodness. You are the only one who can do such amazing work for your children. Continue to be with us this day. Please keep your eye upon us and your loving arm around us. Protect us from all evil, harm, and danger. We praise you, glorify your Holy name, and say thank you once again.

God's plan for this amazing mystery was so we could add more rooms to our home. The car was a total loss. Jurius wanted to replace it with a later model, so he had to make car payments. A few weeks later, a check came to me for fifty thousand dollars. The money to add on to the house. "Why is my name not on this check also?" he asked. "That's a question you need to ask God and the insurance company," I told him. He paused for a bit, then said, "We really need more space, with the family growing bigger."

I didn't say anything else about the money. He got busy finding contractors to do the work. A cousin of his was a brick mason and had a business of building beautiful houses and other buildings. His work stood out amongst many others. One could say this house was built by 'Tom Miller' and would be right. He picked a very expensive and beautiful brick at the company brick store, where there were many designs and patterns. I had already picked one in mind but had not mentioned it to anyone. He asked about the price and found out that my pick was discontinued because of the high price. The owner had reduced the price so it would sell faster. "You come on the right day," the owner said, "I just marked the price down today."

Tom showed Jurius the bricks that were selling at a lower price, and they were the ones I had chosen when we first started to look. Tom also gave us a discount on his work. It was a family business, with his three boys and a brother. They were willing to work whenever there was no pending work for them, and we agreed to do the cleanup. Tithes from fifty thousand dollars was a big blessing to the church. This made it a blessing for financial means, and it eased stress for many members. All things come from the Lord, and of thine own have we given thee.

Our house was finished with the beautifications, inside and out. We dedicated it to God for his glory. People were amazed at the work done with much love and expertise. That's what a caring and loving God can and will do. With the money left over, we furnished the room that was built and replaced some of the old furniture we bought years ago. I was careful to use this money for our home, so I decided to help Jurius with his car payment from my salary.

Even though his salary was twice mine, he was always struggling to keep up. I paid two payments ahead, so when he was late, there would not be late fees. I tried to encourage him to talk to me about his needs, and we could work together to fix them. He seemed to think that we needed to keep things separately. "I'll be happier that way," he said. "When we married, the two of us became one," was my reminder.

"I'm glad you are still feeling that way. Maybe I'll get that feeling back one day. I'm trying hard." "I'm praying that you will not confess to me, but the only one who can help you is our Father in Heaven, who knows all about us, wrong and right. He is always waiting for us to humble ourselves and come to him for help.

"God is so merciful and loving and will always forgive anything we have done against his will. There are things we cannot do by ourselves because we don't have the ability. That is why God sent his son, Jesus, to the world. He knew the world needed a Savior, someone without sin, to atone for our sins. Jesus finished his work on Earth by giving his life, suffering pain and agony. He was made to carry his cross up a hill while still being beaten and mocked. He willingly did all he could because he loved us, you and me. He hung on that cross, nailed by his feet and hands, until he gave up the GHOST and asked his Father to forgive them for they know not what they do.

"Jurius, God the son, Jesus the Christ, has already paid the price for your sins and the sins of the whole world. Your sins have been forgiven. You must admit that you sin, confess by faith, be sorry that you have sinned, and intend not to do the same thing again. No matter how many times we sin, our debt has been paid in full. Just believe God's word in the holy bible and what you've been preaching, that Jesus is the only begotten son of God. He was dead and buried, rose from the grave, with all power in heaven and earth in his hands. He ascended into heaven and is now sitting on the right hand of his father, making intercessions for you. You shall be saved.

"No weapon that is formed against
thee shall prosper."
Isaiah 54:17

# CHAPTER 27

## *More controversy in the workplace*

Going back to work, after six years of being out from work, due to an accident at my workplace I was given an ultimatum by the head office in Washington, D.C. I was placed on workman compensation and told that I qualified for retirement. The government sent me to a doctor of their choosing because I had to have a personal doctor. Both of these doctors stated that I could not go back to work. Most of the time, my condition required walking with crutches in the house and going short distances, where I could use a cane. My pelvic and tail bones were broken in the slip and fall. The pain was excruciating ninety percent of the time, day and night. It was painful to sit as well as standing and walking.

At that early time in medicine, I was told that there was not much that could be done. Sitting on a rubber donut would help me sit for a short time but not for long. Shortly after, or before the injury healed, arthritis developed and caused another problem. I was very sensitive to most pain medicines and could only take mild ones, which didn't help me very much. I went to physical therapy, but the treatments were too harsh. The ultimatum was to retire or go back to work.

According to my head office, retirement meant that I would retire from the day of the accident. They said the workman compensation did not take out any taxes, so that didn't give me any reason for the cost of living or raises when my peers in my same rank received it. I knew this didn't sound right, but when I contacted someone to advise me, I was told that I could not go against the government laws. I had been praying all along, but now I remembered that some things only come by fasting and praying, as Jesus said. I told Jurius about what was happening and asked him to fast with me until God worked out this critical situation that I was facing.

First of all, when we began to pray, the pain that I had been going through lessened. I had heard that you can't hurry God. Sometimes you have to wait. A lot of times, he would say no. My suffering was easy compared to what Jesus went through. God answered by saying, "Go back to work." This was alright with me since I trusted God with my heart and soul. This didn't go so well with the office in Washington,

D.C. They were all set to retire me and take advantage of my life's work and welfare. However, God was in control of the situation.

I went to work when the school opened for the year. My doctors agreed that I could not do the kind of work I had been doing. At the time of the accident, the principal at the school I worked with didn't want to have me come back. She knows me well and could not do what they expected her to do to me. I was sent to another school on the base, where the principal was a woman I worked with at my previous job for several years.

She was very willing to work with the office in Washington, D.C. The first attack they made on me was to hold my paycheck until I signed the retirement papers they sent, and the retirement payments would be deducted from my pay. I let it go by because someone much greater than me was on my side and was advising me on what to do. I heard him say, "Stand still and wait on me."

God set me free from stress, worry, and pressure. My doctors gave me a list of things I could not do and the privilege of moving when needed. The school Superintendent let the doctors who thought I should not be working know there were no positions available for this worker. The doctors replied, "You must create one." The list of dos and don'ts was given to the principal to make sure the rules were followed. The principal, Mrs. Wallace, called me into her office to brief me on the doctors' orders.

She read their letter and their discussion, then told me I would be assisting the secretary and her whenever needed. My main job was to update all students' permanent records and send the record when a student transferred. I would be using the room next to the secretary's office. A telephone would be installed so I could answer the phone when necessary. This sounded like something that I could easily do without walking very much and sitting for a long time.

Before she dismissed me, she said, "I have something to say that I've wanted to say from the beginning." She looked straight into my eyes while I was smiling and said, "What I'm about to say should wipe that smile off your face." "Oh, I did not know I was smiling." Truthfully, I was not aware I was smiling because that is my natural expression. God gave it to me, and nobody can take it away. She stated sternly, "There's nothing wrong with you. You are just putting on an act, trying to fool everybody, but you can't fool me. I know you." I started to say to her, "If you know me, you would not doubt my condition-" She harshly interrupted me. So I quietly listened to all her rudeness and abusive complaints about my "not being hurt."

I stood up to leave, and she ordered me to sit back down. "You're holding the letters from the doctors in your hand," I said, trembling, "what else do you need to prove my condition? One of these doctors was hired by the federal government. My doctor is one of the best in the county for his orthopedic work. I have not said anything about this situation, and there are people speaking for me." I knew she could hear the humbleness in my shaking voice as I spoke. Yet she yelled loudly, telling me to go to work, "Get out of my office!" I didn't go to work. I disobeyed her ruthless command and went to the restroom to pray.

Praying was not permitted on the school property, so I asked God to forgive me for breaking the school's law, and to please hear me, for I needed comforting right then. She followed me into the restroom and said, "Traitor! Traitor!" I didn't respond. I just continued fellowshipping with my Heavenly Father and asked him to help her. "We will have to work together. Please let it be better than today."

The weekend came, and I was completely exhausted from working a few days. Monday morning came, and I was passing through the secretary's office to get to my room when she stopped me to say, "Did you hear the news?" "No," I answered, "what news?" Her voice did not sound sad, so I expected to hear good news. She continued, "Mrs. Wallace took a fall in Centerville Saturday. She and two of her friends were leaving a cafeteria where they had been to eat lunch. She fell off the sidewalk onto the street. She got badly broken up, her shoulder, leg, hip, and ribs. She is in the hospital in traction, waiting for surgery. She will be out for a while."

The first thing that came to my mind was what she said about me. The next thing was, "Lord please have mercy on her." My mind went back to the day I slipped and fell. I couldn't imagine being hurt as badly as I was, especially after driving myself to the base hospital to be checked out by them. Even though they never told me how bad it was, they must have known because my husband was called to drive me to another doctor.

My prayers for mercy continued for her. That was the only thing I could do. I knew God loved her and would give her the comfort she needed. I continued to smile and ignore all the rude remarks and slanderous actions intended for me. One remark I took to heart was when three of my coworkers wanted me to hear their remarks and I pretended not to hear.

I entered the group that I was invited to come and participated in planning activities for the first-grade social event. "She is so stupid that she doesn't even know she's being attacked." As I approached the group, I heard what was said, but I complimented all of them instead of being hurt and upset. "You girls look like a bunch of refreshing flowers, your clothes are as beautiful as you are, and oh, your perfume gives the same refreshing fragrance." Now, who do you think is stupid?

No one could reply when they knew I heard what was said. All of them choked on their own tongues. I was very quiet during the meeting, sitting there taking notes. One would start talking before the other had finished, like they had already rehearsed. I had not one ounce of investment in any suggestions, but I tried to figure out their reasons for inviting me.

Finally, one of them brought up the subject of the principal's fall. I had no interest in talking about that either, so one of the girls asked me what I thought about it. "Accidents happen," I replied. They all looked at each other in disappointment, and one said, "This didn't seem like an accident. This was a payback for what she said to you." I still didn't remark as they hoped I would, but I wondered how they knew what she said to me since there were only two of us in her office that day.

Did she brag about what she said to me to one of the girls in that meeting? I mentally asked God for patience and self-control and also asked that nothing more would be said about the principal in the meeting. I said, "I need to close out my workday and ensure all is properly put away." Others agreed that they had to do the same. It was a very strange meeting, and the agenda was not what it was supposed to be.

Four first grade teachers, meeting about something that only pertains to first grade, why did they need me, an office worker, to give input? There was never anything asked of me about the plans of the social event. "Thanks to my God Jehovah for hearing me." He knows our hearts, all that we think or do; ever-present one, who is with me always. "Please help me, help someone who needs help, use me anywhere, anytime, the way you want to use me according to your will. Help me, Most High God, to please you always and keep me fit for your kingdom."

Mrs. Wallace was in the hospital for six weeks, all this time, the secretary, with my help, carried out the office business without any complaints. The Superintendent came to check to see if he needed to send a temporary principal until Mrs. Wallace was back at work. He talked with me for the first time since he had been asked to make me follow D.C. made up laws. I think he was impressed by my smiles and attitude, and he mentioned that to me.

"I expected to see a bitter person resisting and rebelling authority. That's the kind of person I was told we were dealing with." "Mr.

Peacock," I answered, "I work for my pay and I love what I do. I will give one hundred percent to my job every day. I would not be able to do that if I am angry, rebelling, upset or fighting authority or the people who have charge over what I do. Perhaps you could call one of the ones who want me to retire.

I'm not of retirement age yet. I need to work as long as I can to build up my retirement. As you already know, I'm not getting credit for the time I was out because of the accident, and now I am told I will not be paid. Let me tell you, I'm not working for pay from any man. I'm working for pay from my Heavenly Father. That's the reason I can smile and go about my work with all my might.

My work satisfies me because I'm going to do my best. I'm not convicted in any way. That is something money, even pay, can't do for anyone; that is Freedom. Only Jesus Christ can set you free." He got in a hurry to leave, but not before he said, "Mrs. Miller, I'm so happy to meet you and to know you better. I'll see you later."

The secretary was back from lunch, and I was happy she went while he was there so that we could have a private talk. Even the telephone didn't ring. No child came in to borrow lunch money, nor did any teacher passing by stop to tell him her problems. The secretary, Mrs. Towns, reminded me, "It's your lunchtime now; go on and relax from this rat race." "I'm just going to eat right here," I told her, "I need to be alone."

I brought my lunch from home. The phone rang, and she was busy on the phone. Everything went as usual. Nothing changed, even though the Superintendent said I was different from the person he was told I was. I never had intentions of causing any problems. My Heavenly Father advised me to go back to work to fix the problem that caused me not to be treated fairly. I will always be obedient to him, no matter what he tells me to do. He is my helper and hope, so why should I not trust him? I have no reason to be bitter, upset, or fearful. He is my advisor, protector, and everything I need, nothing exempted. Matter of fact, he had already provided all the money I needed to carry me for a little while.

A couple of years before this, when I was going into a grocery store, the corner of the floor mat in the store was bent upward. I did not see it, and walking with my crutches, I stumbled over the mat and fell. The store clerk looked at my knee, which was scraped a little and bleeding a little, took all my information, and advised me to see a doctor. I told her that if I had any swelling, I would go to a doctor; otherwise, I think I would be alright. At home, I did get first aid, and there was no swelling, and the knee was not stiff or painful, so I didn't go to a doctor.

I had forgotten the incident until two years later, about the time I got the letter from the office in Washington, D.C., giving me an ultimatum to retire or go back to work. They had been getting regular reports from the federal government, as well as from my personal doctor. God is so mighty. He knows the future. A lawyer representing the store where I slipped and fell called me about the same time I got the letter from D.C., telling me we need to settle the case.

I'm blessed to have kept a copy of the forms from the grocery store. The lawyer wanted to talk with my lawyer, which I didn't have at that time. However, a young lady who went to college with my son had just graduated as a lawyer and was opening up an office in Centerville, near where we lived.

This young lawyer had depended on God to help her, just as I needed a lawyer. She took my easy case and talked with the store lawyer, who had already decided on a settlement. We both agreed that the offer that was made was fair and sufficient. All we had to do was sign the papers and get the check. That's the way my God works. When God is for you, he is more than the whole world against you.

Even before going back to work, the check I received would be enough to let me hold out on anything the office in Washington, D.C., would try to do. My real lawyer, Jehovah Jireh, has already planned out every detail. All I needed to do was keep praying and looking up. The peaceful expression and smile that my co-workers kept asking me about were as real as the sun is hanging in the sky. Only the creator can do that and keep it there.

Mrs. Wallace came back to work after being pressured by the superintendent's office to go back to work or retire. Like me, she decided to go back to work. She could not walk or use crutches because of the not yet healed, broken shoulder and leg. She came back in a wheelchair, and the janitors, two men, had to get her out of the car and put her in the wheelchair. One of them had to push her everywhere she needed to go.

This was not working well with the janitors because their job was not being done. After a couple of weeks, the superintendent's office got involved and said she would have to hire someone to push her around or retire. It's impossible for her work to be done sitting in her office and much impossible for her to get out of her car into the workplace without help. The janitors were forbidden to do what they had been doing. First, because of the risk of not being protected legally, and second, the government is not paying them to do such service.

Their job is to clean and service the whole school, and that was not being done.

Mrs. Wallace didn't come to work the next day because she had such a long absence because of the accident and used all her leave. This meant she would be absent without pay. She decided retirement was best for her. Another principal was transferred to this school in a very short time. This lady had been assistant principal when I worked at my original school. I had worked there for over twenty years, and she came the last two years I worked before the accident.

I got along with her just fine, recognizing her job description required her to do certain things that would check into the jobs of other workers. It seemed she was always checking me, who had very few negative reports and a lot of positive reports. Now that she checked my work, the reports switched around more negatives and very few positive ones.

I finally had to show her my notes and thank you cards from parents who thought I had done a good job with their children. I also showed her letters from parents requesting their child to be in my class the following school year. These were parents who had younger children that would be promoted, also neighbors of parents who had heard about the job I was doing with their children. She was very critical of the parents, whose requests she read, and made sure the children were not placed in my class.

Most of my co-workers vouched on my behalf, which made her furious, so she stopped checking my work. Every time I saw her from then on, I said a prayer that God would change her evil ways to good ways and that she would not be predetermined. I also prayed for love in her heart. When I saw her at the desk in the principal's office that morning, I felt sorry for her and pitied the conditions she had been placed in.

Stepping toward her office door, I excitedly announced myself, "Good morning, Mrs. Roosevelt, it is good to see you again. How are you?" She got up from her seat and, with both arms opened to embrace me. She said happily, "Glad to see you also." With that lovely greeting from each of us, I began silently praising God and thanking him for the change. Little did I know that the change was only in me. On my way out of the door, I said, "Oh, let me know if I can help you." My heart was dancing unusual happiness beats as I passed through the secretary's office.

"Good morning to you, Mrs. Towns." She looked at me under eyed, not raising her head and said in a voice that was not hers, kind of squeaky! "I hope you have a great day!" Smiling, she said, "All hell broke loose." As I continued toward my office, I wondered what she meant but dared not ask.

My day was going to be a great one despite what my eyes saw and my ears heard. I closed my door behind me, dropped my bag on the desk, and put my lunch in my mini refrigerator that was my own, so I didn't have to go to the teacher's lounge to use the one there. My mind was beginning to run from excitement to disturbance, and I knew that only a little talk with my Comforter, that Amazing Counselor, would be the only way my day would be great.

I couldn't get on my knees, or I would have, so I just started my work. My work time was approaching, and I didn't want to take work time to pray. "God, you already know what I'm facing," as I pulled out the folders from the file cabinet. "Oh Lord, we need you to send help to this school today. Heavenly Father, you know better than I do what we need. Have your way here today, and let your will be done, in Jesus' name I pray.

Thank you, master, for hearing my supplication and answering my call for help."

My day was great, and I continued to thank God throughout the day. My mind told me not to converse with anyone, including the secretary. She was very anxious to talk with me, so I made sure to stay away from her, and tonight at home will be a better time to get in touch with the Holy Spirit for guidance for another day if it is his will. Jurius asked me about my day, so we talked about some of what happened.

"Tell me," I asked, "what should be the best way to handle this situation," I said, trying to let him know I trust his advice, so he can be certain that when members or others ask his advice, he can be confident and sure his answer is with wisdom and trust for God. His advice to me was to let the secretary know, "You rather not hear anything negative about your work, you are trusting and depending on God's help, and that's all you need."

His advice was very helpful, and I did what he advised. Mrs. Towns was understanding and said, "I have a lot to talk about that's joyful and happy." "Me too," I told her, so we talked about our children, church, blessings from God, shopping, cooking, etc. We never ran out of things to talk about. A few days later, Mrs. Roosevelt visited a classroom where the children were making posters of a certain part of North Carolina, which was very interesting.

She asked if she could display them in the auditorium, where all the classes met for physical education so that everyone at school would get to see their outstanding work. She collected the drawing and just before time to go home for the day, she called me out into the hall and into the auditorium, where she picked up the drawing pile and handed them to me. "I would like these papers to be put up on these walls," she stated to me.

I looked at her shockingly and said, "Just put them back on the desk. I will need a ladder to do it." I was thinking if she remembered my do's and don'ts and the ladder was specifically pointed out.

She called one of the janitors to get the ladder, and he asked why she needed it. She stated that I needed to put these drawings on the wall. He had a questionable look at her but didn't say anything. We went home, and my mind stayed on putting the drawing on the wall using a ladder. I couldn't get on a ladder if I wanted to because my leg would not move high enough to get on it. Dislocated pelvic bones and broken tail bone were the reasons I had not worked in six years. What am I going to say to her tomorrow? That question bothered me, for I didn't want to start complaining now, and I hadn't done it before. Maybe I should have nipped this problem in the bud at first.

My prayers were said, and I had a good night's sleep. The problem did not come across my mind all morning. It was as if there weren't any problems, and the traffic was the only one. Driving and praising God for his goodness and mercy were foremost on my mind. I walked down the hall and passed the door I should have walked into. It was like something or someone was leading me, holding me by my hand, and I turned into the auditorium.

To my surprise, the drawings were neatly arranged on the walls. There was no ladder in sight. I don't know if Mrs. Roosevelt had already noticed. My help, the voice that kept me from doing wrong or making terrible mistakes, whispered, "Go in her office and tell her the truth. Find out if she has a copy of the doctor's report."

On my way past the secretary's office, we greeted and smiled as usual. Knocking on the partially opened door, I realized she was talking on the phone. I backed up a few feet and rested on my cane for a wait. When her voice got louder, I could hear she sounded upset. I backed up some more because I didn't want to hear who she was talking to or what she was saying. I turned to leave and the door opened, with her standing there, saying, "Come on in Mrs. Miller." "Let me come back another time, when it's better for you," I explained. "This is a good time," she said, "I need some distractions."

On my way in, she turned and reached out to shake hands, "Oh," I said surprisingly, with my cane in one hand and pocketbook in the other. I quickly dropped the pocketbook to the floor and, changing the cane to the other hand, reached out my right hand, just as she bent down to pick up my purse from the floor. "Well, we will soon get it right," she said. With my purse in her right hand, I said, "Maybe a hug is what we both need." I quickly threw my arm around her neck, and she did the same with her left arm. Happily, we both started to laugh out loud. "This is exactly what I needed," she stated.

We both took a seat and breathed deeply. Then she asked, "How can I help you?" "I hope we can help each other again," was my reply. "Did you see the auditorium this morning?" I asked. "Yes, I went in to pick up the drawing and they were already on the wall. Did you come back last night and do that?" "Oh, no," I replied, "someone else must have done it. That is what I wanted to talk to you about." Her eyes got larger, and a puzzling expression was on her face.

"Do you have a copy of my doctor's report for my job description?" "Yes," she said bluntly, "I'm aware of that." "Yesterday, when you asked me to put the drawings on the walls using the ladder, I thought that maybe you had not received a copy of my working criteria." "Why didn't you retire?" she asked. "To retire was not best for me at that time." She stopped me to say, "They are going to make your life so miserable you will be glad to retire." "Do you believe that?" I asked.

"That this free country will allow someone to be forced out of their work and livelihood and cheat them out of their rights that they had already earned, for no reason when their employee was handicapped doing her job on their property?" "Let's not get into that anymore," she said, standing up to end the conversation.

Handing her a copy of my doctor's report, I stood up also. "Please read this Mrs. Roosevelt," I said, "so there will be no more mistakes made while forcing me to retire." There were no more friendly handshakes or hugs for me because she distanced herself and escaped by another route every time we saw each other. She tried to make Mrs. Towns, her secretary, do her dirty work. She wanted her to tell me to supervise the children at recess, which would require me to stand for thirty minutes or walk on uneven ground. Either way, this was out of my job description. The secretary refused to tell me and started to walk away from her request.

Mrs. Roosevelt, as I was told, grabbed Mrs. Towns' shoulder, and stated, "Don't walk out on me while I'm talking to you." A push, a shove, a pulling hair, scratching face, knocking down chairs, hitting with staplers, fighting, took place in the secretary's office. One of the janitors, who was cleaning the hallway, heard the yelling, screaming, and falling objects, broke up the fight and called for help. Both ladies were separated and sent to different workplaces. A new principal and secretary were transferred to the school. I didn't know the secretary, but the principal was once again someone I had worked with for several years at my original workplace. She came and was not as friendly as she had been. It was as if she had never seen me before. She never greeted me nor I her.

My days were filled with trying to go through three hundred plus folders before the end of the year. Prayers and singing fulfilled my soul and kept me smiling. Most days, there was no reason for me to see anybody until it was time for the secretary to eat lunch. My office schedule allowed me to see a few teachers and students. In less than six months, this third principal would stay until the end of the school year, I hoped.

I needed to visit the federal government office in Clinton for an appointment and then my personal doctor in New Hope the next day. The secretary gave me the letter with this news, and she also gave me the forms I had to fill out requesting the leave. She put the forms on the principal's desk and back on my desk. That way, I didn't have to face her at all. The doctors okayed my continuing work against their will and were in favor of me trying to get all the credit I deserved.

"Why don't you get a lawyer?" one of them asked. "I have one," I stated, "the best in the world." That was all I had to say, for he was a Christian and knows who the best lawyer in the world is. "Keep trusting him," he said, 'and you are alright.' After two days off, getting back to work was like I didn't want to really be there. However, God's lover and mercy were covering my helpless situation, and I was anxious to watch him work on my behalf. My prayers and hope were for somebody, just one person would be made to know exactly who God is and be saved. My heart desires that more than one would be turned from darkness to light. But it will be worthwhile if only one would come to repentance.

I started walking in the halls just to get some exercise. That was what the doctors ordered, and the rude remarks started again. That didn't bother me since I knew who I trusted and depended on, and I know who I am. My smiles helped me stay calm and connected in my whole being and full of the Holy Spirit of God. Nothing or nobody could intimidate me because I knew my purpose for being there. There were still threats from the payroll office that I would 'not' be paid until I signed and returned the retirement papers.

My Almighty, All-wise God, did what he does best, making the impossible possible. It was time for paychecks, and somehow, I got anxious on my way from work. You know that feeling you get all over that makes you wonder, what is it now?

Driving up to the mailbox and taking out the mail, I noticed a leave slip on top of the mail. This was for my husband. I continued thumbing through, and then I noticed another leave slip. My whole body started shaking with glorious praise and thanksgiving for the mighty work of God. My hand was shaking trying to unlock the door, which made it hard to unlock the lock. "Calm down, Hattie!" was spoken out loud, "you have seen this action taken many times before. You know the creator of Heaven and Earth; you know how he works."

Looking through the other mail was taking too long. The leave slip only gave me credit for the time that I worked this year. No mention of the hours of leave that was left to my credit when the accident occurred. Calling the bank was my next step. I wanted to see if they really did or didn't pay me. "There were no deposits made to your account," the teller told me. "Please check my savings account," I said.

"No deposit there either," she told me. Well, that's strange, I thought to myself. When there is a leave slip, which means you have been paid. I apprehensively waited until I got to work to make a call to the payroll office. By this time, their office was closed.

The spirit helped me calm down and trust what I knew God had done. I waited a little while before making the call the next morning. Calling before they have had time to get their coffee and settled at their desks might be too much for them to deal with. The spirit was telling me, "Be positive and use authoritative and experimental knowledge and voice." I really didn't know I had that. Humbleness is what I like to be. However, if the spirit says, do it, I can do it because my help is with me.

Around ten o'clock, when I usually take a break, I made the call. I asked the receptionist to connect me to Mrs. Real, my caseworker. "She is no longer here," she replied. "Well, give me the person who replaced her," I said. "Wait a minute," she said and left the phone. In just a very short time, a man introduced himself as Mr. King. I introduced myself and stated the reason for the call. Mr. King was not a replacement for Mrs. Real. He had worked with me by phone on another matter.

# CHAPTER 28

# Victory at last

"Mrs. Miller," he stated, "you have not signed and returned the retirement papers. You have been notified, and until then, your payment will be held." "Mr. King," I said, as authoritatively as I could, but not depending on me but the Holy Spirit, the third God in the Trinity, "I got my leave slip yesterday, which was payday, but I didn't get any pay. When you are sent a leave slip, that means proof that you have worked and will be paid." I put emphasis on the word 'will.' "Hold on," he said.

Holding the phone while still working at my desk, I could hear discussions in the background. "Hello," a woman's voice sounded upset. "Hello," I replied. "Mrs. Miller, are you sure you got a leave slip yesterday?" "Yes, I'm sure," I said. "Hold on," holding just for a second or two, she said, "Mrs. Miller, we have not added you into our records as being back to work. Your name is not on our computer, so there is no way you could have received a leave slip.

Is your principal available?" "Hold a minute, I'll check. No, my principal is not available." "Is there anyone there with you?" "Yes, Mrs. Towns, the secretary. I had already read what was on my leave slip to Mr. King and the other woman." "Give the leave slip to Mrs. Towns," she snapped.

I could hear the frustration and unbelief of what was going on in their voices, or shall I say what has already been done by God. The secretary read what was on the slip, told her what date was listed, and answered all her questions. "Yes, it looks legitimate to me," Mrs. Towns stated. "We have no way to verify what she has because we don't have her in our records. Put Mrs. Miller back on the phone, and give back the slip." "Hello," I said, as compassionately as I could sound.

"OK, you got that slip by mistake, and since you have it, we will have to pay you this time but don't expect any more pay until you sign and return your retirement papers." I didn't answer because this was out of my hands now. My Heavenly Father was in charge. All I needed to do was praise, acknowledge, and give thanksgiving to his Holy name.

When I got home, I called the bank again, and the money was there. Unlike what they said, I got paid every two weeks thereafter. Another unusual working of the Spirit, I didn't hear about retiring from them anymore. The office of the superintendent didn't give up, they were 'Hell-Bent' on getting rid of me, and hell-bent was what they got. The third principal, who was determined not to face me nor talk to me, did her dirty work undercover.

That didn't work either, for God is not mocked. Whatever a man soweth, is what he will reap. God sees and knows everything. We don't have to call him and tell him what's going on. He knows before it happens. Get right with God, and do it before it is too late. Today is the day of salvation; tomorrow might be too late. God never promised us time; that is in his hand and will. Call on Jesus, his only begotten son.

He is able and willing to save you.

Mrs. Leiden, the principal, had a great reputation with most of the staff, but not all. There were small numbers of genuine Christians who could see her working against me. Thinking about this, and having to write about this, is very hard for me. I'm sitting here thinking about what happened that dreadful day, with tears in my eyes and my heart still going out to her and her family. I said a prayer as I have been doing. Also, her name is on my prayer list, which I offer up to God daily. There's nothing anyone can do to help her now, but there is something we can do for others who are going astray or walking in darkness.

God used Mrs. Leiden, who could not face me because she knew me better than any other co-worker. We would talk about some of our problems at the other school, and I would promise her I would pray about it. She would return the next day and say thanks to me because her problem was not as bad as it had been. She met her demise on the way home one afternoon. The head-on accident was non-survival for both passengers.

I'm still hoping and praying that her soul was not lost, that she had a chance to call on the name of Jesus for salvation. That's the danger in waiting and not taking every opportunity we have to stay protected by the blood of Jesus. The fact that she had left her evaluation reports on her desk ready to be handed out let me know that she could not have been as underhanded as some said she was. If it is God's will that my prayers could make a difference, then I will keep the faith that she still had a chance.

The secretary and superintendent went into her office to pack up her personal properties and handle any school work they could do. They handed them out to all the staff that had already been completed. She had already evaluated me. Upon leaving the office, the superintendent handed me my copy and looked at me, shaking his head and smiling. I often wonder why his actions made such an impression on my feelings.

When I read my report from Mrs. Leiden, I couldn't believe what I saw, and now I knew why Mr. Peacock was shaking his head and smiling at me. She had given me outstanding in every category of work that she had to evaluate me on. She had not completely changed into the kind of monster some of us saw. Deep down, she still was an honest and fair human being. I really believe that God used her as a 'scapegoat.' The whole base schools were mightily shaken up from the day she was killed.

Everything began to change, some for good and some disturbance. Some started looking at me as a magical being with super power, and some just the opposite: my power was for helping God do his work. All power is in the hand of God. There was nothing I did to cause anything to happen; God did all the work.

The superintendent's office called me. The call came from the person who worked directly with the department that kept the records of all time cards, absentees, raises, steps, deduction, etc. She asked me to come to her office after school that day. When I arrived, Mrs. Moguar was standing at the door waiting for me. She ran out to my car to help me get out. Her voice was trembling, and she was shaking like a leaf on a tree. She immediately started telling me she was washing her hands of all this mess. "What mess?" I asked as if I didn't know what she was referring to. She didn't say what mess, because she was anxious to tell me what she had decided on her own, without talking with anyone.

"Today, I'm going to give you what is owed to you, and what is rightfully yours, all your leave, all your raises, your steps, and the cost of living. You are due all of these, and you are deserving of it." "Are you sure you can do this?" I questioned. "I'm sure, and if I get fired, that will be alright, I can get another job. Please forgive me," she said, "for participating in this injustice against you. Too many tragic incidents are happening because of what we are doing; that is not right." "What tragic incident?" I asked.

"You know about it, don't you? Mrs. Real, and now Ms. Leiden, you didn't know your caseworker in D.C. was killed in an auto accident." I was so shocked that she had been killed in an auto accident that I did not answer her, for they only told me she was no longer there. I was very sad that it took all this to make employers do what was right. No wonder some of my co-workers were afraid of me.

I wanted them to take a look back and see that all I did was do my job. Those who think I did something should do what Ms. Maguar did, look at their actions and attitude, do what they can to change them, and get right with God. He will fight your battle, for the battle is not yours; it belongs to God.

My back pay came in a lump sum, and Jurius was ready to get rid of his car and get another later model. "I'm going to get a later model because I want to work until I'm old enough so I can get full retirement. That being God's will, I've already contacted him to let his will be done." He tried to talk me into getting a truck instead of getting another car. "You can drive this car and I will drive the truck," he said. I told him the truck would be hard for me to get in and out.

I didn't want to drive the Cadillac because that is not who I am. It caused me to be embarrassed to drive to work driving that car, and most of the time, it was not clean because we lived on a dirt road. When it rained, the mud from the road would muddy it up, and when it would dry, the dust would mess it up. There was not enough time to keep it clean. The church work and housework were all I could do, and work full time.

Church was enough to keep him busy with a full-time job. I didn't feel bad driving my little old model Toyota when it was dirty. But we finally traded the Toyota for a truck, which was very useful because of the farm. He didn't have to pay someone to use their truck when he needed one.

Jurius had been better about his elusive ways. It pleased me so much. I would do anything to help him along the way, anything that was right. I would make devastating choices to keep him growing in grace and the knowledge of Jesus Christ. I could really wrap my mind and thoughts around this being the last year of work come May. We just celebrated Christmas, and usually, the time went fast until school was a few weeks before closing, then the time would start dragging.

I had what I hoped would be my final trip to Clinton to see the orthopedic doctor, and that would not be my last trip because I would go to other doctors in New Hope. However, I hoped and prayed it would be the last to see the orthopedic doctor. They would conference and let me know what their decision would be. I went to the doctor, and he took off the soft cast I had been wearing for six weeks because of twisting the ankle.

On the way back, I was trying to decide to go back to work for two hours or go home because the ankle was not strong as usual and could not take all of my weight. I decided to go back to work in order to get more work done and not have to rush at the end.

Driving along in a thirty-five mile per hour area and having already set my speed control, there was a 'big' bump in the back of my car. The car went out of control. The steering wheel was turning around rapidly, and the car was pushed forward to the opposite side of the road. When the car came to a stop, a man stated, "I'm a policeman and saw what happened. I've called the rescue squad and the police because I'm off duty."

The car was smoking and making a noise from the dashboard. My head was spinning, my eyes wouldn't focus, and I was nauseous. The off duty police told me to get out of the car because the airbag had not ejected, and that was possibly where the noise was coming from. "It might eject anytime, and you could be hurt badly." What struck me from behind was a dump truck loaded with debris from a storm earlier in the week. I could not get out of the car, so I held on to the steering wheel and called on Jesus for help.

The rescue squad came and got me out of the car, but I couldn't lie down. They explained that they couldn't transport me without me lying down. The police department car came and got information about what happened. He then asked the rescuers to take me on, for it was only a few blocks from the hospital. "I will follow you and vouch for her inability to lie down. At the hospital, the doctors examined and ordered x-rays of my neck. Whiplash is a common injury by hitting the back of the car. They were satisfied that there were no injuries to my neck and that all was well. Despite my vomiting, dizziness, and not being able to lie down flat, I was discharged.

Days passed, and I was not getting better. I went to the doctor they recommended at the hospital to see. He examined me, took another x-ray of my neck, and said, "Mrs. Miller, there is nothing wrong with you." He showed me the x-ray and said, "This is what I'm going to report to the insurance company when they ask for a report." The word insurance struck a big nerve, and I yelled out so loud that Jurius sitting in the waiting room, rushed in to see what was going on.

I yelled out, "Oh my God! Do you think that I'm interested in insurance when I'm literally suffering in pain and can't eat, sleep, or go about my daily occupation? Someone has to care for me with everything I need. Have you tried to see if something else is causing my problems?"

By this time, I reached for Jurius to help me get up and get out of this place. "Mrs. Miller," the doctor said, "I need you to sign these papers." "What for?" I asked. "You haven't done anything to help me." "I'll tell them about this visit when I get forms from the insurance company you are expecting payment from." "The neck x-ray was not necessary. There were x-rays made of my neck already on the day of the accident. What else did you do to find out my problem? Nothing, not-a-thing." I'll sign your papers when the insurance company contacts me since you will not try to find out why I'm dizzy, in pain, and vomiting."

Jurius took me to my primary care doctor, he was booked for the day and for several days. He did take the time to call a neurologist and make an appointment. The first he could get was ten days away. Even though I couldn't see how I could make it that long, we kept the appointment. As soon as that thought passed through my mind, I spoke aloud, sitting in that doctor's office with the waiting room filled with people.

"God has never failed me yet." The man sitting next to me heard what I said, and that was when I remembered I was speaking out loud. Thank God I did, for the man next to me said, "You are right, lady. He is the only reason I'm here today. My cancer was supposed to take me out a year ago. Nobody knows how I am surviving but me. I'm not giving up on God, and he hasn't given up on me.

None of the treatments did me any good. They believed I would be dead a year ago; instead, I'm getting stronger and stronger each day. I'm not taking any medicine, just eating right, taking vitamins, walking as much as I can, thanking, praising, and trusting God. He is keeping me here, and I'm not going to die until he is ready for me."

"Thank you, sir for that testimony," I said. I knew I would be alright, for God has never failed me yet. It seemed like the longest ten days ever, but I decided in my mind, I would not complain; if I suffered, let me suffer. I can love and appreciate Jesus evermore, for what he went through, for my sins and the sins of the whole world. Jurius took off from work to be with me since I could not be trusted to be by myself.

Finally, with revelation from on High, I decided that I could go to work with Jurius. He asked his supervisor, and he said it was a good idea. There was a waiting room next to the mess hall, close enough for him to watch out for me. Most of his co-workers helped him by coming by, checking, and bringing me water and what food and drink I could eat.

God can make ways where there seem to be no ways. Captain Anderson was still there. He came in to talk with me and offered me a bed, but I hadn't laid down since the accident. "If you need anything, just let Jurius or me know." "I really appreciate that," I told him, "and thanks for letting me be here. Thank you for offering to do this, for we were short-handed, and Jurius makes a difference being here. The pain in my head lessened, and the vomiting subsided. I was able to eat more food and was eased from overall misery. We made the trip to New Hope to see Dr. Miso, the neurologist who did an M.R.I. test right away and discovered that the skull had been separated from the bone over the left ear.

He worked to get the skull back in place but could not complete the job in one try. This injury caused the cells in the left side of my brain to die. He quickly told me, "Your cells will grow back in a while." The dead cells caused me to lose memory of all things I had memorized. Most of my memory was renewed as the cells grew back. Still today, my memory of how to use and operate my computer, DVD, and other technology is intact.

The dizziness was gone before I left the doctor's office, and he was happy, and sure he had found the trouble. My visits to him were in Centerville, where he had a second office. This made it better for me because I could drive myself there, and Jurius didn't have to take off from work to drive me.

It took four trips to complete the job, and the last trip was to make sure that all was well. This accident was the third one, which meant an update in Cadillac for Jurius. We both agreed that we should trade for a van so that we could have more space for the foster children we now were caring for. The Cadillac van was disgracefully overcharged. Jurius overlooked the price. He was focusing on style and color. We took a trip to look at other models and brand names.

There were many that captured his attention, and the price was good. He soon dropped these from his mind and tried to convince me to agree to get one of these vans and a Cadillac car for him. This idea of his didn't hesitate to go through my mind. It went from one ear through the other ear without stopping.

We needed three cars like we needed a hole in each other's heads. I got the money from the accident, and it was enough for us to pay a smart down payment on a brand new van and not have a big monthly payment. We both planned to retire next year. Since the accident, I had to remain actively working to use all the leave that I had accumulated over the years. This would take me into another year before I could retire but not have to work. Jurius was getting a bit disturbed about not getting the money for the car. The problem was that some thought the car could be fixed, and others wanted a total loss.

Anyway, we needed a way to get the children wherever we went. So he finally decided to get one of the vans we looked at earlier. The rental car was not large enough, and the time had expired. As soon as we got the van and brought it home, the next day, we got a letter stating that the car was fixable, so they would fix the car back to its original status and bring it back to him. How happy we were that we had already purchased the van. He finally sold the car at the blue book price because they explained to him that the car had been wrecked, and he didn't want to be responsible for any problems they had afterward.

When he retired, he was very glad we made the decision about the van because both our retirement money was less than his salary. Money had never been a problem for me. I can always live on what I have. My daddy taught us how to make do and trust God when he said, 'I'll feed the little sparrow and there is a berry for every bird. Aren't you more precious than a sparrow?' Yes, my Heavenly Father has always made me feel more special than anything. I can truly trust him to take care of me and do my best, even when in danger or live with a cheating, abusive husband.

God let me know that his protecting arm was around me. When in danger of contracting a sexual disease, he protected me. He kept that .45 pistol from firing. You might think that was the most awesome action he took, but wait a moment. Look back at that old rugged cross, with his only begotten son hanging there. He was bearing 'my' sin, your sin, and the sin of the world. That was the most amazing and mighty act for me. The bullet could have killed my body, but not my soul. My life had been saved for eternity, forever, and everlasting. Thanks be to Almighty God, for his marvelous plan for salvation, not for me only, but for all who will come to him and believe. Praise be to Jesus, my Savior, for including me then and forever.

I lived all my life to live always. That's why nothing was going to separate me from the love of God. Like Job, God has given, and God can take away. Still, I'll say, "Blessed be the name of the Lord, The Most High God. The only one True Living God Most High, nobody but you Lord, nobody but you can make me holy and heal me too. When I was in trouble, you brought me through. Nobody but you, Lord, nobody but you. The life and death situations that I went through four times has sealed the bond. The three total lost car wrecks that could have been fatal tightened the screw bolts that holds us together, Lord, God Almighty.

God reminded the Israelites, wandering in the wilderness, how he delivered them from the Egyptians across the Red Sea. Don't forget he said it was me using Moses as the leader to bring you thus far. I can never forget what he has done for me. He is my God who has kept his promises, and I will always remember to keep his commandments. The first one says, thou shalt have no other gods before me. I try to keep all the laws, but I am sure to keep this one.

I learned that when I was in Sunday school at a young age. We had to remember them to say as bible verses in school. We also had to say them at our family gathering every Sunday morning. We couldn't say the same one; we had to learn some different one to say each Sunday.

To know what God expects of you, you have to be obedient to him, as to your parents. Let God's word grow in you, and there will be no problems in living according to his word. Train up the child in the way he or she should go when they are young, when they are old, they will not depart from it. I'm so happy my parents trained and taught us at an early age, for we are still following their guidance today. For that reason, my life has been happy and peaceful. What God gives you, no one can take it away. No situation, problem, or trouble can make you depart from it.

Jesus is all this world to me, my life, my joy, my all. He is my help from day to day. Without him, I would fall. He sends the sunshine and the rain. Life has not always been easy, but I've always had a helper all along this tenacious journey. When my ways were dark, he gave me light to see where to go. When the way got rugged and I could no longer make it, he picked me up and carried me so I wouldn't fall, placed my feet on solid ground, renewed my strength, and showed me the way.

There have been times when I didn't know what to do; when he told me to preach his gospel, he told me to tell my dad for advice. He couldn't advise me, he didn't trust God or me. He only remembered the church's rules, and when my husband didn't want a preaching wife, this is when I struggled and couldn't find my way. However, God never gave up on me, for he knew my heart's desire to please him. This is one of the times he picked me up and carried me to where he wanted me to be.

The church in my community needed my help, teaching Sunday school, bible study, and singing in the choir. I expressed my joy through the song "How Great Thou Art." They listened to the sweet melody of 'when through the woods and forest glades I wander, and hear the birds sing sweetly in the trees, when I looked down from lofty mountains grandeur….' For the first time, somebody heard that Jesus was not a baby anymore but had decided to come here and give us much needed help.

He gave his life for you and me, and when it was sung with great expression, they had to decide and yielded to this serious cry. They heard that when Christ shall come with shouts of acclamation, and take me home, what joy shall fill my heart. Then I shall bow in humble adoration, and there proclaim, my God, how great thou art! Then sings my soul, my Savior God to thee, How Great Thou Art, How Great Thou Art!

Then sings my soul, my savior God to thee; How Great Thou Art! How Great Thou Art!

God will use you if you just have a mind and desire to be used by God to help someone. Somebody is out there wondering, lost in sin, and can't find their way. God is calling you to turn on your gospel light and let it shine. Be brave and trust God to give you courage and strength to help someone find their way. God will always be with you, teaching you what to say and do. You are never alone.

The Holy Spirit will be with you. My ministry has mostly been a teaching one. In Sunday school, when I was twelve years old, shortly after being saved and giving my life to Jesus, the first teaching I did was with my doll babies under the house where I made my playhouse. Teaching was what my heart desired to do first. I would also teach my siblings what I learned in school each day and could go step by step, just like the teacher did in class.

In high school, right after the call to minister God's word, there were many opportunities to teach. First, the greatest came when I was asked to monitor the Glee Club, when there was no teacher available. Then there was the Drama Club and the annual end of school social activities to entertain parents and the community. Also, there were filling in for teachers when they couldn't be there for any reason. The principal and teachers had no problems knowing that I could handle disciplinary problems that showed their ugly faces to me. That's the way my parents taught us from the beginning. Respect others as you respect yourself.

I didn't tell anyone about my call from God to preach, so I'm sure that was not the reason they treated me with love and respect. My clothes didn't speak for me, and certainly not my looks. I'm just an ordinary plain Jane, who wears her hair and homemade clothes the same all the time. I didn't "flirt" or tease anyone. I hoped the humbleness was outshining my true feeling of being a poor nobody. Sometimes I was embarrassed to let my classmate see what I was eating, except when one of them had nothing to eat. I was happy to give them one-half of my baked sweet potato and share my biscuit and sausage link with them.

Loaf of bread was a delicacy in those days, and we never had money to buy it. Some of the classmates would have sliced bread, with whatever inside, always wrapped in paper napkins or wax paper. Neither of these was in our category of things you need. My lunch was put in a tin bucket that originally had Karo syrup in it. It was a good lunch box because it didn't get cold when the food was put in hot.

Most of the girls, to my surprise, were envious of my lunch. We never went hungry growing up. We ate what we grew on the farm most of the time. We also bred chicken for meat and eggs, hogs also for meat, sausage, smoked hams, etc. My dad was a schooled man in all categories except education; he knew just enough to be able to read and write. His other learning and wisdom were outstanding. He was always prepared for the winter months when the snow came and no work to be done, 'preparing and saving' were his motto.

When I was younger, I thought I would drop these two words from my vocabulary. However, they were "deeply rooted" in me. There was no way I could get rid of them. I'm now teaching these rules to my great-grandchildren; prepare ahead of time and save all you can. I'm so glad God gave me this teaching ability. Now I need it more than ever because the younger generation has helped fulfill the prophecy; every generation gets weaker and wiser.

Some may give up on them, but I have no intention of giving up. The more they rebel, the louder and longer I teach. My prayer has taken another direction toward those who think they know it all. My prayers for patience and courage has been put on the back burner. I know how to do what God has allowed me to go through these many years. So young one, I am on the battlefield fighting for you to turn to God. I realized there's not much I can do, but I'm not going to give up on the little I can do. I will keep hunching you until I'm satisfied that you are wide awake and realize where you are.

What's facing you can only get you to come to my God, your Heavenly Father. Look and live like Jesus Christ. It's recorded in his word how you should live, so just look to Jesus; he will show you how to live. He is the only way to meet our God in heaven. I'm sure we can get there if we apply his Holy Word to our lives. God gave me talents, like the Master in his Holy Word. He went away to give us a chance to work and use these talents to increase his kingdom.

He is coming again to see what we have done with his gifts. Don't let him catch you with your work for him undone. We don't know when he is coming. He didn't let anyone know, not even his Son Jesus the Christ, our Savior. Get busy, everybody; get your house in order, and do your best for the Father, the Master of heaven and earth. Work, for the time is coming; work through the morning hour, work while the dew is sparkling, work the mid springing hour, work when the day grows brighter, work in the glowing sun, for the night is coming when man's work is done.

Fill the brightest hours with labor; rest comes sure and soon. Give every flying minute something to keep in store. Work, for the night is coming, when man works no more.

God gave me the task of writing this book so that it would greatly impact the world. He wants people to know who he is. This is another effort he had made to help us to be prepared for his kingdom. He has given me revelation from on High and has told me what to write and how to write. Even though I didn't feel worthy or capable, I had to obey his call. My daily prayers include my life's desires to help someone who needs help. "Use me, oh Lord, anyway, anywhere, and anytime. Use as much as you please until you can't use me anymore." My life is filled with unspeakable joy, peace, happiness, contentment, satisfaction, the word of God, faith and trust, and when I need courage and patience, my request is made known to our God.

I was born a premature baby, but I'm not sure of how long before the time. Matter of fact, it has just been confirmed as the truth. My older cousins who live in our neighborhood would tease me about certain things, which made me know that there was some situation that was not normal. They would say I was very small when I was born. "At six months, you were walking, being about a foot high. You were such a tiny little thing.

You were always chattering about something. We could not understand what you were saying at first. Then in a little while, everyone could understand what you were saying. We understood the words and the emphasis you put on them. You were a very determined, smart and definitely speaking, courageous little girl. Even though we somehow charted your destiny, you would be an oracle and be able to communicate with a multitude of people.

"Our prediction has been proven by what you have become over the years. Our prayers have been and still are that Almighty God will continue to use you for his Glory and increase his kingdom building. He will not save and enrich your life, and then let you fail. Your name means "one who sees god" and with our faith in the Holy One, who never does wrong or makes any mistakes, we know he sees you. There is no doubt in our minds that your life was spared many times because our Lord God, the creator of heaven and earth, knew you would not deny his trust.

We both are old and are happy to see this day when we have already experienced many great things that only God could perform in our lives. We bless the Lord for not giving up on you and us. And we promise him that we would keep the faith and be willing to hold fast and strong until that perfect day when his son Jesus Christ will come back for his True Church.

"We expect to meet him in the sky and reign with him forever. We would love to see one of our children in the position you are in continually being used by God to help others. In as much as this was not his will, we are happy and rejoicing that he saw it fit to use one of our family members, who has proven to us that we have been a mother to her, and she is our daughter. Our sincere prayers will always be made to our heavenly Father on your behalf. Our love and adoration will continue to follow you all the days of your life."

My dad or siblings never talked to me about when I was born. They probably didn't know why I was such a small baby. In the older days, adults didn't talk to children about certain things such as sex, menstruation, childbirth, or the permanent and real-life or the 'birds and bees.' These talks were considered for adults only. Parents would omit teaching their children for the lack of education and the proper use of words. My mother probably would have taught us more had there been time for her.

One of the doctors who had seen a lot of unusual happenings in my life, and also from my medical chart, which none other had told me about, wanted to go back to the archives to look into all my medical records. I had to give written permission for him to search and find out all the unusual health actions in my life. He worked with my records for several years and finally came to a conclusion.

My birth was surely premature, and his guess was about three or four months. He also found that my organs, including my brain, were not fully developed. When a sleep study was done, this function was mentioned to me because my breathing would stop during sleep. This report jotted my memory of when I was a child and my sibling would remind me to stop holding my breath. I would not be conscious of such actions. But I would start breathing deeply to correct the matter.

The report found that my brain did not tell me to breathe in the sleep study. Also, since I'm older and can't hear as well as when I was younger, I was given the same reason for not being able to hear well. I was told in both cases that there was nothing that would help me. Even though I have a CPAP machine, it does not keep me from not breathing, but it does give me continual air to keep me from suffocating.

Nothing has helped me or can help me 'except' our Heavenly Father, who can do all things at his will. With the CPAP, I still don't breathe deep enough to get enough oxygen, so when this happens, I wake up with the help of God and take deep breaths until I fall asleep again.

I thank and praise God. He has allowed me to live a peaceful and happy life free from sickness and stress. I continue to glorify and adore my Lord and Savior Jesus Christ for his wonderful works. The first time I had a chest x-ray in my early thirties, I was told I had an enlarged heart on one side. At that point in my life, I did not have any medical conditions except allergies. I thought that was due to the enlarged heart on one side. Later by my mid-thirties, I started having high blood pressure. The blood pressure had been at a normal range since I was treated for low blood pressure. There were some sickness and awareness at all times. High blood pressure was much different.

When Doctor Bearfoot told me my pressure was high, I had no symptoms at all. I had gone for a medical check-up for work release. I've been taking medication for high blood since that time. Dr. Bearfoot was a very kind and serious doctor who made me believe I could trust his advice. He told me, without batting an eye, smiling, or taking his eyes away from my eyes. "If the sun comes up, you take this pill; if the sun doesn't come up, you take this pill. Every morning you wake up, take this pill for the rest of your life." Since that day, I have not taken that exact pill because there have been some upgrades in medication. But I have taken a high blood pressure pill every day since.

Over the years, other forms of illness have crept up on me, but none that I know that Jesus Christ our Savior had not already taken stripes on his body. He was beaten all night by cruel unbelieving men who tried to make him deny his deity. The stripes on his body were for 'our' healing. I don't have to stay sick when the devil sends sickness into my body. I will suffer at God's will while claiming my uttermost healing through the stripes of my 'Chief Doctor' Jesus Christ, God's only begotten Son.

I believe what the Word of God says, that I can move mountains if I have faith as small as a mustard seed. I believe what the word said, "Surely he has borne our grief, and carried our sorrows; yet we did not appreciate his worth, he was struck and wounded, smitten of God and afflicted. But he was wounded for our sins, he was bruised for our wickedness and lack of righteousness, the punishment of our peace was upon him; and with his stripes we 'are' healed."

We are like sheep that have gone astray, "We have turned everyone his own way, and the Lord our God hath laid on 'Him' the sins of us 'all.'" Yes, I have peace, that peace that Jesus suffered that I could have. Joy unspeakable joy, Joy that this world didn't give me, and this world can't take away. I'm free in the midst of trials, trouble, harassment or war, bound with chains and bondage, I'm free. When the Son of God makes you free, you 'shall be' free indeed. And thanks be to God, that we were the servants of sin, but you have obeyed from the heart, that form of doctrine which was delivered to you. Obeying God's word has made you 'free' from sin; you became the servants of righteousness.

Jurius could not break my spirit with his punches, kicking, cursing, cheating, and threatening and trying to take my life. The husbands of women whom I was housekeeping and cleaning didn't break my spirit, for I was not in slavery. I had been set free by the Master of Masters, Jesus my Savior. They offered a lot more than my salary, which could not buy my freedom. Their strength and power couldn't make me yield to temptation. God spoke for me in the midst of struggling and being overtaken.

I said this to every one of the men who were almost overpowering me. "When you are finished with me, I'm going home, and call your wife and tell them why I'm not working for them anymore. This is the reason your work did not get finished. He came at his lunchtime and offered me this amount of money. When I refused to take it, he overpowered me and committed rape."

There was no need to call the law officers. Who would believe me? One of them told me this was what was expected of me when I do this kind of work. "My wife is already accusing me, so I might as well benefit from her beliefs." "Let me tell you," I said, "unless you kill me first. This body belongs to God, the creator of Heaven and Earth. And I know he will not let you take advantage of me and get by with it.

You might as well leave right now while you have a chance and never let me see your ugly face again. You better start looking over your shoulder, for God's got your number, and he knows who you are. He said in his word, it is impossible but that offences will come, but woe unto him through whom they come! It is better for him that a millstone was hung about his neck, and he cast into the sea than that he should offend one of my little ones, take heed to yourself."

I was never afraid of dying because I knew that meant going to my Father's house. There will be life eternally, where peace, joy, and happiness shall reign. Every day will be Sunday, while we worship and praise our God with shouts, and singing Hallelujah, salvation, glory, honor, and power unto the Lord our God. I know because I lived right, and I know that heaven belongs to me. I don't know about you, but I know that Jesus said, "I'm going away to prepare a place for you, that where I am there, you will be also. In my Father's house there are many rooms and if it were not so, I would have told you."

I didn't have any more problems with that man and none of the others. I always gave them the message God gave me while struggling for my dignity, self-possession, and self-respect. Let me say again, to remind myself and you, if you will, when Jesus sets you free, you are free indeed. No 'devil in hell' can take your freedom. God, my Heavenly Father, soon moved me out of this situation to a better one with more pay and a better opportunity to use some of the talents he had given me. I'm a witness that God will make ways where there seems to be no way. He will provide for you if you only accept his plan for your life.

We have a Father in heaven who loves us all and wants us to live in harmony. I know God is not pleased with the people who mess up his beautiful world. And Jesus, his son, sitting on his right side in Heaven, is giving us another chance to make things right. He is making intercession for us, pleading and depending on us to stop our evil and selfish ways for a chance to have mercy on us. God made us all in his own image and likeness. None is better than the other, regardless of what nationality we were born in or what color we are.

We are all sinners. The Bible says that all have sinned and come short of the glory of God. Our hope is to confess our sins and ask God for forgiveness. Repent, accept Jesus as the Son of God and Savior of this world. God has been giving me a revelation of what to write in this book, to help all those who do not know to get a chance to know "Him" and let knowledge rule in our hearts as children of God. God loves you and gives you another chance to get right with him by getting right with your fellow man. He wants you to fill his kingdom. He does not want the 'devil' to have you and send you to hell.

God has not given all his power to any human, kings, queens, popes, or presidents, no matter the leadership title or ability. He still and always will rule this universe until the end of time. God is honest, true, righteous, loving, and faithful. He is good, merciful, and almighty. Let me say again, he knows everything; you can't lie to him. You can't hide anything, for he sees all you do and knows exactly what you think before you think it. I haven't told you all about God, but if you grab hold of these few characteristics and truly decide you want to know more in your heart and mind, you will learn all you need to know to live a clean and righteous life.

Sincerely call on the name of God the Son, Jesus Christ, and he will hear and answer you. Jesus has sent the Holy Ghost to earth to be with us and do whatever we need. He will comfort you and change you from all your wrong and evil ways to become a child of God because Jesus came to this world and gave his life for all humanity; we have a chance to the right of eternal life. I pray that the simplicity of this book will make you understand who you are and who's you want to be.

Because Jesus lives, I can face tomorrow. Because he lives, all fear is gone because I know he holds the future. My life is worth living because Jesus lives. God sent his son. They called Him Jesus; he came to love, heal, and forgive. He lived and died to buy pardon. An empty grave is there to prove that my Savior lives, and then one day I'll cross that river. I'll fight life's final war with pain, and then as death gives way to victory, I'll see the lights of glory.

He never left me alone when the storm of life was raging. When the hurricane winds are blowing, he tells me I can speak peace to that wind and it will stop blowing or change its direction. He has given me faith as a grain of mustard seed, and that's all I need. I know that God is with me, and that's more than the 'whole world' against me. God specializes in things thought impossible. He can do what no other power can do. Missiles, bullets, planes, rockets, satellites or any man-made objects can't go where or do what our God can do. I know that our God's power is indescribable. There is no power on earth that can be equal to his power.

Political powers in this world have greatly been misused. The people never intended to give their votes for personal purposes. Elected officials are to represent all the people, not just a few who are of a special party. Jesus helped everybody that he saw that needed help, rich, blind, sick, intelligent, or ignorant, and that is the plan he wants this world to abide by today. We all will have to give account to him one day. It behooves all of us to get our house and life in order to be ready to meet God one day, when we have to stand before his Judgment Bar and give an account of all we have done, good or bad, right or wrong.

Today, my prayer is for you to wake up and consider your worth; an eternal life in heaven or hell. This life on earth is but a short time, no matter how long your life will be.

As you are already aware, my birth was premature, and there were some immutable, internal medical deformities discovered when my first baby was born. It was such a rare condition that the doctors thought this child was a miracle to be here. And for sure, the discovered condition would not allow us to have other children. This deformity was diagnosed congruently by three doctors located in three different cities who didn't have any contact with each other. I am so glad that God ruled over medical science, or I would not be writing this book today.

The midwife was so sure of what she saw at my birth that I would not make it. She reported to the registrar's office that I died at birth.

When I needed a copy of my birth certificate, there was not one for me. I was standing in the registrar's office with my driver's license in hand to prove that I was not dead and very much alive. The clerk took all the information I could give her about my father, mother, siblings, and all the physical information, address, and schools I attended.

She even allowed me to show my baptism certificate; still, this was not enough.

I had to go to the county's superintendent's office, look through the files, and get my first grade report card and last year's attendance report. She also needed the birth certificates of all my siblings. My husband and I made a trip to Raleigh to the state registrar's office to have this information I secured certified and my name added to the registrar records. We came home not knowing if they would accept me as being alive or dead. It took almost a month until I finally received a birth certificate.

All this is proof to me, and I pray it is proof that our Lord God is a God of love and has no respect for a person, as his word tells us. According to our society, I consider myself a 'nobody' but look at what my God can do. He can take a 'nobody' and make 'somebody' out of them. Yes, I am somebody, you may not know it, but I surely can claim my status, position, rank, and standing, believe it or not.

I'm a child of a King. My Father is rich in houses and land. He holds the wealth of this world in his hand. He created the heavens and earth and all there is. He formed the mountains and scooped out the oceans and sea. He slung the sun, moon, and stars in place. He made the flowers and the trees, the birds and the bees. He has ownership of all the cattle on every hill, and if I was hungry, he fed me, naked he clothed me.

When I'm sad, he makes me glad. He gives me the blessed assurance that Jesus, his son, is mine. If I'm down, he picks me up and places my feet on solid ground. He's my light in dark places, a shelter in times of storm.

If you think you're 'nobody,' my heavenly Father will stretch out his mighty hand, saying, "Come unto me you that is heavy laden. Call on my name, the name of Jesus." He will claim you as his own and make you his loving child. When this world puts you down, look to God from whence all your help comes. He will never forsake or leave you alone. This world had treated me mean and tried to block my way. My conquering King took a procession and let the world know he was in control. He's the General of every army. The Head of every situation.

Your problem is not flesh and blood, but you are fighting hopelessly against principalities, against powers, against rulers of the darkness, against spiritual wickedness in high places. Know that there are no powers on earth that can take down God's anointed. He's the Alpha and Omega, the first and last, the beginning and the end. If you want to rule, first let God rule in your heart, your mind, and behold the tabernacle of God within you. Let God's incarnate word be your ruler, your guide, and your protection.

Sanctify yourself and give God charge of your life; you will see men as men, people as people, right as right, wrong as wrong, you will know not to judge anybody except yourself. Your main issues will be to get right with God and to love everybody, for we all are God's children, and he loves us all.

Wake up, world leaders. You have a charge to keep, a God to glorify, and a never-dying soul to save and fit it for the sky. You were elected to serve this present age and to do only your "Master's Will." World leaders, state leaders, country leaders, county leaders, city leaders, town leaders, church leaders or wherever your leadership role may be, God wants to use you for his glory. Stop all your evil ways and realize that God sees all you do and everything you say he hears.

You can't get by. He's got your number. He knows where you are. My God is a Jealous God. He will not allow any other God to rule his universe. Our God, Jehovah, demands exclusive loyalty. It behooves you to get right with him and do it "now;" tomorrow can be too late. My prayers go to God on your behalf.

After retiring from the school system, my night's sleep was not restful, and dreams overpowered me as I slept. I would still teach and interact with the children as I did at work daily. My intermingling with children allowed me to reach them when they had problems or difficulties. Working with children made me want to reach out to them even more than my job allowed. I applied to social service child care to become a foster parent several years before retiring and was told I was past the parenting age, but look what God can do.

Ten years later, I received a call from the same office, asking if I was still interested in becoming a foster parent. Well, the right request, but at the wrong time, I thought. I had just had an operation to remove my gall bladder and was not feeling up to par.

The class for parenting would start in a week, and my surgeon had not dismissed me for anything, waiting for more healing. To my astonishment, the need for homes was so great that she was willing to let me start the class late and make up all the work later. My daughter, who was there attending to me until I could do what was needed myself, encouraged me to do it. Another consideration was that married couples were required to attend. I had to take this situation to God. He was my only help.

Jurius had planned to retire, and I wasn't sure if he wanted to give his free time without children in the house to help some other children. When the situation was brought before him, he was as sure as I was that this was what God would want us to do. "He has given us a second chance," were his exact words. Praises and thanksgiving to our amazing Lord for hearing and answering my prayers. He was willing to attend the class and worked hard to learn the requirements of becoming a foster parent. The children adored him, especially when they could ride on the lawnmower and that big green John Deere tractor. Most of the parenting was left up to me because the only way he parented our children was what he learned as a child, whipping.

Children do live what they learn is a very true and necessary phraseology. It befits parents to be careful of their actions and reactions when raising a family. I'm still benefiting from my training and teaching when I was a child. My dad was mother and father to his ten children. Even though he used the whip, we were always aware of his reason. The bible teaches, "Spare the rod, and spoil the child." My daddy could not afford to spoil ten children, so his best actions were to train us in the way to go, and when we are old, we will not depart from it.

God gave us help through the Holy Spirit to be able to catch up on all missed classes and to 'ace' the class with flying colors. Almost everyone was eager to see our performance when we had to demonstrate by acting out what we would do in a certain discipline situation. There is no room for mistakes or fumbling when God is directing and guiding you. Just keep your hands in his almighty hand. Most of the children God sent to us were very much in need of help. We trusted God that he would help these children learn the value of life and the importance of being a fruitful citizen to humanity.

Our first child was a three-year-old boy. The caseworker who brought him to us was carrying him as he was screaming and kicking. She handed him to me and then handed me his jacket that he had taken off in the car. She tried to talk over his noise but could only get out that he couldn't talk. He had been in therapy for a while. Finally, she gave up trying to talk and told me she would call the next day to inform me of other matters that would better help me deal with him. He struggled to get away from me and ran to the closed door to try opening it. He kicked the door and beat on it with his hands. All this time, I was calling on my God for help.

This little one heard my soft plea to God and immediately turned around and reached out both hands for me to pick him up. "Let's put your jacket on," I said, "and go outside to see the chickens." He obeyed without any fuss, and we proceeded to go out the back door. He walked with me holding his hand. "Thank you, Lord," I whispered.

At the fence that surrounded the little chicken coop, all the chickens had gone to roost because it was late evening, and they had already been fed their food for the day. When the chickens heard a voice, they all began to fly off the roost and come toward us. I thought the excitement of them running toward us might frighten him, and it would be too much for him to deal with. Instead, he started laughing happily and said, looking up at me and pointing toward the rushing chickens, "It that cicken?" Well, for someone who had not said a word before, I understood all he said. "Yes," I said, getting gloriously excited myself.

Maybe I misunderstood the case-worker, Noraman. What I thought she said was that he could not talk, even though his words were not plain, I understood him. We watched them go slowly back into their coop and walked back to the house while God was glorified with all the praises I could muster up. "God, you came quickly. Thank you for hearing and coming to my rescue." What puzzled me was what I thought I heard, but I didn't want to not believe that God worked in such an ultimate and marvelous way. I don't really know why there is even a shred of unbelief in my mind, for I know that God has done much greater things in my life before. Why should he not do the same again?

When Noraman called the next day, I questioned her about Jamie not speaking. By the time she called, he had been saying several words, all getting plainer. When I asked him at dinner time if he wanted to eat, he repeated "eat" he could say "no" and "yes." He repeated prayers when I told him I would say prayers for him. Noraman didn't believe me that I heard him talking or saying understandable words. I realized what was going on when he refused to say anything while Jurius was present.

The next morning at breakfast, when I made what my ideas of a good breakfast was, he threw the plate of food onto the floor and demanded cereal. "Okay," I said, "you can say another word." I put the cereal in a bowl, which was Cheerios. He looked at the box and began to name the cereal he wanted. All of which I didn't have and all very sweet, Frosty Flakes and Trix.

I never gave sweet cereal to my children, so this was a big challenge for me. He didn't want the cereal even when I showed him I put sugar in it. I offered him peanut butter and jelly; he wanted nothing but Trix. He kept repeating Trix and crying until the phone call came from Noraman. He got very quiet and stopped crying while I was talking on the phone. "Okay, you are a very smart little fellow," I said to myself, "just in the wrong way." I have never let a child outsmart me and I'm not about to let this one do it either.

I took him out of the high chair and put him on the floor. Let me remind you that the plate of food is still on the floor where he threw it from the beginning. The plate, thanks to God, was one of those unbreakable plastic ones made especially for small children.

"Come on," I said in a joyful voice. "Let's pick up Mr. Hoppy and put all his food back in it." I always made up names for everything when dealing with uneasy children. "Mr. Hoppy don't like being on the floor; let's hurry and get his food back in him so we can make him happy." I handed him the spoon that was on the plate for him to eat with. I got another spoon from the drawer and proceeded to pick up the mess of food that was splattered on the floor.

I noticed that he could handle the spoon very well. He had gotten adapted to eating the cereal all by himself and could easily pick up the food. "Bet I can pick up more than you," I said while pretending to speed up my pace when for sure, he was getting most of it on the plate. I finished by getting the part that was too hard for him to get.

"Who got the most?" I asked. "I did," he responded. "Well, let me see who can clean the floor better, you or me. I got two paper towels and put a little water on each from the sink I had used while making breakfast.

By now, he was very anxious and excited to do a better job than me. I handed him one of the towels and reached for the towel rack to get another one for drying the floor. When I stooped to help, I shouted very loud and disappointingly, "You have already finished, and all I can do is dry it." He reached over to me to give him the dry towel. When he finished, he yelled out a very loud, "I beat you with everything." "Wow!" I said, "you did, and now I am sad that you didn't want to eat Mr. Hoppy's food or my cereal. You will have to be hungry all day. I'm sad that you don't like any of my food."

He reached for the bowl in which I had put the cereal and a little sugar. I picked him up and put him back into the high chair and pushed it up to the table. "Do you want milk?" I asked. "Milk in my cereal," he answered. This is two times he has made a sentence using four words. This little guy has really been doing an amazing job fooling everybody. If it was true that he couldn't talk, God has done an amazingly miraculous, speedy transition these two days.

What else can one's heart desire but to live Holy and true, pleasing in his sight? I told Noraman about the talking, and she still didn't believe me. I had no witness from Jurius or anyone, for he would not make a sound in the presence of others except to cry and point his finger.

The bright idea came to me to tape him talking. I got a small tape recorder that I told him would record singing and all good things. My singing and talking were recorded and played back to him, so he could hear me when I was not near him or in the room with him. He thought that was fun, so he wanted to do it. I asked him a few questions, and he answered using the tape recorder. My first question was, "Jamie, where am I?" "Right there," he answered. "What am I doing now?" I asked. "Shaking your head." "Jamie, where are you?" "In my high chair," he stated, using four words this time. I played it back to him, and he liked it and said, "That's funny, that's me talking."

I played this recording to Norama when she visited the next time. She commented that it could be any child's voice. I was wondering why she thought I would lie about such an insignificant matter. I stopped agonizing over the lack of belief from all the social service staff that were interested in this child. I was satisfied that he was not mute and prayed in his own time, he would know that it is very important to communicate with others. My prayer went up to God, and he lifted my burden and gave me satisfaction that I would not let what anybody say or do keep me from being the person God is pleased with.

Jamie finally let Jurius hear him speak when Jurius told him to ask me if he could ride on the lawnmower with him to cut the grass. I was standing right there, and he knew I heard what Jurius said. He looked at me, wanting me to consent, but I said to him, you will have to ask me what grand-dad told you to ask. Jurius started the motor of the mower and pretended to leave him. He said what was expected of him to say, but I pretended not to hear him.

I asked that the motor on the mower be turned off so I could hear him. The motor was turned off, and he spoke very softly. I said, "I still can't hear you." He raised his voice, and both of us heard without any more coaching. He always talked to both of us from that day forward, calling me grandma and Jurius papa.

Eventually, he would talk to other members of the church. Now, I had to ask him to be quiet. No one ever found out why he chose to keep silent. He was a healthy joy to have as a grandson until his mother was rehabilitated and could have him back. While Jamie was in our home, we were assigned two brothers, one twelve and his younger brother ten. These brothers lived with a family who decided they wanted to exit the system for a while. For us to meet the boys, we were invited to the home for dinner one Saturday evening. The home was a mess, with clothes on the couch from the dryer.

We had asked to set the kitchen chairs next to their family room. Most of the clothes on the sofa belonged to the boys in care. My concern about the clothes disturbed me, and I asked Marcus, the oldest, why not fold his clothes and put them in his room. His reply was, "That is not my job. Mrs. Waters is being paid to take care of us." His answer made me want to get up and walk out of that house. Then another thought came to mind. This working mom and dad don't have the patience to deal with this twelve-year-old or don't care about them. The foster parents were of a different nationality and didn't know how to handle the situation or were afraid to be accused of mistreatment.

Mrs. Waters was in the kitchen making dinner and didn't take the time to talk with us about the boys or anything else. When she announced that dinner was ready, Jurius and I were already sitting near her two-year-old in his high chair. Mr. Waters was not present at all, and there was no mention of him. It was very strange that we came to meet the family and learn something about them, and all we learned was what we saw. Everyone was at the table waiting. Marcus was in the living room with a frown on his face. Mrs. Waters called him a couple of times, and he didn't move. She decided we would eat without him.

After all were served, Marcus came to the table, stood there looking at Mrs. Waters, and said, "I thought that you might have enough common sense to have a decent meal since you have invited guests." "Marcus," Mrs. Waters said, "please sit down and eat." Marcus' voice rose to almost a loud yell when he said to us, "She has been giving us sandwiches every day since we've been here for two months. She upgraded to tuna instead of peanut butter and jelly, and we have potato chips and tea instead of water." She tried to make Marcus stop talking, but she had no success. I was glad to see there were some reasons the foster parents wanted us.

We had to stay outside until they got home from work, at six o'clock. When we came here, it was to be for the better for us, but we have found out that nobody cares. We stood up to leave because we had heard more tonight than we knew what to do with. Mrs. Waters said, "We will have them ready to go tomorrow at about twelve o'clock." "Twelve is too early for us because our church is not near and it will take until at least three o'clock for us to get here." Marcus spoke up and said, "That will be fine then.

We can make it to our basketball games. We've had to miss most of them because no one would take us. Do you want to see the game? We both are on the team but never get to go."

This visit gave me mixed emotions. These boys desperately needed help, love, and guidance. "Oh Lord, please help us to be able to help these young men to know there is help and hope for them. I would surely like to know what the other family they lived with before the Waters had to say about them. Also, it would be a great enlightenment to know more about the case that brought them into care. As you can imagine, sympathy had already taken hold of my feelings, but sympathy is not what these boys needed.

Marcus had already taken a role to be the spokesperson for his brother Ron, and I was not sure if this was a performance just for us or if this was a way of expressing or fighting. There is a hard task for all involved, but never is there anything too hard for God.

We have already involved the Chief Teacher and Master Trainer. While listening and receiving the serious conditions this household had been living with, we saw selfishness and greed raise their ugly head. We saw self-respect and respectability run out of the house. We saw obedience and discipline hide in dark places. We saw hate, envy, and malice manifest and grow like a tall tree. My silent prayer was, "Oh Lord God Almighty, have mercy on all of us." I needed to do something or say something, but nothing came to mind, so I sat silently.

I looked at Jurius, who had his eyes closed, and I knew he was also praying. We had both heard enough. What needed to be done or said is unto the Master of Mankind, the Master Maker of Heaven, and Earth. The wise King of Glory, the Holy one, Omniscient, All-Knowing God.

Before making an agreement to care for these boys, the Waters should have considered and counted the cost. What do these boys need that I can supply? Their age makes a difference in their requirements. Why are they coming to live with us? Do I want to make the sacrifice? Give up my free fun time to attend to their needs? Who are these boys? Can I love them as my own, even though they don't look like my son?

Can I swallow my pride and keep it down? Is this small amount of money enough to really help us out? Will all they give be enough to help us care for the boys' needs? Where can these boys stay after school until we get home? For sure, not outside our house. What about if it rains, snows? They have to use the toilet? Who will advise them not to ride their bikes to the shopping center? Who will tell them where to get food when they are in the store where there is plenty to take?

Who will come to their rescue when the police are called because they took candy from the store without paying?

Mr. and Mrs. Waters didn't count the cost before making a decision as serious as the lives of two young boys. Please don't try to benefit yourselves at the expense of another's life. We prayed all the way home that God would help us to help these boys, and would teach them to be obedient and cooperate with us as foster parents. After Sunday service, we both were renewed by the Spirit of God and were very hopeful that God could use us to undo this neglected work.

We picked the boys up from the Waters at three o'clock as promised. Mr. Waters was absent again; Mrs. Waters had very little to say to us or the boys. There was no hug from the boys or her, but the boys showed their true feelings of appreciation to us with hugs as we got out of the car.

We went to the school where the basketball game was held, and was told that the boys could not play because they missed many practices. "Don't worry," I told them, "we can see what you can do when we get home. We have a basketball goal, and we are going to challenge the two of you." "Wow, you two can play basketball?" Marcus said, "I know we can beat you two old folks." "These two old folks had not forgotten what we learned early in life. We also got plenty of practice with our children and grandchildren." The boys relaxed, and it was a pleasure and joy to have them as members of the Miller family. They got to go to church every Sunday, bible study, and Sunday school.

On vacation to Maryland to visit our daughter and her family, they visited Washington, D.C. and got a look at all the historic sights there. The social service system tried to replace the children with families within one year. These boys stayed with us two years before being released to their grandfather in Florida. Jamie, the three-year-old, stayed for two years also. Our home was never empty, though. Before they all left, others were waiting to move in. The next little six-year-old had a brother that was four who was beaten by his aunt, who was their foster parent and caused him to be paralyzed. The four-year-old was in the hospital in a critical condition, not expecting a full recovery.

We came home from church on Sunday, and a three-month-old baby boy was waiting for us. This little fellow was very tired. He and his older brother, ten years old, and sister, six years old, had just flown from Nebraska. Another family near where we lived took the other two but didn't want a sick three-month-old. This little one named Joseph had a condition that caused him not to be able to keep milk down. He was very tiny for three months. As sick and tired as he was when

I reached for him, he gave a big smile with his big blue eyes looking even larger, for he was so tiny. As usual, I was silently asking God for help and mercy. All of us were also tired because we had attended two services that day.

Jamie was very excited to see the little one but was too tired to interact. He went right to bed. The information we got about Joseph's health that day was that he couldn't sleep lying down flat. He has been sleeping in the car seat. I got him ready for bed, giving him all the special treatments I learned throughout the past years: warm bath, hot oil rub, oatmeal for the diaper rash, and warm water with karo syrup and ginger.

All the time I worked with him, he was smiling and looking so weak. My heart and prayer went to God as tears ran down my cheeks. I held him wrapped tightly as a newborn until he fell asleep. When I put him in the car seat, he yelled and started crying. "He had been in that car seat all day; why won't he yell?" Jurius said, "let me hold him while you take care of yourself and get ready for bed."

For the next four to six weeks, we took turns holding him until he was hard asleep before we would try to put him in the car seat. None of the medication the doctors prescribed did him any good because he couldn't keep it down. The different kinds of milk, almonds, lactack, etc., didn't do any good. God revealed to me to cook a certain fruit and give it to him. When I started feeding this to him, gradually, he was able to keep food and milk down.

His body weight increased, his complexion improved, and he began to crawl. By one year old, he could walk. Before he was one year old, I got another 6-month-old who had a 'rag doll' syndrome, which meant he had soft bones and no muscles. He came with a rash all over his body, and he was not crying out loud but a soft whine.

He came to us at two a.m. God showed me right away to get the oatmeal, sprinkle it all over his body, and just leave him undressed until he gets relief. I had to buy a double stroller for the two babies about the same age. The mom wrote me a long list of dos and don'ts, none of which I gave attention to because if these suggestions she gave me worked, why is the baby still in this condition?

My Chief, Master Doctor, knows exactly what to do. My faith in him allows his authority to do just as it is his will. Thank you, God, for I know I can depend on and trust you. Somebody else has begun to know what to do, especially with these unhealthy children. A call from social service landed me another three year old who seemed to be healthy but spoiled. He wanted to tell me what he would eat and wear.

He was hung up on Spiderman. He brought all Spiderman toys, clothes, pillows, bowls, plate fork, and spoon. He wanted to carry around a full-size Spiderman blanket. The blanket would drag on the floor, knocking down everything in its path. When the end of the blanket would get caught under the door or stuck under a chair, he would not try to unfasten it. He would stand there and cry, yelling on top of his voice.

He was an only child and bi-racial whose parents didn't make it, and the court awarded the child to social service. He was not potty trained and had no knowledge of what that was. My training was not as hard as some others because I had the six-year-old who took him to the bathroom when he went and encouraged him to do what he did. We prayed about the hang-up with these Spiderman characters with Mack. He would get seriously frantic and frightening to the other children, stomping and hitting the walls and would not let me touch him. Well, my normal healthy child may not be physically sick, but I sure judge this one wrong.

I was beginning to thank God for one who would be easygoing. "Lord," I said, "you already know even before he got here, but I'm going to say it anyway, I NEED HELP FROM YOU, in the worst kind of way. This mental condition is worse than the physical one." Jurius heard all the yelling and screaming and rushed in to help. He picked him up as he was fighting and kicking, and took him in the driver's seat. That calmed him down for that time. Jurius got a revelation from God to take away all the Spiderman images and box them up until he left. In a few days, Thank God that was what we did.

The first time we took all the boys to the shopping center, he threw a fit for us to buy him a Spiderman. Perhaps that is why he had so many characters when he came to us. I simply took him aside and said, "We did not come here to buy toys; we have plenty of toys at home. I want you to stop all this crying and noise and do what these babies are doing and hold hands with papa. If you don't stop making this noise, we will take you back to the car." That did it, he got alright, and we finished our shopping.

It took a few more days before he was over the Spiderman phase. He was kept busy interacting with the other children and his 'new' toys. Mack became a joy in our family, easy to potty train and a great helper in letting me know what the other children were doing. I didn't want to see anything else in his life as a problem, even though the continuing telling was more than anyone could handle. I had to grab patience with one hand, endurance with the other hand, and stand on a determination that this would be healed. Our Heavenly Father never fails or forsakes us. He was always so near that it seemed that he was there with an answer before we called.

We make a great mistake in thinking that we can be wary of God. But what peace we often forfeit, what needless pain we bear, all because we do not carry everything to God in Prayer. Are we weak and heavy laden, cumbered with a load of cares? We should never be discouraged; take it to the Lord in prayer. God is so good. He enhances the calls, prayers, and praises of his children. He is waiting just to hear your earnest request.

I take everything to God in prayer. He has made my burden lighter and my way brighter. He gave me this work to help these little ones to a better way of life, so I keep calling on God Almighty, King of Glory, who never fails. He brought me from a long way, from despair to cancellation, from death to life, from sinner to salvation. He is my God, Lord, Master, Savior, the Rock on which I stand. He's my dearest friend.

Blount, the "Rag Doll Syndrome" baby, was a jolly and determined little fellow. He would try and keep trying; he didn't want to give up. He wanted to do what the other little ones could do. The doctors' diagnosis was that there was nothing to be done until he stopped growing. "Oh Lord, what will this child do for this period? My Lord God, I know you can do it if it is your will. Whatever I can do, please let me know." I didn't hear from God like I had been hearing.

But the message came by way of Joseph, who was a few months older than Blount. Joseph would be on the floor on a blanket near the playpen where Blount was lying. Joseph wiggled over to the playpen and started to reach his hand inside as I walked in the room to see the sight. I took Blount out of the playpen and put him on the blanket with Joseph. The two boys were so happy they immediately started to wrestle.

Joseph would pull him by his leg, arms, and turn him over and over. When Blount's arm or leg was caught under his body, Joseph would pull them out. Tears ran down my cheeks as I stood and watched. I thanked God for the answer; somehow, even as cruel as it looked, I knew this was the way to do what God wanted.

Both boys worked hard, Blount trying to get his hand on Joseph's hair, both boys laughing like I'd never seen before. When they both separated and on their stomach, I knew it was time to stop. They both ate a big lunch, and I got them ready for a nap. After nap time, they wanted to play again. A few days later, I could see a huge difference in Blount's strength. He could move his legs and arms and hold them in a certain position. Worship, praise, and thanksgiving were offered to my God for his wonderful works to the care of his children. I knew God could do it; also, I knew he would do it.

Blount continued to develop little muscles around his joints. He could get his hands to Joseph's curly hair in a few more days, and I heard Joseph yell stop. One of the few words he could say. I rushed where I could see what was going on. Blount had both hands in the hair, what he had been trying to do since the first day. There was something about that hair that Blount wanted to get his hands onto. He had enough strength to make Joseph feel him pulling.

I picked up Blount and started shouting around like I was at a revival meeting. I was praising so sincerely I had not noticed he was reaching for my hair. Joseph was reaching up for me to get him. Both of these babies were underweight, so it was easy for me to carry both of them at once. But guess what, not for long.

The next morning when I went to get Blount out of his crib, he was standing there holding onto the side of the crib. I ran to get my camera to take a picture, for the social workers did not believe what I said about his progress. All I did was rub and massage him using blessed oil and ask God to have his way and will. To God be all the glory for the amazing and wonderful works that he had done. We visited the social service office after the court date, where a discussion would be made about custody for the baby. The court could not decide because neither parent had reformed as expected. And another reason was the baby had made progress in his recovery. The court decided to leave him with me for further improvement.

Blount's mother decided to move back with her mother, who had to be investigated and approved before she, the grandmother, could be responsible for the child. Two years later, the decision was made to reinstate the child to the grandmother's care, with both his parents agreeing to go to counseling and work out the marriage process. When the parents saw their little boy for the first time since he was put in care, standing there with me holding his hand, with his long pants, shirt, tie, and jacket, and a little black and white gabardine cap on, they were so astonished; I thought they would faint. They expected to see him being carried or in a stroller, for they had heard from the doctor's report of the time it would take before any improvement.

I believed that this miracle made this whole family believe in God. It also gave hope to his mom and dad that they could make their marriage work for the sake of their child and their sake also. Neither one wanted to give up their right to not be there at all times. The grandmother was an unbeliever until this day when all of them witnessed the mighty works of God. You have heard so far that all the children I had in care have been boys.

That was my request from the beginning. You see, my hands had been damaged from other works that I had done through the years: looping tobacco, having to hold the string tight enough so the tobacco leaves would not fall from the sticks, washing clothes on a washboard, cleaning house and wringing out cloth, typing on a manual typewriter for many years, holding a baseball bat, playing softball in school, and oh yes, I believed catching a basketball, may have contributed to some of it also.

My hands got so painful at one point that I could not hold a pen to write. When I used instruments during the workday, I could not sleep at night because of the pain. The orthopedic doctor suggested surgery on both hands. Arthritis had become a problem likewise. The surgery was a success, but there was nothing to help the arthritis but less use of the hands and pain medicine, which I had to use sparingly because of hypersensitivity. I requested boys because of the hair combing.

Finally, there was a brother and sister pair, both with red hair. The girl's hair was below her shoulders, very thick and curly; also, the brother's was very thick and curly. I said, "No! No!" The boy Aaron was six, and the girl Robin was eight. "This is the last home we have to put them in," they begged, "they have been in many homes and also our group home, and nothing has worked out." "I still can't do hair," I explained.

"Also, Robin can do her own hair, and Aaron can get his cut closer," they suggested. "Well," one of them said in a very pleasant and pleading tone, "will you keep them for tonight and we will find a place tomorrow. We will have to send them out of the county if we can't find one who will take them." "Just for tonight," I repeated. One asked, "Can we leave their belongings here?" "I have clothes for them tonight, and I will wash the clothes they're wearing tonight."

I didn't want their clothes left because that would give them a reason to stick me with them. Jurius came from work and engaged in the conversation about the clothes. "Why not put them on the porch where it will be easier to remove tomorrow." I couldn't get a chance to tell him what I suspected if the clothes were left. I lost the battle. There were toys, bikes, skateboards, balls of all kinds, shoes galore, and clothes. The porch was overcrowded. There was no way my house could hold all this stuff. Jurius started to tell me they would come back tomorrow to get it. I told him what I suspected, and he was so sorry he made that suggestion.

They left, and I noticed Aaron crying, and when I asked why, he didn't want his hair cut. I told him he would not have to get his hair cut because he would not be staying with me. "Are you hungry?" I asked. "Have you already had dinner?" We had already finished eating and Blount, Joseph, and Mack were ready for bed, except for their story and a little exercise to tire them out for a good night's sleep. Jurius went into the kitchen to eat and share with our two new guests. I took them to the bathroom to wash their hands before eating.

The brother and sister walked into the kitchen, where Jurius made three bowls of homemade chicken vegetable soup with crackers and three glasses of cold fresh milk, which we had learned we should drink at dinner time. They both stood a couple of feet from the table, and Jurius was encouraging them to sit, pointing to the chairs. "We want McDonald's," Aaron said in a very whining voice. Robin stood there, nodding her head in agreement. Jurius took his seat and began eating, and both Robin and Aaron started yelling, so I stopped reading to the boys and ran into the kitchen.

I stooped down in front of them and said, "We don't have McDonald's, but we have this delicious chicken soup, crackers, and good cold milk." Before I could finish talking, one of them said, "You can go to McDonald's and get some." "We are a long way from McDonald's. We can't go there tonight. Have a seat and just taste it, you will like it, for it is very good."

Jurius was quietly eating without saying anything. Shortly, he stood up to get another bowl full for himself. Looking at me kneeling on the floor and the two standing there crying louder and louder, Jurius said to me, "Go ahead and get them ready for bed." I stood up, and both of them took a seat at the table. They sat there for a few minutes staring at the food. "Go ahead," I said, "it's good," encouraging them to eat. "Go ahead and take care of the other children," Jurius said to me. I turned around and started out of the room. The other boys had already fallen asleep, so I put them into their beds. I heard Jurius putting his bowl into the sink and I went back into the kitchen, hoping to see the children eating.

By the time I reached the area where I could see, the bowls were being removed from the table by Jurius. He turned to the two children and said, "Get ready for bed." "Come," I called out; they both started to cry, "I'm hungry." "You will be alright till morning," Jurius stated, putting the dishes into the dishwasher. I ushered both of them toward the bathroom without saying a word and started filling the bathtub with water. "This is where you will sleep," I said to Aaron, "this is where Mack is sleeping, so you will need to be quiet." I gave Robin nightclothes and hurried her out of the bathtub.

I put my hand on Aaron's shoulder to tell him to go right in. He shrugged his shoulders then rushed away for me. I turned on the water, making sure it was the right temperature and put it in the bubble bath. He said, "I can't take a bath by myself; Robin needs to help me." "I'll help you," I said.

I showed him how to wash his face, and in walked Jurius, who took over the job, showing him how to do it. For sure, I was right. God will not let you have many surprises when you depend on and trust in him. We got stuck with these spoiled, untrained children, who were much in need to be at our house. God knew they needed help, skill, and training for life. I don't know where they had been living, and I'm glad I didn't know.

No matter where they had been, they had not been treated right. They should not, at this age, know to use the words they used to us, calling us niggers and take your black hands off me. When I helped pick Aaron from the ground where Robin had pushed him down, tears ran down my cheeks for the damage done to God's little ones.

When we went to move their belongings from the porch, we could not bring them into the house. Jurius had called the exterminator because roaches were crawling up the wall outside the house. These little ones didn't know what was best for them, but we began to approach the throne of authority to seek forgiveness for my slackness in trusting God's will in our work for the betterment of humanity. We had to come together as we had done many times before we could ask anything more of our awesome King of Glory.

Confess our lack of dependence on the one and true God Almighty who never makes a mistake. Who knows everything, right and wrong, who had already done so many wonders in our lives and the lives of these precious ones. He has answered our prayer, for which we are eternally grateful and appreciative.

Our request and determination from Jehovah God is to help someone every day and show them how to live right and holy. The day these children were brought to our home was the answer to our prayers, but for a brief period, we wanted to allow the storm that had been raging in our lives to calm, or maybe I wanted it to pass by. Jurius evidently saw God's intention when he agreed to put the children's belongings on the porch for the night.

I knew God's watchful eye was on us all along, for I felt pity and compassion for the social workers when I agreed to help them through the night. I also knew that I didn't have to face this battle alone, for God had never left us alone or failed me from my early existence of life until now. I knew that this battle belonged to God and not ours. We had to acknowledge that all this belongs to God, and he knows what to do.

Six children and two bedrooms, for the first night, I had to pull out from the utility closet, a fold-up bed for Robin, the only girl. How will we solve this problem? "Oh well," I said, "we have a closed garage that God gave us when we needed more room for our three grandkids when they were teenagers visiting us during summer vacation." We rarely had to use it for anything but storage and vehicles. Just look at God working miracles again.

"Jurius, let's talk," I said, after going to bed, but knowing that we would not get much sleep. One of the reasons I wouldn't get much sleep was I still wanted to blame my caseworker for not keeping her word of leaving them with us for just one night. Even though I had already heard from God, this thing you call getting the satisfaction of "being right" still lingered. This precise feeling was able to rule over me for a little while.

I was lying there frantic, allowing that great enemy of man and goodness to play around with my conscious, governing who was "right and wrong". My thoughts were running rapid, and for an instant, I lost control of all that God had provided to help me know whom I could depend on.

Jurius was waiting quietly for me to start the conversation of what we needed to talk about. I moved slowly back to reality with the help of the Holy Spirit and continuous help from God's amazing grace. It was like I had gone to a strange location against my will, and now my guardian angel has brought me back where I belong. Jurius and I talked about how we would accommodate these six little ones without breaking foster care rules. Girls and boys had to have separate rooms, and each child should have their own bed; even siblings could not sleep together. I told him that I had an idea that we could use the garage, which was enclosed as a part of the house. We needed to see if that was possible.

We decided to make the garage our bedroom and rearrange the other room, including our bedroom, to accommodate the children. The arrangement was faulty because we were too far away from the children and could not hear their movements and words. All the moving was a waste of our time. "God, we need you, we can't do without you. We need your Wisdom, directions, guidance, and help." We stopped and admitted. The arrangement was put right before our eyes in just a twinkling of our eyes. "Would it be approved by the official of the service?" Jurius laughed aloud and said, "The officer knew how much room we had from the beginning, so why will they pass judgment now? What do they expect us to do with God's little ones?"

I heard God speaking, and we are the ones who will be making a sacrifice. We had to give up our privacy to accommodate someone else. The plan was to keep the younger toddlers in their cribs and move them into our bedroom. The law did not say that they couldn't sleep in our room, for they are our babies and we are their parents. Complain all you like, but you cannot alleviate God's plan. This plan also made it easier for us because we were closer to the situation that needed most of our attention. Thank God and his son Jesus for their unselfish love to all humanity. God Almighty, the Most-High does not discriminate against nationality, sex, race, age, or color.

Everything began to smoothen out and bind together. Our oldest one, whom we had almost a year, started to tell Robin and Aaron, "Don't you talk to my mom like that anymore. She is a good mom, and I love her." When Eric came to us, he was very frightened, devastated, and couldn't stop talking about what happened to his brother. God heard our prayers and had mercy on him. Talking to him made him understand that we are God-fearing and will love and care for him. "You are our child now, and God will take care of you and your brother." He would get upset with Aaron and Robin every time they acted disrespectfully toward us. He would let them know how they should act.

Finally, with all our convincing and showing love to them in the midst of their rebellion, God changed their minds and hearts to accept our care and love. At this time, they had only eaten enough to stay alive. We refused to give them junk. Both of them came to us severely overweight, and I was not going to keep giving these kinds of food to add more pounds. This was long enough to give them time to know who we were and where they were.

Praises and adoration to our Savior Jesus Christ, for he is not only a Savior of souls but he will be there any way you need him. We already knew that he would come on time. Sometimes he waits to see if we will keep the faith and wait on him. Mary and Martha gave up on him when he didn't come immediately when they sent for him. But I have learned that he may not come when you want him, but he will be there on time.

After they learned to stop fighting us, Robin and Aaron became part of our family because the harder they fought, the calmer we became. They had to learn to be children, listen to our teachings, and accept our caring and love. Junk food was forbidden, and we gave them another chance to sit at the table and eat the food put before them.

They finally learned to say a bible verse and were extremely happy about that. After three months of wrestling, they became beautiful and loving children who were still learning how to be obedient and accept the rules of our home.

Our trip to Maryland for vacation, a tour of Washington, D.C., and seeing the White House and learning of its greatness and importance showed that they were very appreciative of our care. "We never had a trip before," they said, "we have never been anywhere but Centerville." My daughter and her family responded to them as my children. I can't take credit for training these little ones, for my love for them and all we do comes from above. No matter the problems or circumstances, our Heavenly Father will solve them all. Under no conditions will God ever leave you if you only give him an opportunity.

Rubin's hospital reported to the social service office that they could not keep him any longer. He was our new intake and suffering from paralysis. All they had done had not been effective, and they didn't think he would get any better. Of course, they looked at our home, saying we have his brother. "We think he would be more comfortable with his brother being there." They placed Mack in another home to make room at our home for Rubin. They brought him by medical transportation with a special wheelchair designed for him. This chair had a removal part to make getting him in and out easier. Even though he had been at the hospital for about a year, he was still wearing a soft cast covered by ace bandages to keep it in place.

The next day, they would bring us a special bed for him. My problem was what I was going to do for tonight. We decided to put Joseph into Mack's bed and use his crib for Rubin. That worked out all right for one night because Joseph was such a hard sleeper; he would not roll out of bed or miss his crib. We were happy they would bring a bed that Rubin was used to sleeping in. Something familiar at our home would be a big help for him to transition easier from his hospital stay.

Rubin was a big chore for us because he had to be fed and depended on someone for everything. He was like a newborn in every way, except he was not sleeping most of the day as a newborn child would. His continuous squealing noise and banging his head on the bed were very annoying to the other children and us.

Aaron asked me to call someone to come and get him. That's when God revealed to me what this helpless child was going through. I called all the children together in his room and explained how uncomfortable Rubin must be, that he cannot walk or use his hands like we can. He has to stay in one place, day and night. While I was talking to them, he was very quiet and seemed to understand what I was saying. "Let us pray," I suggested. We all held hands. Eric held one of Rubin's hands and I held the other. Most of the children were too small to reach over the top of the crib. My prayers were very short and to the point.

First, we prayed for his healing, of which everyone repeated 'healing.' Then we prayed for him to be happy and thankful to be at our home. "We thank you, our Heavenly Father, for hearing our prayer and giving us the victory in Jesus' most Holy Name we pray, Amen!" We also decided that all of us would help him. He would never be in his room alone. We decided what each of us would do when we were with him.

One decided to read a book, another to make funny faces, another to tell jokes, and the little ones will dance. Rubin laughed really loud hearing that. Aaron, who was standing behind everyone, had not said what he would do. "What are you going to do, Aaron?" I asked. "May I help him to eat?" he asked. "That's a super suggestion," I stated, "I will help until you know what to do." Rubin had a big smile on his face, the first time he had smiled since being here.

Jurius walked in and wanted to know what was going on. Everyone told him what they would do to help Rubin. "You didn't leave anything for me to do," he said, "well, I didn't hear anyone say they would rub and massage him, so that will be my way of helping him." "What will you do, grandma?" one of them asked. "He needs to be able to talk better, so I will help him say some words." He had been scheduled for physical therapy and speech therapy, which we would enforce with daily practice.

We all left the room except Eric, his brother, who said he would read a book to him. I helped him pick out one that would keep Rubin's attention and was easy for Eric to read. We all were ready for lunch, except Aaron. He was very excited to help him eat. "Why don't you eat first?" I said to Aaron. "No, I want him to eat, and then I will eat."

Jurius was helping everyone at the table, so I put food on the tray and drank a sippy cup. As Aaron wanted to carry the food tray, I said, "Be careful," I explained, "because it is a little heavy for a six-year old." He took the tray, and I reached for the sippy cup to lighten the load. I went for a TV stand to put the tray on, "Aaron," I said, "watch me to see what you need to do to help him." After the napkins were tucked under his chin and I reached for a pillow to prop him up a little, the voice of God said, "Get the chair and let him eat in the kitchen with the others." "Oh yes!" I said out loud, rushing to the chair's hallway and pushing it into the room.

"What are you doing?" Aaron asked. "She can sit up and eat at the table."

Everyone was happy when Aaron came in carrying the food on the tray and placed it on the table, and I followed, pushing Rubin in his chair. Even though lunch was disturbed and everyone was making a lot of noise, we didn't let it bother us because, as Jurius said, "God has already started his plan working for Rubin." We asked for another blessing for the food and thanked God for being our provider and helper, our leader and guide. The little one, Joseph, didn't understand us saying another blessing and was exceedingly astonished to hear Robin, the one who pretended not to accept us as family and was always saying, this is not my family, spoke quickly before anybody else could speak. "We had to say another blessing, Joseph, to thank God for being good."

Our hearts were humbled that we could once again see the mercy of God and his Grace. "How excellent is thy name in all the earth. We glorify and adore thee. We magnify thy Holy name." We could actually feel the presence of Almighty God and his wonderful power, and we knew we had nothing more to wonder about, for his work was done.

Not wanting the children to see tears from my eyes, I silently slipped out of the room to praise and worship God.

When I heard Aaron yell, "Grandma," I rushed in, wiping my eyes. Then I saw why he yelled. Rubin had taken the spoon out of Aaron's hand and was trying to pick up food with it. I quickly supported his hand, helped him get the food into the spoon and guided it to his mouth. All eyes were upon him in awe, and the children started clapping their hands in praise to God. I knew he would do it but didn't know it would be so soon.

While the children were clapping, Jurius stood up from the table and started toward me, but the Holy Spirit overtook him, and we shouted all over the room. Even the children were overcome by God the Holy Ghost. We all worshipped and praised God until we were full and wanted nothing more to eat. I called the caseworker to tell her the good news, thinking she would want to know. It was like I just had to tell somebody. The words hit me like someone had thrown a bag of ice at me. "I don't believe it," she said, "this little boy is completely paralyzed, and there is no way he can move a finger, let alone his hand and arm. He has not been to therapy yet to be evaluated.

"Mrs. Coleman," I stated, "I'm so glad God heard me, and Rubin didn't have to depend on people like you," hanging up the phone and shouting some more. In a little while, I heard bumps on the table legs and on his chair. I peeped under the table, still shouting. I could see his feet moving against the table and chair. "Look," I said to Jurius, who was still praising, until he saw what God had done for this paralyzed child.

"We don't care if nobody believes this. God has performed another of his miracles in our lives. Many are the afflictions of the righteous, but the Lord will heal them all. Our God is a Right Now God, and we cannot know his mind or will. Almighty God, let your will be done on Earth as it is in Heaven."

The hospital sent the bed made of steel, but it was too big to fit through any of our doors. "Take it back," I asked. "We can't take it back because it was made just for this little boy. The bed was designed like a crib for an adult. The hospital doctors and staff believed he would never overcome this condition, and the bed would accommodate him for life.

Seeing what we saw today – hand and leg movement - I knew this was from the Spirit of God. We were all shouting, and the spirit was stronger than any paralysis condition. Believe it or not, my God can and will do anything 'he wills' at the twinkling of an eye. He can make ways out of no way, open doors closed before you, and close doors no man can open for you. The Almighty God can make the impossible possible. You have heard me say this before, and I will say it again until you believe.

I already told you what God the Everlasting, the Beginning, and End has done in my life. Let me say again, he brought me through sickness, pain, death, danger, trouble, trials, and abuse, mental and physical. While I was going through my afflictions, I was determined to make it by holding on to God's Unchanging Hand. What he did for me he will do for you, just decide in your mind to live right and accept Jesus, God's only begotten son, as your Savior. His word said, "None but the pure in heart shall see God." He will not alter his word or take it back. His word will stand until the end of the earth.

A few days later, the children and I were relaxing in the yard. Rubin was in his wheelchair and I was in a chair too. The other children were busy playing tag, running and laughing. Rubin unfastened the seat belt that held him in and was trying to wiggle out of the chair. He had some motion in his legs but was not strong enough to walk. The second time he unfastened the belt, I decided to put him on the grassy ground; that was what he wanted to do.

He started scooting on his hip and legs in a sitting position, using his hands to push himself forward. He was determined to be able to play with the other children. They noticed him on the ground and started interacting with him and coming close so he could tag them. What a glorious sight to see and to know that it is all about our God's love, compassion, and caring.

A couple of days later, he was on the ground and pulled himself up, holding on to his chair. I jumped up quickly and held him by the shoulders to guide him. Before the day was over, he was walking and falling alone, not wanting help to get up. God wants all his children to be just as determined to please him in our daily lives, and he will supply our strength and courage to help us on our way.

By the time his appointment date came, he was walking and talking very well. The therapist was astonished about the progress he had made on his own. I had to let her know this was not on his own or with my help. "From the beginning, this is all about our Creator, the Maker of Heaven and Earth, the Maker of Man. His will, power and authority did this." Everyone looked at me strangely but had to agree that it was not possible for man or medicine to do.

One unbeliever is all I need to make my time and faith worthwhile. I need one person to be fit for God's kingdom; one soul saved, just one to give God glory, praise, and thanksgiving for his amazing plans and work.

When we made the monthly trip for the appointment at the hospital that kept him for the initial treatments, he recognized the doctor and the doctor recognized him, even though he could not talk at that time. He called the doctor by name, which was unexpectedly surprising. He was in a wheelchair when he left the hospital because he was not strong enough to walk the distance to the ward where her appointment was scheduled. Rubin continued, "I can walk too." The doctor stated, "Can walk?" He didn't answer, he just unfastened the seat belt and went out. The doctor took him by the hand and started walking in the hall. "I can run," he announced, and off he went. The doctor chased after him, calling him to stop. Doctor Chad was afraid that he would hurt himself.

Others who heard the commotion rushed in to see what was going on. Rubin was calling everybody by their names. "We didn't think he was comprehending anything. This is amazing," one of them said. By now, I had gotten my voice back and said, to the doctor who said it is amazing, "You are right. What happened to Rubin is God's amazing miracle. No one can explain what happened or how it happened. We were there and saw it happening, but it is still a mystery to me.

All I can tell you is the power of God came through the Holy Spirit and Rubin was healed." All began looking at me strangely, and one asked, "What did you say?" I repeated what I said before, but they didn't believe me. One said, "But what else could it be?" Some nodded in recognition, and others shook their heads, still not believing.

The doctors walked away for what their eyes had seen and what their ears had heard was impossible for them to accept. Dr. Chad did an examination and found him in very good physical and mental health. He wanted to see him again in a month. He wanted to know whether this was a gradual recovery or not. "It was almost instant; once he got the first movement, everything else just came into place within a week," I said. "He was extremely determined to heal, so God helped him." If we just have the faith of a grain of mustard seed, Jesus said, we can say to the mountains, remove to yonder place, and it shall remove, and nothing shall be impossible unto you. Rubin continued to get stronger every day and was almost normal while under our care.

The brother and sister pair Robin and Aaron, who didn't want anything to do with us when they came, wanted only MacDonald's to eat and didn't want our black hands to touch them. After a year and a half, they started calling us just as everyone else, grandma and papa. Along the way, Robin coached Aaron to do dishonest acts, such as lying, stealing, breaking other children's toys or destroying their property. The most damaging was to lie on me to say I had bruised his wrist.

She was the one who hurt her little brother but didn't want us to know. She would threaten him with leaving him alone by asking to not keep them together. The social worker saw the bruises and asked what happened, and he told the social worker that I had done it. Robin agreed with him. When I had to be investigated and told that I had to give up all our children, Aaron changed his story, told the truth about everything, and convinced the counselor when she didn't believe he was telling the truth.

Robin was removed from our home and put back in the care of her dad, who was in rehabilitation under supervision. Robin didn't want to go back to her dad's home and begged me to keep her. I explained to her that it was not my choice that she leave. But I would ask to keep her. Her caseworker decided that it would be best for Aaron that they were separated. This problem was a continual difficulty for him. A space was made at our home for another brother-sister pair.

Pudd was a five years old boy and Callie was a three years old girl. These children lived in a home where their parents were making methamphetamines (crank, crystal or ice) inside their home. These little ones were in bed all day. They could barely walk without falling. In fact, they were drunk from the fumes they were exposed to night and day. Their parents had not realized the reason they slept night and day. They were happy, and the children were not a problem for them.

When law officers raided them, the children were discovered just in time to save their lives. They were hospitalized for a week before being sent to our home. They came looking almost like zombies. Their eyes were disguised, their walk was almost like penguins, and their bodies formed like penguins. I cried and prayed for God to take control because I didn't know anything else to do. They couldn't keep food down. Their stomachs were affected by this terrible illegal drug they were exposed to for a long time.

They were trying to talk, but we couldn't understand what they said. We never gave up on God. We trusted him now more than before. It took a while, but God brought them to a normal state. I thank the Lord for sparing these two beautiful children. They were very appreciative of our help, never mentioning their parents. When I would tell them their names, they acted as if they had never heard of them. As far as they were concerned, we were always their parents.

There were many more children we parented from age zero to twelve years old, forty-two altogether.

After Jurius passed on to glory, it was too much for me to continue with the younger ones. My decision to stop fostering was not allowed for me. The department needed our home in the worst kind of way. They asked me to become a respite parent, to help whenever there was an emergency need. This meant that my home would be available twenty-four-seven. I tried to wiggle out of this plan, but my Father in Heaven would not let me.

I'm so glad he didn't. The teenagers I would be working with needed me as much or more than the younger group. Almost every one of the forty-five young men and women who came to our home didn't want to leave. My destiny to help everyone paid off in such a rewarding way for them and me. Most of them called me grandma. A few called me Ms. Miller, and three of them called me mama. These three and one more are still keeping in touch.

Some of these teens only stayed at my home for one night. Long enough for the caseworker to find a home for them.

There were times when there were as many as four at a time, all girls, which made it easier for all of us. I didn't have very much trouble with the girls, but most of the boys didn't want to learn to cook, and the majority of them were lazy, not wanting to do anything except play with the toys they brought with them. I can understand their problems with the other homes they were assigned to. They didn't want to keep their room tidy, wash dishes, or do any chores.

I had to let everyone know from the beginning, no work, no eating. Some of them argued about my job and what they did at their homes. I told them that is the reason you are at my home now. To teach you some life skills and remind you that you are part of a family. Families all work together; there is a part for everyone to do.

For some, I took away cell phones and video games until they left my home. The voice of God recommended this through the Holy Spirit, and it worked. I tried to teach each one who was sent to my care at least one life skill and some of them learned more than one. Most of the teens learned that there was an authority figure when they recognized that the only place they could go from here to stay for the night was incarceration. I explained to each of them how blessed they were to be sent to my home. My love for children wouldn't let me be any way except in their best interest. I was determined to help everyone who entered my doors through the help of the Lord. My rules schedule was posted so everyone could see.

Bedtime and breakfast time could be altered if behavior and cooperation were followed. There was definitely a fellowship formed during every stay. Some of them wanted to have this as their permanent residence. Jesus will always work out any and every situation that comes your way when love abides. Over the period of sixteen years, the total number of children in care for me was "eighty-seven" and I know that eighty-seven blessings and more were given to my family and me.

I also pray and hope that each one of them received at least one lifelong blessing. I'm still praying for God's rich and choice everlasting blessing for each of them. I love all of them as my very own. I had to give up foster care for no reason of my own. God said I had done enough. So he caused my license to expire, and no one could renew it but him. I give him thanksgiving and praise every day for his wonderful marvelously fruitful work in my life.

When the death angel wanted me dead at birth, God said, "Live, you are my child." When the automobile struck and knocked the breath out of my six-year-old son, he was not killed, for God Jehovah had already given him eternal life. Jurius laid on his sickbed and prayed that God the Father, God the Son (Jesus), and God the Holy Ghost would forgive him of his many sins, by word, thought, deeds, by commission, and omission against the Thy Divine Will.

He knew the only way to claim that mansion that his Savior Jesus Christ had gone to prepare for him was to make everything in his life right with God. He also had to make things right with all those he wronged. He was mightily blessed with God's mercy and grace throughout his adult life. Don't hear this incident and try to do likewise, for there is no promise that you will not meet your end and have the opportunity to ask for forgiveness.

If you know you are not living according to God's Holy Word, the Bible, you need not put off today until tomorrow, for tomorrow might be too late for you. God did not promise us tomorrow, so why wait? Do what you need to do now to have salvation and everlasting life. You can live and not die when your time comes to leave this world. When this world can't afford you a home any longer, you will have to meet Jesus at his Judgment Bar. You want to hear him say well done, enter into Eternal Joy.

This morning is a bright sunny day. A fearsome thunderstorm rolled over our community last night, bringing lightning and wind. I thank God that he protected us and let us know how mighty he is. Only he can do awesome work as that. We need to only trust him for our lives, safety, provision, etc. We all have crosses to bear, sometimes the same but mostly different. The cross we carry is different in shape and material from the cross Jesus bore.

Jesus carried his cross on his shoulder up a steep hill. He needed help, for the load got heavy and too much for him to continue onward. He fell on his knees, and the answer came in the form of help. Our cross comes in different kinds and stages, periods or degrees in a development process. My cross, unlike your cross, may be sickness, habits, a wayward child, deformities of the body or mind. Sometimes your cross is sin, trouble or affliction that tries one's patience or thwarts you.

Crosses are not supposed to be easy to carry or to get rid of, but there is help for us along the way. It is an uphill battle; a weakened state, a rude and cruel situation, a harsh journey, a bitter course of depression, or oppression by unjust or cruel use of authority. Jesus, our Lord and Savior, didn't give up. When he fell to his knees, he still tried to get up and keep going. Don't give up my brothers and sisters, don't quit, for help is on the way.

Keep pushing and calling for your assistance; he is always near. He may be a family member, neighbor, preacher, child, wife, teacher, friend, kinsmen, co-worker, stranger, or angel; no matter who it might be, it is always our Father in Heaven. It is always the Holy Ghost. It is always Jesus our Savior aiding and giving what we need.

This cross you carry don't belong to you, it belongs to Jesus, and he has already paid the uttermost sacrifice for you. He gave his life to pay your debts and mine, also for the whole world. He bought you with his shed blood. He paid a high price for you. You belong to "Jesus." Don't waste your life, come to Jesus right now, don't let another day go by without calling and asking him to help you, save and free you from the cross you're bearing.

When you can't sleep at night, God is waiting to hear from you. He wants to lift your heavy burden. Call him, he wants to take away all your sorrows and give you peace and joy. I can truly and sincerely say that my God has made a way; he never failed me yet. My brief glimpse of Heaven was enough to let me know that 'there' is where we would want to be. There are no mortgages or rent, no price to pay.

Jesus has already fixed everything. He is waiting, pleading for us to come. Come all ye that labor, that are weary worn and defiled. Bring him your burdens, seek his favor, tell him your sorrows and confide in him. Don't waste a moment. Your precious time is fleeting by. Won't you try Jesus after you've tried everything else? Jesus will satisfy you. My journey never took me to a place that led me to quit or give up; never was I weary or unsatisfied.

I don't feel tired. I've come too far from where I started. Nobody told me that my way would be easy, but Jesus brought me thus far, and he will never leave me.

In the early 1930s, after the battles with hard and fickle economic struggles, my parents made it through with God's love, mercy, and grace. He provided for our community by giving them love for each other as well as wisdom and knowledge. They learned to live off the land and to share with one another. God also provided wild animals and fish in the rivers for food. Wild blueberries and strawberries and other wild berries and grapes were plentiful. Nobody needed to be hungry even though money was not available to them.

Smarts and willingness were necessary survival skills in those days. Anyone then, just as today who trusted in God for his grace and mercy and was willing to seek, find, and knock on Heaven's door, it was opened unto them. I can say that God never fails. He is waiting to hear your call.

I was born during this severely harsh period. Prematurely, as I learned in later years. I realized it was all for the glory of God that somebody would know his mighty power and love. I was taught from a child to be guided by God's word, the holy bible. My heart's desire was to please God and live right. The bible said, "Thou shalt not commit adultery," so I vowed to keep all the commandments. The Lord had been good and caring to me. He had done everything I asked of him from my early existence in life, as far back as six years old when my mother went to Heaven. He was a mother to me using my older sisters, my aunts, and older cousins. He always gave us food to eat, warm clothes, and a house.

When we worked in the fields, the sun was bright and hot on the farm. I would whisper to him to help me make it to the end of the row so that I could get to the shade trees. A brisk cool wind would immediately blow and give me a fresh renewing of strength. No one can make the wind blow but you, Lord, and I give you thanksgiving and praise. You see, the premature birth caused my body to not fully develop internally. There was no maternal care as in today's time. But thanks to a loving, caring Heavenly Father who knows his children. He always knows what to do, when to do it, and what you need.

Out in the sun's heat, near twelve o'clock, just before time to go to lunch, when the wind is resting and not blowing, my undeveloped body and brain, yes I said brain, would not tell me to breath. Hallelujah, for mercy and grace and a loving Savior, who loves me so that his eyes are on me no matter where I am. In the midst of the tall vegetation lapping over my head, gasping for air, I would remember where my help comes from.

Looking up beyond the sky, got in touch with the maker of this Heaven and Earth, my all-wise Almighty Heavenly Father, whispering help! Oh Lord God, only one true God. I didn't have to tell him what to do, for he already knew what I needed. He sent the north wind our way, reached out of the sky, and pulled down a cloud to cover the sun to make everything comfortable for me. Blow wind so she can breathe fresh air and blow away all those harmful odors from this field.

In order to glorify God, I couldn't complain or tell anybody. I believed my only help came from God, and he never let me down or failed me yet. God gave me the energy and strength to do my share of the work and chores. He proved his love to me. When my body got weak, he gave me power, toughness, and durability. When I was sick, he healed my body. He sent strength to raise me when I was down.

He sent his marvelous light to shine before me and show the way when I was in darkness. All the glory to God! He brought me back to life four times and possibly five times, only there was no doctor there to say what happened. I passed out and went to the floor on my dog bed while caring and attending to her. When I became conscious, Sheba, my five-year-old thoroughbred German Shepherd, was breathing and licking me all over the face.

Sheba was breathing near my nose and mouth and taking turns licking. Her front paws were placed beneath my breasts, pressing in a rhythmic motion. All my strength was gone, and I could not move for a while.

She continued the CPR treatment until I was strong enough to move and press the button on my life alert system to call the emergency rescue squad. The time was nine a.m. when this incident happened and one p.m. when the medic got the alert. Sheba never gave up on me, which made me believe that God was using her to do his work through the Holy Spirit. Please be mindful that I went down, face forward, and she turned me over still on her bed. I heard nothing, felt nothing, and was unconsciously out of this world for four hours. Only God knows what happened, and I'm so glad he cared enough to use what was available.

Praises and thanksgiving to Almighty God for being available to all his children. He loves and cares about all of us. He does not discriminate based on race, color, national origin, age, disability, or sex. He will hear and answer your cry for help. He is a forgiving and loving Heavenly Father, waiting to hear from you. I was told that our first baby son was a miracle, and there would be no more children. Believe me when I say only God can add and multiply your blessing for you.

He gave us four children, just in the order he knew was asked for. He didn't have to do it, but he did. He could have decided that I would give you what I wanted, but he didn't. He was honored, and I was privileged he gave us special rights. Only a loving and righteous Father will grant his children their wishes as they ask. He allowed us to trust and depend on him even more.

Our second son, the one who was hit by an automobile when he was six years old, was named after his paternal granddad, Mark Christopher. He was characterized by being excessively brilliant and keenly intelligent. He was extremely happy and friendly toward all he came in contact with. When we asked him not to talk to strangers, he would smile very widely with eyes wide, look into your eyes, and say, "He is just a man or she is just a woman." He was always asking questions of anyone he met.

The amazing part of all this was he always got a polite answer for his questions, then he would say, "Thank you, sir or mam. I just wanted to know." Sometimes we would be embarrassed with the questions and would try to stop the process. Strangely, the person he approached would seem to think they needed to answer. Their attitude was that he needed to be rewarded. Both of us, his parents, knew he was a different child and had a kind of attractive magnetic power over his own self and toward all he spoke to.

His personality was such to make everyone think and be happy. Being extremely curious, he wanted to know all about nature and how it worked. "How did the trees get planted in the forest?" I used the word God so many times I would pray and struggle for a better explanation and come up with an answer like, the trees all have seeds and the seeds are carried by birds, animals, and the wind. "Alright, mother," he would say, "you got it right this time, and all of that is because of God." Working in the garden with us, he wanted to know about all the vegetables. "What part do we eat? When will they be ready to eat? How do they taste? When will the green beans be ready to cook?"

Working in the garden and learning about the vegetables made him eager to eat them. Once we cooked food from the garden, we had no problem with him tasting and then eating them. His older brother would try to discourage him from tasting some of the ones he didn't like. He would say let me taste it first. There was nothing that he didn't like, even okra, which most children have a problem with. This little one was only given to us to prove that God will always keep and honor his word. The other three children gave us seventeen grandchildren, forty-two great-grandchildren, and four great-great-grandchildren. Oh! What an amazing supernatural miracle God Jehovah has performed in this era.

We thank you, adore you and give you, oh Lord God, our precious Heavenly Father, all glory. God has been with me throughout my entire life, working miracles and doing the impossible. Three of the four children had surgeries when they were very young. The youngest of the children was born at six months of pregnancy, premature. In two of the births, the girls were born by caesarean section. Jurius had three hospital stays during this period and two were surgeries. I had two hospital stays, one for surgery. After all of these, there were many follow-up appointments.

My point in writing this again is to tell you that our Eternal Mighty God did not let us pay one cent for all these treatments. Our doctor paid all the hospital charges so that we could be discharged and go home. He also recommended that we get a tubular pregnancy corrected to give our first daughter a chance to live. Let me say again that all our children were miracles that our Holy Father of Heaven loved us so much and did not want us disappointed, but faithfully trusting in the name of Jesus. My family is dear and precious to my Father in heaven and me. I pray that God's desire for you to know him and his intentions to all mankind, will be rightfully justified.

I am worshipping Jehovah, our God, for trusting me to write such an important dialogue and to be able to honor his command. I feel so unworthy, but I continued to make supplications unto him and ask for revelation of what I should record of my life's story. One of my greatest blessings was given to me when I was eight years old. The day when God stopped me from taking my classmate's life. She was nearly dropped in an outhouse toilet by me.

In an instant, she would be dead, except the mercy of God had her sister call her name. I know it was God who knew exactly what to do, when to do, and how to do everything. This voice I heard stopped me from taking a human's life. I learned who God was on that day, when the Spirit of the Holy Ghost ministered unto me, to let me know how I could have ruined two families' lives. Thank God for knowing where I was and what I was doing.

He saved us from pain and misery.

My second greatest blessing came a few years later, at eleven years old, on my knees at our church revival, the first Monday in September 1944. God, through the love of his son, Jesus, who suffered, bled, and died on the old rugged cross, rose again from the dead, for the sins of the whole world, saved my soul from hell, which gave me eternal life. What an experience that was to have EVERLASTING LIFE, PEACE, AND JOY. You can have this same experience when you sincerely and truly repent of your sins and ask Jesus to save you.

You need to do it now, for time is not promised to us. There is no chance after death. Don't wait and try to get right. You can't save yourself. Trust and depend on Jesus to forgive you of all your sins. If this world could realize what a difference it would be, when men, women, boys, and girls bring into being the facts that things you 'want' cause most of your troubles. Wants cause, GREEDY, SELFISH, LASCIVIOUSNESS, WANTON, JEALOUSY, DISCRIMINATION, CHEATING, HATE, STEALING, ROBBING, KILLING.

Your wants can give you a miserable life. Your 'NEEDS' are all you need. God, our Heavenly Father, promised to supply all your needs, according to his riches in heaven. Can you remember that everything belongs to him? He owns the cattle upon a thousand hills. You need not store up your treasures on earth, where moth and rust eat and corrupt, and where thieves break through and steal, but lay up for yourselves treasures in heaven, where they will be kept safe.

Strive for what you need, and don't try to satisfy your wants. You will befit yourself for heaven and God's Divine Glory. Peace, joy, and happiness will be your first steps toward Heaven. You will be lifted from all your care and worry. Your burdens will be cast upon Jesus, for he cares for you. Freedom will be your buckler and shield, for when Jesus sets you free, you will be free indeed! Prestige, the power to command esteem, money, houses, land, cars, and all excessive material things for your pleasure and joy, you will need no more.

Set your heart and mind on things in heaven, not on things on earth. Ask God for a desire to help and love someone who needs your help.

My third greatest desire is that everyone who reads this book will see, hear, comprehend, grasp mentally, and understand exactly what God's will for you is. Everyone will get a better understanding of his Deity; his love for all, Heavenly Father, foreknowledge, wise, Most High, Only One True God, Ever-Present, Powerful, The Creator of Heaven and Earth, All Caring, Never Failing. What my God did for me, he will also do for you. Trust him and let him know you depend on his help. Worship daily and pray for forgiveness. Love everybody; don't just say you do. Remember, he knows when you're right and wrong. You cannot fool or lie to him. Be prayerful when you read and expect whatever blessing you need.

<div style="text-align:center">~~~</div>

The names of people and places all are fictional according to God's will. "Tell the truth," he said, "about what you have been through. I will be with you still, never leaving or forsaking you. Your family will help you also." The writing is not written in detail but by the revelation and spirit of God.

# A Final Word of Gratitude and Faith

On my way home from Nashville, Tennessee, after attending my great-grandson's college graduation, I boarded an airplane as a handicapped passenger and was allowed to board early. When the rest of the passengers began boarding, the seat next to me was filled by a woman who seemed hesitant at first to sit beside me. She later told me she felt a strange sensation, as if her hair were standing up all over her body, and that feeling made her comfortable enough to take the seat.

She became curious and began asking me questions about my life. She asked what it was about me that made her feel almost compelled to sit next to me. I told her, "Nothing about me. Maybe God was speaking to you." That answer excited her, and she asked why I believed it was God's way of getting her attention.

As she continued what she jokingly called her "interview," she realized that I was glorifying God more than talking about myself. She began taking notes and asked if she could take my picture. She said she needed to show her audience that I was a real person—someone who had survived death four times after being pronounced dead by doctors, and who had even faced a moment when the trigger of a .45 pistol was pulled, only to jam.

After that experience, God spoke clearly to me and told me to write this book, so the world might come to know Him. I thank God the Father, His Son Jesus Christ, and the Holy Spirit for choosing me to tell my life's story. I have been richly rewarded with spiritual growth and healing because He knew I would trust Him and depend on Him as my source of help. Throughout this writing, my thanksgiving, praise, and prayers were continually offered to Him.

Knowing that I could depend on God's revelation and wisdom kept me faithful. I have written according to the understanding He has given me. The majority of the scripture references in this book are drawn from my lifelong remembrance of the Bible. The songs mentioned come from the unification and prompting of the Holy Spirit. My days have always been filled with singing, praying, and reading, even while tending to daily chores.

Now, I listen carefully for God's voice, trusting Him to send the revelation needed for my writing. This is my sincere belief, because only in this way can this book be pleasing to Him. It is His will that the world be given another opportunity to know who He is and what He is able to do.

My prayer is that everyone who is led by the Spirit to purchase and read this account of my life will be richly blessed with knowledge and understanding of how mighty, powerful, loving, and caring our Heavenly Father is and always will be. As you read, listen for His voice, because He will speak to your heart what He knows will be beneficial to you.

I also pray that your spiritual life will be activated with love, joy, peace, long-suffering, gentleness, goodness, faith, meekness, temperance, and a determined mind to make heaven your home—even here on this earth. Be determined to help someone every day, and to show some weary, weak soul the right way.

# About the Author

Hazel Grace Mitchell-Mattocks has lived a life marked by faith, perseverance, and an unwavering trust in God. Raised in humble circumstances, she learned early in life the importance of family, hard work, and relying on God during both good times and difficult seasons.

Throughout her life she has faced many challenges, yet her faith remained the guiding force that carried her through trials and allowed her to experience God's grace and provision in powerful ways. Her story is a testimony of how God's presence can sustain, strengthen, and bless a life devoted to Him.

Through this book, she hopes her journey will inspire others to trust God, remain faithful during hardships, and recognize the many blessings that come from walking in faith.